Where's the Abundant Life?

Living in the Fullness of Life Jesus Has For You

by
Christopher Long

Cover design by Christopher Long. Main cover photo by Tobi.

DISCLAIMER: Among other topics, this book deals with the subject of health from a Biblical perspective. This book is not meant to be a substitute for a medical opinion from a licensed doctor or healthcare practitioner, nor is the purpose of this book or any statements in it to dissuade you from seeking medical advice or attention. If you feel you need medical attention, you should go get it! God can definitely work through doctors.

ISBN: 978-1-7348457-4-7 (Paperback)
Paperback First Edition. Core Text Version 1.0 (April 2020).
BodEquip Publishing
www.bodequip.org

Dedicated to the Body of Christ –
May she walk in the fullness of life Jesus died for her to
have.

Contents

Acknowledgements

It's a given to say that the foremost acknowledgement has to be God, because I most definitely could not, and would not, have written this book without Him. With that said, the following individuals have in some way, whether they knew it or not, influenced my life in a way that without them, this book probably would never have come about or would not be what it is. My thanks to each of them for their ministry in my life – I love you dearly in Jesus!

Mike Webb, Andrew Wommack, Ryan May (Ryan Paul Ministries), Joyce Meyer, Joey Buran, Chuck Smith, Craig Lockwood, Caroline Walton, Judy & Ray Prouty (your encouragement has meant more than you will ever know), Tony Rhee, Bayless Conley, Carlie & Ashley Terradez (Terradez Ministries), Mark Burgoz, Michael Newnham, Greg Mohr, Barry Bennett, Daniel Amstutz, all the wonderful Charis peeps, and of course Vince & Vicky DeMartino (words can't even express....thank you...)

And finally, I must acknowledge my mother for her wonderful influence and modeling what it means to have a childlike faith and trust in Jesus. I look forward to our reunion.

It is my prayer that this book will be used to elevate the Body of Christ to a place of walking in victory in all that is ours in Jesus. To God be all the Glory!

*Note: The above list is of course neither meant to imply that I completely endorse every teaching/thoughts etc. from everyone listed nor that they do so for me, and that includes the content of this book (though I hope they do) :)

Chapter 1 – The Disconnect

You know what would be an awesome way to start off a book? Why, with an awesome Bible verse of course!

> The thief comes only to steal and kill and destroy. I came that they may have life and have it abundantly. (John 10:10 ESV)

These words were spoken by Jesus to His disciples. While encouraging and hope-filled, for a long time they were a source of confusion for me. In this passage, Jesus tells us that the purpose of His coming to this earth was to bring life to people. But not just life – *abundant* life!

If you, like me, have understood that Jesus came to this earth and paid the penalty for your sin and rose again, and have accepted this by faith and trusted in Him, you have become "saved" or "born again" (as Jesus described in John 3) or whatever terminology you prefer. [sidenote: If you are not in this category or don't know what I'm talking about, please see Appendix A]. Many of us have been taught (correctly) that because we have accepted Jesus, that we will go to Heaven and will live forever with God. So, there is a sense in which we all as believers in Jesus Christ know that Jesus did indeed come to bring us life.

But Jesus didn't say that He came to bring us abundant life in the future when we die and go to Heaven. Notice that Jesus said that He came that we might *have* abundant life. It's present tense. He came so we could "have" – now. Not only that, but I just can't get away from this word *abundant*. Jesus could have left off that adjective and just said that He came to bring us life, and it would be absolutely true since the Scriptures teach that before Christ we were dead in our sins (e.g. Eph. 2:1). But He seemingly really wanted to emphasize something – that He wasn't just bringing life, but abundant life. And it's clearly implied that this abundance is available to us now, not sometime off in the future.

And here's where I have long had a problem. Because what I can look around and see is the experience of the average follower of

Jesus does not bear this out. Even seeing evidence of life can sometimes be a challenge, let alone *abundant* life.

Let me back up for a minute.

In the book of Genesis, we see that everything God created He declared was "very good" (Genesis 1:31). There was no sickness or death or pain. Adam & Eve lived in perfect fellowship and communion with God – they had fullness of life – abundance of life. But, when they disobeyed God and thus sin was introduced, this whole world – including all subsequent humans – have been under a horrific curse, which can still be seen all around us today. Death, hurt, pain, disease, sickness – all a result of sin. It was never God's plan for us.

We've all felt and seen the effects of it to one degree or another. If you've watched a loved one die as their body wastes away, suffered or know someone who has suffered childhood sexual or physical abuse, or witnessed or experienced any of the other myriad horrible things that exist in this world, then you've seen the effects of sin in the most brutal, ugliest way.

We try to hide it, put on a "happy face" and pretend all is well, but the reality is that it is HORRIBLE. Death is HORRIBLE! Cancer is HORRIBLE! Sicknesses and diseases of all sorts are HORRIBLE! Starvation, loneliness, lies, hatred, fear, torture, murder, terrorism, pain that cuts so deep – it's all HORRIBLE!

It's so BAD that most people spend much of their lives trying to live in pretend worlds where they can escape the reality of life, even if for just a little while. It's easier (we think – though usually not consciously) to avoid reality, because the reality HURTS. Television, movies, music, video games, surfing the Internet, and social networking are just examples of things that often we can become absorbed with in such a way that we really are avoiding living in reality as much as possible. Spending hours watching TV or movies or sports, hours writing and posting superficial blurbs on social networking sites, or even just scouring the 'net – all of these can easily be methodologies where, though we might not realize it, we're looking to escape having to deal with the real issues of our lives, because that means having to face real pain. Alcohol, pornography/sexual pleasure, drug use, overeating, and other addictions of all shapes and sizes, often (if not always) are fueled by a desire to avoid feeling pain and to "feel good", even if only temporarily. Of course, such addictions just end up creating more pain and the cycle continues.

Or then there's those that pour themselves into their work or fill up all their free time with a specific hobby. Underneath, it could just be that it's a subconscious attempt to stay so busy that they avoid having to face key realities of life.

Reality hurts. A LOT.

We look around and can easily see the effects of sin in our world. And if we're really honest with ourselves, we'd have to admit that this world hurts.

I don't know what your church experiences have been, but I've been in some churches that have had weekly prayer lists where during the service the pastor leads everyone in praying for those on the list. Week after week after week, at least 90% of the prayer requests dealt with people that were sick or had died. And you know what? It was downright depressing! Because week after week, it just seemed like a never-ending flood of sickness and stories of defeat. With one of the main ministries I've run for many years, I've also provided an opportunity for people to post prayer requests. And without a doubt, the vast majority of those requests were in regards to sickness.

It seems like just about everyone is sick or has some ailment or disease. Where I live, there's been a noticeable increase in the last 15 years of medical and urgent-care centers popping up. I've heard it said that the medical sector is one of the largest sectors of the U.S. economy and I believe it. Every other ad on television it would seem is an ad for some drug. And every other news report seems to be warning us of some health issue. Basically everywhere we turn, we see sickness or see reports of sickness.

As I am typing these words, at the moment the big thing is the COVID-19 (Coronavirus) pandemic. Mass disruption worldwide has occurred due to this flu-related bug. In addition to the physiological component of the sickness itself, it has produced incredible amounts of fear and anxiety in people over the prospect of possibly getting sick and dying from this new virus. It also has produced a bunch of major secondary effects in people's lives around the globe such as financial hardships. This bug has even disrupted many churches gathering together as public officials have declared gatherings to be a health hazard.

The simple reality is that whether we're talking about some new flu strain or any of the other countless physical maladies out there, there are sicknesses and diseases of all types in our world.

In addition to physical health, there's the area of emotional health. Everywhere you look, you find people frustrated, angry, sad, lonely, anxious, hopeless, and discouraged. Basically you find little joy and little love. People seem to be mad at just about everyone and everything. The battle lines get drawn over every little thing and people are quick to come out swinging. And the amount of addictions that people deal with is incredible. It seems most everyone is dealing with some addiction or another. Some common addictions include overeating, cigarettes/vaping, alcohol, recreational drugs, prescription drugs, video games, and pornography/sexual pleasure. This last one is absolutely rampant, with studies showing that a majority of men (and an increasing amount of women) have admitted to regularly viewing porn. And actually, the lines between what's even considered "porn" now have gotten somewhat blurred because many popular television shows (especially on cable and streaming services) now regularly feature nudity and sex scenes (in addition to plenty of violence and bad language of course).

This is our world when you look around. But, the thing is, I'm not just talking about those in the world that are unbelievers and could care less about Jesus. I'm talking about the church. I'm talking about believers.

This is where I've long had a bit of a disconnect. I see Jesus talking about His followers really having abundant life. But then I look around and I see His followers every bit as sick, broke, discouraged, angry, lonely, fearful, and addicted as the unbelieving world. When 43% of **pastors** admit to viewing pornography[1], you know there's a problem. When believers in God Almighty, who created this world and knows every hair on our head and who is the One we say we trust, cower in fear because of the latest health threat the same way unbelievers do, you know there's a problem. There's a disconnect somewhere. Something is wrong.

Did Jesus come to bring us abundant, victorious, joyful life, or not? Because if I'm just looking at the evidence I see in most churches, I would have to conclude He did not. And my guess is that so would you if you are honest.

Everywhere I turn I see Christians living in defeat – always "struggling" with sin, "struggling" with sickness and disease, "struggling" with their emotions, "struggling" with finances. Struggling, struggling, struggling.

Can you identify? I can. For most of my Christian life, I would say it's been a struggle. And I would find myself looking around and saying to Jesus: "Where IS this abundant life?? Because I sure don't seem to have it, and most all these other Christians walking around don't seem to have it. Where is it?"

I knew I was missing something, but for the life of me, I couldn't figure out what it was.

In Romans 5, the Apostle Paul, speaking of Adam, says: "For if by the one man's offense death reigned through the one, much more those who receive abundance of grace and of the gift of righteousness will reign in life through the One, Jesus Christ." (Romans 5:17a NKJV)

Paul tells us that death (and by extension all the stuff that comes from that including sickness/disease, etc.) reigned through Adam because of his sin but that those of us who are believers in Jesus and have received an "abundance of grace" are to REIGN in life through Jesus Christ. Again, I have to ask: how many believers do you know that you could honestly say seem to be REIGNING in life – showcasing that they've received an "abundance of grace?" My guess is probably not many. I think it's time that we all start asking "why?" It's time we start questioning where the disconnect is.

You see, I am convinced that Jesus never intended for His followers to live defeated by anything – whether sin, sickness, or whatever. There is an abundant life that Jesus came to bring us that we are able to walk in, and that is what this book will be exploring.

Many churches have tried to address the obvious disconnect by just reminding us of Jesus' words about how in this world we will experience trouble but that we are to take heart since Jesus has overcome the world (John 16:33). This line of teaching has basical-

ly been used as a cop-out to say: "Yes life stinks here, but it's supposed to be just as bad for believers as unbelievers – Jesus said so.
The key is to just adjust your attitude, have joy anyway, and hobble
along 'til Heaven."

But, what if, while acknowledging that there are troubles in this
world, that precisely BECAUSE Jesus has overcome the world, we
can walk victoriously – not just in attitude, but in actual reality –
through, and yes, even around, troubles that are here? What if there
is an abundance of life that we can walk in where we live victoriously in every area of our lives?

I know you may be skeptical and are possibly even already having objections rise up in you. That is completely okay! Believe you
me, I've been plenty skeptical too. I had been taught all sorts of
teaching that countered this notion. But, as God kept showing me
things and revealing things to me in His Word as I dealt with my
own personal sin and health issues, I came to a place where I realized I couldn't get around some of the things God was showing me.

When I first started having some of my long-held theology chal-
lenged, I prayed a bold prayer. I'm going to ask you to consider
doing the same. If you are willing, would you honestly from your
heart pray the following?

> "God, I want to know Your Truth, whether it contra-
> dicts teaching I may have been taught and believed my
> whole life or not. I want to know the truth. I'm asking
> You by Your Holy Spirit to show to me and confirm to
> my heart what is true and what is not. I don't want to
> believe any lies and I don't want to be misled. I want to
> truly live a victorious, abundant life in You. Please re-
> veal your truth to me. In Jesus' name I pray, Amen."

As you progress through this book and you run across statements
or concepts that challenge your beliefs, I am just going to ask that
you reiterate this prayer between you and God: "I want to be open
God. Show me if this is true or not." I prayed a prayer like that
many times, and I still do. Sometimes He would show me what I
was hearing/reading was true. And sometimes He would show me it

wasn't. I don't blindly just follow the teachings of others, and I hope you don't do that with me either. First and foremost, our teacher is to be the Holy Spirit. He can work through other believers to speak to us, but we always want to check things out for ourselves by talking to God in relationship with Him and by studying His Word for ourselves.

I think you will find that I am not a shill for any specific "camp" in the Body of Christ. While the theological perspective of this book definitely is more "in line" with certain parts as opposed to others, in my Christian journey, I have personally been in and around many different parts of the Body. And for over 20 years, I've run a ministry to Christians worldwide with believers from many different parts of the Body. In other words, I like to think I've got at least somewhat of a broad-level perspective of the Body as a whole. And one thing I have universally found to be true is that pretty much every part of the Body thinks they have all the truth and that those that disagree with them on things are misguided at best to being heretical or of the devil at worst. I think part of this is just human nature – people tend to be fearful regarding what they don't know. And many just listen to what people have told them is right and what is wrong without fully researching it themselves.

Some of the things that I'll be sharing in this book are things that I was either actively or passively taught against in some Christian circles. I was taught to stay far away from certain parts of the Body (i.e. the more charismatic, "tongue-talker" types) and was taught that certain teachings were wrong and certain prominent people from other parts of the Body were really "wolves in sheep's clothing" etc. I am not naive enough to not know that some of you reading this may have heard or been taught similar. I'm not saying that there might not be at least a basis in truth in being wary of certain people/things, but I have found that often things get painted with far too broad a brush. Without a doubt, I am convinced that one of the devil's greatest ploys is to sow discord and disunity within the Body, and this often happens from within – where one part attacks another part under the banner of "defending the faith." While there are times where division sadly might be necessary over significant issues, it is also true that sometimes what people think is significant really isn't. What people don't understand they tend to criticize and demonize.

All I ask is that regardless of what part of the Body you might identify with, that you are open to what God might want to say, even if it contradicts things you may have heard before. It's more than okay with me if you approach this book with a healthy degree of skepticism, as long as you are also willing to approach it with a degree of openness where you are willing to adjust beliefs if God reveals that needs to occur. Does that sound fair?

We all come with certain judgments based on our experiences and things we've heard. As we make this journey together in the pages ahead, may we adopt a posture of openness with the Lord, being willing to look at Scripture with as little "pre-judging" as possible.

This book shares and references a lot of Scripture because Scripture is the foundation for this book – NOT emotion. One of my pet peeves is when I see people blatantly applying a portion of Scripture in a way that isn't supportable, so I don't think you will find such in this book, but I always encourage people to check it for themselves. You will find that I primarily use three different Bible translations throughout. I know people have their Bible preferences and that some people feel very strongly about this subject. I'm not going to satisfy everyone, but all three translations I have chosen are common and popular and generally well-respected. These are the KJV, NKJV, and ESV. Typically which one I choose to use for a specific passage comes down to which one seems to do the best job at getting the concept across in the most understandable way. But, as mentioned, you are welcome to look any of them up in your preferred translation.

You've no doubt already been able to figure out that this book isn't going to read like your typical book. It's not polished or flowery in any sense. I think for far too long in the Christian world we've put on a good show, but we've neglected really dealing with the real issues head-on in a straightforward manner. Some of the "pat" religious answers that have been parroted for years just don't cut it. I'm not trying to impress you with my knowledge or theology or build my own kingdom. I'm a fellow human being that's trying to understand my humanity in light of the Bible and believe God has shown me some things that He wanted me to write down to be a benefit to others. But whether you end up agreeing with me or not, I hope you will find this "real style" refreshing. There's enough nonsense going on in the Church – it's time to get real and be honest and take a fresh look at the Scriptures, and if that means busting through some religious traditions of men, then so be it.

[Note: The way this book is constructed, each chapter is truly meant to be read at one time and not in pieces if at all possible. This is why, with a few exceptions, you won't find subsections listed within the chapters as many modern non-fiction books do and is why this book is formatted more like a fiction book is. Some chapters are fairly short and some are pretty long, but most of them build throughout the chapter and thus the flow can be notably disrupted if portions of a chapter are read at different times.]

[Note: Throughout this book, be aware that while I sometimes use italics to emphasize something, I do NOT do so in Bible verses and any italics you see in Bible verses do NOT mean I am trying to emphasize something in the verse. The NKJV and KJV translations utilize italics as a part of communicating to readers words that the translators felt were necessary to be added in English in order to make the meaning clear for English readers. If I emphasize something in a Bible passage, upper case letters or bold styling are used and I will specify that I have provided emphasis after the passage.]

Chapter 2 – Who's to Blame?

If I asked you the question: "Is God good?" – how would you respond? I can't imagine any Christian not answering "yes" to this.

However, I have found that for many people this is an "intellectual yes" – that there actually is great confusion on the heart-level with many Christians as to exactly what this means.

Awhile back I watched a Christian movie put out by a popular Christian movie studio[1], which had great reviews on Amazon by other Christians talking about what an encouraging movie it was. It was definitely exciting and well-made. Unfortunately, it had a major flaw with it. In the movie, the main character witnesses several deaths where it is clearly implied that God caused those deaths in order to get this guy to surrender his life to God. Indeed, in probably what would be considered the critical scene of the movie, the main character finally "gives in" to God in surrender and begs him several times not to take his wife too. In other words, this movie basically portrayed that the loss of his child, a friend, and others, was basically something God did and used to get his attention so that he would surrender to Him. This guy didn't turn to God because He heard all about Jesus' love for Him and God's kindness (i.e. it wasn't God's kindness that drew him to repentance – see Romans 2:4). He, rather, turned to God out of fear of God because he was afraid that God would continue killing people close to Him. At least that's how it was seemingly portrayed. It seems to me this would make it hard for such a person to ever have any real, loving, deep, intimate relationship with God.

Although this movie is a very blatant example, it is not an isolated one. I have seen numerous other Christian movies, read a variety of Christian books, and listened to countless sermons that to varying degrees all portray a similar message.

Again, the reviews for this movie from other Christians raved about how great a movie this was and how encouraging it was! And I've come to a conclusion. I've concluded that many people are actually more comfortable in having a distant, angry God that's "out to get us", instead of having a close, loving, intimate God that is FOR us. And in a strange way thus finding films or books that portray the former more "encouraging" than the latter.

I believe a lot of the reason for this is because there is a lot of confusion in our Christian churches about exactly how to reconcile this world of pain and sickness and death with a God of love.

The perspective of logic that undergirded this movie is extremely common in many Christian circles, and it goes like this:

– God is God, we are not, and He is sovereign over all.

– Therefore, since God is sovereign over all, any bad thing that happens goes through His hand.

– Therefore, any bad thing that happens must be His will for us.

– Therefore, if it is His will for us, since we know that the Bible says God is good, God must want to use this bad thing in our lives to teach us something or cause us to grow.

– Therefore, to resist or fight against the "bad thing" means we are actually fighting against God since it is God's will for us.

Often people with this worldview don't make the leap to this last logic step, but that is where the logic leads. Because this type of logic puts all the emphasis on God's sovereignty, people that either consciously or unconsciously think this way, will put all or most of the responsibility back on God when discussing a tragedy, sickness, death, etc. For instance, if a friend gets cancer, someone that has this type of worldview will be prone to saying things such as: "Who knows why God has allowed this to happen? His ways are not our ways. We just need to trust Him. Maybe God is trying to teach you something."

Such people are quick to quote Isaiah 55:8–9 where we're told that God's thoughts are not our thoughts and are higher than our thoughts, and His ways are not our ways and are higher than our ways. They latch on to this scripture because they feel it bolsters their view that everything is just all up to God and there's not really much we can do about it. That we just need to submit to what is obviously God's will since He is in charge of all.

The best answer this worldview offers to the question of why something bad is happening is a murky, vague, "well, God must know what He is doing" type of response.

This theology is all very "distant" feeling. On the one hand you are told that God loves you and wants a personal relationship with you through Jesus and wants to speak to you and guide you on your life's journey. That He wants you to talk to Him and Him to you and have this deep, intimate relationship with you. But then as soon as you develop some serious sickness or a loved one dies, you are told by the same person that we really can't understand because God is so much higher than us. All of a sudden this God that was supposed to be so close to us becomes clouded in mystery – He becomes much less approachable – He becomes "distant." Rather than trying to understand what's happening, we instead adopt a "God's the only one that can know" attitude, which renders us absolutely passive.

It comforts people to think that everything that happens in our lives must be God's will for us, because that then means that we have no responsibility in the matter. It allows us to "explain" why bad things are happening without really having to explain it at all, and without it requiring anything of us. We can just put it all on God.

The net result of this is a schizophrenic view of God. On the one-hand people believe that God loves us and will talk of how Jesus died for us and loves us deeply, but on the other hand, they will then blame God (directly, or more commonly, indirectly) for bad things that happen in their lives. This keeps people in a state where they really on a core level aren't sure what to make of God and whether they can trust Him, which actually keeps people from really drawing close to God into a deep intimate relationship with Him (even as they will say they believe in Jesus and love and trust God). It's this schizophrenic view of God that I believe is one of the key reasons that many Christians are not walking in more victory in their lives. They know they are supposed to trust God and love God deeply, and they will often say they do, but on a core level there actually is doubt about God's goodness that keeps them from really pushing in too close.

I'm just going to be blunt here, but this theology I believe is one of the most damaging and dangerous lines of thinking in the church today. It's a total cop-out. It puts all the emphasis on God's sovereignty and ignores or minimizes two other major factors: the devil and ourselves.

In the last chapter, I mentioned that when God created everything in this world, including us humans, He declared it "very good." If you read through the creation account in Genesis and all that God created, you will not find one mention of God creating sickness or disease or death or lack of any kind. What you will find is that the first two humans (Adam & Eve) lived in a perfect state in a union with their Creator, but then something went very wrong.

God gave Adam & Eve everything, but He told them there was one thing that was off-limits: "And the LORD God commanded the man, saying, 'Of every tree of the garden you may freely eat; but of the tree of the knowledge of good and evil you shall not eat, for in the day that you eat of it you shall surely die.'" (Genesis 2:16–17 NKJV)

God told them if they ate of this one tree, they would die. There's a whole lot packed in that right there. They didn't even experientially know what death was. How could they? They had never experienced it or seen it! Yet, they apparently did understand that this meant they would cease to exist here on this planet since we don't have any record of them questioning God about this – and the text assumes their understanding. But I'm quite comfortable in saying they probably had no idea the full ramifications of what "you shall surely die" would mean not just for them, but for everyone that came after them. But they knew enough to know that they had a choice: to obey God and live in fullness of life in perfection with Him, or disobey Him and suffer death.

God wasn't being cruel and He wasn't being harsh. He gave them everything, but He left one thing that they could not do so that they would have a choice. If God did not do this, then they would have merely been robots without any say as to whether they wanted to do things God's way. I like how James Dobson puts it: "God gave us a free choice because there is no significance to love that knows no alternative."[2]

Right away after the creation account, we are introduced to the devil, referred to as "the serpent." In the first verse in the Bible about him, we are told that he is "cunning" and he offers this lovely question to Eve: "Did God actually say, 'You shall not eat of any tree in the garden'?" (Genesis 3:1b ESV) In other words we see him right off the bat trying to get Eve to doubt God and His Word that He gave. He then goes on to question God's goodness by claiming that God lied to them and was holding out on them (Gen. 3:4–5).

Well, we all know what happened, right? Long story short, the devil lied to her and she listened and ate. Then she gave some to Adam and he ate. And the next thing you know, everything's changed. They immediately felt shame and tried to cover themselves and hide. You can almost hear the breaking heart of a Father as God asks Adam: "Where are you?" (Gen 3:9b ESV) as Adam & Eve try to hide from Him. We're introduced to the concept of pain (pain in childbirth, painful toil in work) and death (the first murder occurs in the very next chapter!) In regards to the pain in childbirth and painful toil in work, those were a part of curses that God pronounced as a result of their sin.

But can I ask you a question? Who caused that pain? Did God cause it because He pronounced it? Or was it Adam & Eve that caused it by listening to the devil in the first place and disobeying God? Who's to blame?

I know some of this might seem like Christianity 101, but I'm going somewhere here, so stay with me.

When Adam & Eve disobeyed God, they committed the first sin, and their sin brought forth death – just as God said it would – in every conceivable area. It brought death to their previously unbroken fellowship with God in their "spirit man" and it brought death to them physically. It did not immediately cause them to die, but it put death into motion; their bodies started the "death process" – started decaying. In their case, it took a long time, but eventually they did indeed physically die. If they had not disobeyed God, they would still be in the Garden today!

Because of their disobedience, death became a reality. All of us from the moment we are born are moving towards physical death. Whether we like it or not, death is physically at work in our bodies.

Sickness and disease are merely the natural byproduct of this death process. In other words, sickness and disease are the natural by-product of Adam & Eve's disobedience.

God never intended us to be sick and He never intended for us to die. Yet, here we are today, and we can look around now and see lots of people sick and lots of people dying. Who's to blame?

Did God cause all this sickness and death we see? Or did us humans cause it after listening to the devil? (Hint: this last one is the answer).

It can all ultimately get traced back to Adam & Eve choosing to listen to the devil over God back in the Garden of Eden.

Their sin not only opened the door to sickness and death to occur to us down the road, but it introduced those concepts into our very being – the DNA of our being and our world, creating mutations. This is why some babies are born with diseases. The thought of an "innocent" baby being born with a disease causes many to question the goodness of God, and I get that. However, it was not God that caused it, but humanity. I'm not saying that is a particularly satisfying answer for our emotions, but it is the truth. That fact also causes people to question why what Adam & Eve did should even be affecting us at all – because after all, we are so sure we wouldn't have disobeyed like they did!

Adam & Eve's spirit connection with God is part of what kept them in a state of perfect Life and health because those things spring from God. When they disobeyed and they lost that, the natural result of that showed forth in their bodies, which then naturally affected their offspring since their offspring was a product of biological processes in their bodies. In order to keep their offspring (and eventually you and I many generations later) free from these newly introduced effects, God would have had to nullify the results of their choice. God takes the whole choice thing that He gave humanity so seriously that He wouldn't do that. We can gripe about it all we want, but like it or not, Adam & Eve are humanity's parents and they did make a choice that has affected all of us. The good news is that though it can seem like a raw deal that through their sin we all are affected, God also has provided an answer and in similar fashion His answer came to us through One, but is available for all.

Jesus, God's Son, came and paid the penalty for not just our own personal sins here and now, but for the sins of humanity going all the way back to that first sin in the Garden. In other words, Jesus paid for all sin, for all time. Now just because Jesus did this, it doesn't mean that every person accepts this gift and makes it applicable to them. We may not have had a say as to whether we were born into this sinful world, but we do still get to make a choice. God never took back the gift of choice He gave humanity. We still get to choose whether to look to God and believe Him or not. Jesus' sacrifice for humanity was a global human act and yet, it is very personal in application. If we do not WANT Jesus to pay for our sin, God will not force it.

This whole choice thing is actually the reason why our earth even still exists right now in a sinful state. Had God removed our choice, then when Jesus paid for sin, it would have applied for all irrespective of what they wanted and all would be "saved" and God could just usher in a new earth unaffected by sin right now (as will happen later per Revelation 21:1). The whole reason why our earth is actually still as it is right now and we all are still here in it is precisely BECAUSE we have choice. In 2 Peter 3, Peter addresses this and explains what the "holdup" is; we are told that God is patient (longsuffering) toward us and that He is "not willing that any should perish, but that all should come to repentance." (2 Peter 3:9b KJV). The fact that we are even still here right now living in this sinful earth is the greatest proof against the false doctrine of universalism (which says that our choice for Jesus really doesn't enter into the equation). It all comes back to choice. God wants as many with Him for all eternity as possible. If He stepped in and just righted everything now, then with it goes the hope of any additional men and women being saved.

This is standard Christian belief – I haven't said anything radical in saying any of that. However, many Christians have taken what was accomplished by Jesus as only affecting us in a "spiritual sense" – that we are set right with God – that the "spiritual connection with God" is restored. But that there's nothing whatsoever in what Jesus did that affects us in any other way. But I intend to prove that everything that was lost as a result of the fall is re-gained in

Christ – it is available to us. This means that since being born into sin and being a slave to sin came as a result of the fall, that in Christ we are set free from sin and can walk victoriously over it. This means that since health is one thing that was lost in the fall, in Christ, I believe this is available to us. This means that since anger and hatred and lack (of all types) came about through the fall, in Christ we can walk in love and joy and blessings. As I make the case in the chapters to come, I ask you to weigh the evidence and render your own verdict.

You see, I propose that our experience today isn't really that much different from Adam & Eve in the sense that we still have God's Word to us, we still have a devil that is lying to us and trying to deceive us, and we still have choice.

The Bible tells us that the devil is a liar (Jn 8:44), deceiver (Rev. 20:10), murderer (Jn 8:44), oppressor (Acts 10:38), destroyer (Jn 10:10), thief (Lk 8:12), devourer (1 Peter 5:8), and sinner (1 John 3:8).

God on the other hand is portrayed from start to finish in the Bible as the one that created us and loves us and is for us. We are told that God is "merciful and gracious, longsuffering, and abundant in goodness and truth." (Exodus 34:6b KJV). We are told in 1 John 4:16 that God not only loves us, but that "God is love." If you remember from your math schooling, "is" equates to "equals." In other words, the mathematical equation is God = Love. Have you ever paused to really think of the ramifications of that? That means that the very essence of God is love. That also means that the definition of love is God. We think we know what love is based on human love that we see, but actually our human love is but a reflection of God's love – and often a very poor reflection at that. Even though many don't realize it, because God is love, any genuine love that we may experience in some way can be traced back to God. If we could really grasp this 'love' component of God's very nature, we might finally dispense with this notion of a distant God that is always angry or out to get us. Our God is love. And love is for us, not against us.

James 1:16–17 tells us: "Do not be deceived, my beloved brethren. Every good gift and every perfect gift is from above, and comes down from the Father of lights, with whom there is no variation or shadow of turning." (NKJV) God is the one that gives us good things. "What then shall we say to these things? If God *is* for us, who *can be* against us? He who did not spare His own Son, but delivered Him up for us all, how shall He not with Him also freely give us all things?" (Romans 8:31–32 NKJV). God is on our side – He is for us. He has already proven His love for us. He is a giving God that seeks to do good for us – He's not out to harm us or hurt us. The picture all through the Bible is one of a God that deeply cares for His own.

The mistake that people make is in mixing God and the devil up. It's one of the devil's greatest tricks, actually. The devil hasn't changed much from how he operated with Eve in the Garden. He tries to get us to question what God has said and doubt God's goodness and believe that God is holding out on us or may not really be for us. If he can get us to pin the blame for sickness or suffering or death on God, well nothing pleases him more.

We want to watch ourselves that we don't repeat the same mistake made back in the Garden. Let's get this lesson down once and for all: "God is good. The devil is bad. Do not confuse the two."

The reason for all the suffering and hurt and death we see is because we humans mucked it up way back in the Garden and basically submitted to the devil's plan for us – and the result of that sin still plays out today and affects us all. But God loved us then. And He loves us now. God is on our side and the fact that Jesus came at all proves this!

One might ask, "If God is so good, then how do you explain accounts in the Bible of Him putting sickness on people or causing people to die?" It is true that there are several accounts in the Bible of this occurring – mostly in the Old Testament, but there's a few related in the New Testament as well (e.g. Herod being struck by worms). And we do need to be honest about this. I have heard some well-meaning pastors that in trying to defend God or defend their view that God never has put sickness on people, they'll claim this isn't true – that these instances aren't translated correctly etc. But the problem is that there are so many examples and they all say similar things – at some point it just becomes ludicrous to claim that the numerous passages interwoven throughout the entire Bible aren't saying what they clearly at face value say.

Yes, you will find examples in the Bible of God putting sickness or disease on people. And yes, you will find examples of God in the Bible causing some people to die. However, this does NOT mean or imply, as some interpret it to, that God isn't good. Just like the curses that were pronounced by God on Adam & Eve after their disobedience, when you look at the judgements where God did this, you will find that it was a response to sin on the part of the people in question. People disobeyed God, and sometimes God just plain had enough, usually after we see Him being extremely patient for a very long time – extending mercy and grace, time after time after time.

There is an EXTREMELY important point about all of this though. You will NEVER, not once, find God EVER putting sickness or disease on a genuine believer in Jesus Christ. This will get explored more in a future chapter. I know some of you are also already having some things pop in your mind like "what about Paul's thorn in the flesh?" etc. Hang tight – we'll get there in a few moments. But for now, I'm just making the blanket statement that in the Bible you do not see God interacting with believers in Jesus that are under the New Covenant in the same way that He did under the Old Covenant. Under the New Covenant, when God looks at you, He sees Jesus and His righteousness – and He is not about to inflict you with sickness as a believer. Again, I know I'm opening up a can of worms by making that statement – stay with me – I promise we'll come back to this more at a later point in this book.

Many Christians wonder why it seems that there are "two God's" in the Bible – the one in the Old Testament that seems to be harsh, and the one in the New Testament that seems to be so loving. But the truth is that it is the same God. The difference is that in the Old Testament, God related to humanity differently because Jesus hadn't come yet. Under the New Covenant in Jesus, everything is different because God is relating to us through Jesus – He sees Jesus's righteousness when He looks at us. I know these statements are revolutionary ideas for some. But even in the Old Testament, when you read it in order and you see the entire story unfold, you don't get a picture of an angry God who's out to hurt people. From the very beginning, we see a loving God that loves His creation and we see His mercy and grace and love portrayed all the way through. By contrast, we see humanity constantly rebelling and turning away from God and committing terrible evil. We see humanity time after time repeating the same sin that Adam & Eve did – listening to the lies of the devil over the Word of God.

God is good. The devil is bad. Do not confuse the two.

Another common mistake that people make is in assuming that because God is God and is so mighty and powerful that therefore everything that happens must be His will in our life. Remember the question I asked earlier about who was to blame for the consequences when Adam & Eve sinned? Let me ask it this way: Was it God's will for Adam & Eve to disobey Him? Was the fact that they disobeyed proof that it was His will for them? Theologians have been batting around questions like these for centuries, but it's all so ridiculously silly. Of course God didn't want Adam & Eve to disobey Him. Just because God, being God, knew what would happen does NOT mean that He WANTED it to happen. That's a significant mistake in thinking that people make. God gave His creation choice and He honored that choice. No matter how much we might want to complicate it, it really is that simple.

Likewise today, God has never taken away the gift of choice He gave us. And you know what? He still honors our choices – in MANY areas of our lives, not just in what we do with Jesus.

We do know that God is over all in the sense that He is still God and we are not, but God allowing the choices of humans and letting things play out in our world is not the same thing as God actively choosing to cause someone to get sick or die. There is a HUGE difference between God causing something and God allowing something. Many people equate them as one and the same, but they are not. They assume that just because God allows something, then that must mean that it is His will. Just because a loved one gets sick doesn't mean God wanted that loved one to get sick. Just because a little baby dies doesn't mean God really wanted that little baby to die. We are living in a world that is still reeling from the effects of the Fall – and there is sickness and there is death and hurt and pain in this world.

I know this is really hard for people because we all know that God is powerful and so if He's powerful and could intervene, the question is "Why doesn't He?" I understand why people ask this. But let me throw this out for consideration: If God always intervened and put a stop to every sickness and disease and death and any number of other "bad things" that were a result of the Fall, what would we have now? Would it not be perfection now, heaven now? And what would that say about God's honoring of our choices? See, friends, God still honors our choices – and not just ours, but of those around us as well. And, I've already alluded to the fact that I believe one of those choices can be to take hold of things that are available to us in Christ – I'll be making this case further in the chapters ahead. But in the absence of this, to just put everything all over on God and ask why He doesn't always intervene on His own to do things we want, just plain isn't fair to God.

It is true that God sometimes miraculously intervenes in circumstances on His own – He does have that prerogative since He is God – the Creator. Our prayers can definitely affect things, but why God sometimes intervenes on His own or doesn't is up to Him, and this is where it is true that God's ways are indeed higher than our ways and His thoughts higher than ours. It frequently seems that God just kind of lets things play out. Just because God does not on His own intervene in a specific circumstance, or does not intervene in the way or timing we would like, does NOT mean that He is any less good, or any less loving. That's where many people make their mistake in their logic. They assume that if God really loved them then He wouldn't have let "X" happen in their lives. That's faulty logic. They assume that if they beg God a whole lot, and then God doesn't "fix" their situation, that must mean God doesn't love them or isn't a good God after all – that really He's just a giant "meanie" out to get them. Or at least that's what it seems to them.

But God choosing NOT to supernaturally on His own intervene in a certain situation doesn't mean He isn't good. In the final analysis, God is not to blame. He never was. And He never will be. He didn't cause our problem – we human beings did – either on our own or by giving place to the devil in our lives. It wasn't God's fault. So if He doesn't on His own intervene and correct it, that doesn't mean He's not good. It means He's allowing things to play out in their course. Again, if He did always intervene, then there would be no significance to our choices at all (including in our choices or the choices of those around us to listen to the devil on things instead of God).

Let's take a "for instance." Let's say there's a guy who chooses to listen to the devil and get drunk and then chooses to get in his car. He then proceeds to hit another car with a woman in it who is seriously injured in the accident to the point of being on the brink of death. Consider this: If God intervenes, what would this say about the man's choices? It would mean that He puts a block to the natural ramifications in our world of the man's choices, correct? If God does NOT intervene, then it means He lets the results of the man's choices play out, including their ramifications on someone else. If He doesn't intervene and put a block to the natural ramifications of the man's choices, does that mean He's not good?

Now, let's suppose the woman's family are Christians and they pray for God's intervention for miraculous healing. If God intervenes, He again is blocking the natural ramifications of the man's choices. Who among us can really weigh whose choices in the grand scheme of things are more important to let play out? Just to throw another wrinkle to make another point: What if while that woman's family is praying for her miraculous healing here, she herself on her heart level is thinking how with the pain she's in, she'd just like to go home to Heaven to be with Jesus. Perhaps she already has loved ones that have passed and she's so longing to be with them again that she would rather just go home to Heaven. Perhaps the family doesn't even know what she's thinking on her heart level. Again, whose choices does God go with? The man's, the family's, or the woman's? Whose choices are "worth more?" Do we really think we're smart enough to figure all that out?

Again, if God always intervened in the way we wanted, then there would not be any point in anybody having choice since God would just always step in and right everything here. But God HAS given us humans choice – and He does honor that. And we need to be careful that we don't think we're so smart to think that we know which way God should always act in these kinds of things – there are often variables we don't know. With that said though, I do just have to say this (which will be fleshed out more later): God honors His Word and I'm just telling you from practical observation and personal experience, that when we exercise our choice to act in faith on God's Word, God honors that.

The whole discussion of God's sovereignty has gotten skewed in many circles to the point that it's pretty much "what will be, will be" – God's just in control of everything. While it is true that God is sovereign in the sense that He has no equal and is the Creator over all, He has given His human creation the gift of choice. He gave it to us in the Garden and He has never taken it back. And He does honor our choices. It is commonplace to hear Christians anytime something seems overwhelming or beyond our control, to just say things like "Well, God has a plan and is in control." And in a sense that may be true, but He works with our choices.

For instance, I heard many Christians in the U.S. make comments regarding the outcomes of the 2008 and 2012 presidential elections (or on the flipside, in some circles, the 2016 election) by saying "Well, God's in control – though we don't understand it, God must have some purpose." I'm not going to get political here, but I'm just going to say that God isn't the one who voted! His human creation that He gave freewill choice to are the ones that voted. And they got what they voted for, plain and simple. It's not fair to turn it back on God and say that because it happened the way it did, well that must just be God's will. We have to dispense with this notion of a God up there that's just a puppet-master weaving and ordering everything as He sees fit. It may be comforting to think of God that way because it eliminates us from having any responsibility, but it just plain is not true. All through the Bible you see God interacting with and responding to the choices that people make. As a nation, America has been going down a certain path for a long time and over and over again has been making choices that do not line up with God's Word. This isn't God's will – His will is for people to look to Him and trust in Him – to live in accordance with what He's told us in His Word, not turn away from Him and rebel against

Him. But if that's what people want, He will let us. And we'll reap the results of that.

On a personal level, people love to quote Jeremiah 29:11 where we are told that God has wonderful plans for us. And Amen to that! But those plans don't just magically come to pass as we sit back and do nothing. No, we have a part to play. Now God works with us, for sure – but we still have a part to play. God may have a plan for me to write this book, but if I don't actually sit down and write the thing, it's not going to happen. We have choice. Just as He honors people's choices regarding whether they want to believe in Jesus, He honors people's choices in any number of areas.

This all should be blatantly obvious, but unfortunately it's not, as many Christians have bought into this weird theology where God is actually up there arranging every last detail of our lives and everything that happens is because He wants it to happen to us. This theology for all intents and purposes completely serves to nullify our choices and responsibility for our choices and allows us to put everything over on God.

This is no more true than when it comes to "bad" situations that occur in our lives or of those we love. As already discussed, we make a mistake if we just say that "it must be God's will." Just because someone close to us gets sick or dies doesn't automatically mean that it was God's will. Now, as a believer in Jesus, we have bedrock promises such as Romans 8:28 where we're told "And we know that for those who love God all things work together for good, for those who are called according to his purpose." (ESV). As believers who love God, we are told that God does work all things together for good – and we can rest in this promise. God definitely specializes in taking bad situations and turning them for good. God can use the results of a death or sickness and bring great good out of the experience (which we may not even see initially). But that's a whole different notion then saying that God must have wanted the event to occur in the first place.

It is my testimony, as I'm sure it is many of yours also, that God has taken me forward from some very hard and painful and tragic situations and has brought good from them in my life. The mistake that some people then make though is in assuming that God must have wanted them to go through those things all along just so He could teach them things. For instance, some argue that God puts sickness on people sometimes so that we will learn to trust God more or develop more patience. Now a person may be sick, and they may indeed learn things – God may indeed teach them things through that experience such as learning to rest more in Him and look to Him. But that doesn't mean that it was actually God's will that they got sick. God doesn't have to teach you through sickness. But He will if that's where you're at. Again, He specializes in turning bad to good. But we need to be careful that we don't fall into the trap that many fall into in assuming that everything that's happened in our lives happened because God wanted it to.

Many years ago, I took a multi-year sidestep with the Lord where I got involved in some relationships and situations that were not right before God. And as usually happens when we do things that aren't right, I ended up bringing some incredibly intense pain on myself that took me a long time to work through. A great deal of the suffering and pain that God is often blamed for is actually the result of us or other people doing the opposite of what God says. That may not be a thought we like to entertain, but it is true. I can look back though and see all of the valuable lessons I gathered and all the ways I grew through that experience. But that doesn't for one second mean that God intended for me to take those paths and do things that went against His Word. It wasn't His will, but God will work with us where we're at in the situations we are in. As His children, He will take us forward as we look to Him – and we can learn from our mistakes. But just because we learned from mistakes, doesn't mean God wanted us to make the mistakes in the first place!

Now, when dealing with the whole subject of God's sovereignty specifically in the context of sickness or disease, there are usually two major Biblical narratives that come to the mind of many Christians. The first is the story of Job and the second is Paul's "thorn in the flesh" as detailed in 2 Corinthians 12.

Without fully delving into the entire book of Job, let me just say this: In the first chapter we see a behind-the-scenes exchange between God and the devil. Here's a critical portion of that exchange with the devil speaking to God:

"... You have blessed the work of his hands, and his possessions have increased in the land. 11 But stretch out your hand and touch all that he has, and he will curse you to your face." 12 And the LORD said to Satan, "Behold, all that he has is in your hand. Only against him do not stretch out your hand." (Job 1:10b–12 ESV)

Notice that it is the devil that wants to attack Job, not God. Notice that God was doing GOOD for Job. The devil tries in verse 11 to get God to attack and afflict Job, but God isn't about to do that. He does, however, allow the devil to do it. And actually, even in that, He initially doesn't even allow the devil to do anything with Job himself – that doesn't come until later when the devil basically insists on it.

Now, again, many people equate God's allowing of the devil as the same thing as God doing it Himself. But that is not true – there is a huge difference between the two. God isn't the one that afflicted Job, the devil is. It wasn't God's WILL for Job to be afflicted. God's will was obviously for Job to prosper in all areas – this was proved again at the end of the book of Job where we are told that "the LORD gave Job twice as much as he had before." (Job 42:10b). It was the devil that wanted to go after Job, not God.

"But wait," one might say, "didn't Job himself say the Lord caused his calamities?" Why yes he did. In an oft-quoted part of the book, Job says: "Naked I came from my mother's womb, and naked shall I return. The LORD gave, and the LORD has taken away; blessed be the name of the LORD." (Job 1:21b ESV). People that love to use the book of Job to defend their theology that God is a puppet-master who might just decide to afflict you love to quote these words Job uttered. They will say: "See? Job said God did it and God does do these things to us but we just need to trust God that He knows what's best." There are indeed some statements in the Book of Job that could lead one to this conclusion if you don't balance those statements with what is shown at both the beginning and end of the book.

As mentioned above, the book opens by giving us the behind-the-scenes commentary of what was really going on that Job did not know. Job was not privy to the conversation that we are privy to between the devil and God. There are plenty of statements in the book of Job (particularly the middle as Job and his friends try to make sense of things) that are bad theology. The Bible records them for us as a historical record and to show us some of their foolishness, not so we will hold every statement made in high esteem!

With the verse quoted above where Job says that the Lord gave and took away, the Bible records in the next verse that at that time Job did not sin or charge God with wrongdoing. (Job 1:22). But here's the thing: Job did not know what he did not know (I will prove this in a moment). He made a statement which he absolutely believed (that God caused his problems), but that was an incorrect statement. With the information Job had available to him, it was what he believed. Yet, even though he had a wrong belief, he did not (at least at that juncture) hold it against God. And thus, based on what he knew, the Bible tells us he did not sin.

A little later, while discussing with his friends, Job uttered another line that has become famous: "Though he slay me, I will hope in him; yet I will argue my ways to his face." (Job 13:15 ESV). In the first part of this which is commonly referenced and touted as great theology, Job says that God did this to him and yet he would still have hope and trust in God. He then goes on to say that he will defend his ways to God. So Job said it was God's fault and he will freely argue with God and defend himself to God. But guess what? You know what really happens when God speaks with Job as recorded at the end of the book? Not Job arguing with God, but rather Job repenting.

Before Job really even gets to say anything, God asks Job a massive amount of questions, including these two doozies: "Will you even put me in the wrong? Will you condemn me that you may be in the right?" (Job 40:8 ESV). My take on what God asks is something like: "Job, are you really going to blame Me and condemn Me in your prideful arrogance for what's happened in your life?" And I think God might ask the same of many today who are likewise pointing fingers at Him.

When Job does finally respond to God, he repents: "Therefore I have uttered what I did not understand, things too wonderful for me, which I did not know. ... I had heard of you by the hearing of the ear, but now my eye sees you; therefore I despise myself, and repent in dust and ashes. (Job 42:3b, Job 42:5–6 ESV). Likewise, many people today also need to let go of what they have HEARD about God being the One causing their problems to try to teach them things or punish them, and instead need to start seeing God as He really is: One that is for them and on their side.

The Bible also records in Job 42:11 that his brothers and sisters and others came to comfort him because of "all the evil that the LORD had brought upon him." (KJV). Again, I suppose if we didn't have the benefit over what they had, of actually seeing a glimpse into the behind-the-scenes conversation between God and the devil in chapters 1 and 2, it could be easy to just blame God and assume God was the one responsible.

Despite what Job thought and had uttered in his lack of understanding, and despite what his friends and family thought, it was NOT God that had caused his problems, but the devil. Now while we've established that, the question still remains: "Why did God allow the devil to do it?" I do understand that to some people, if God allowed it, it's no better than if He did it Himself (and perhaps that's what Job or his family were even thinking when they uttered some of their statements), but that really isn't fair. God's clearly revealed heart in the book of Job was to bless Job, not to hurt him. It was the devil that wanted to hurt him. But there still is the question of why God would even allow the devil to do that.

I think there could be any number of possible explanations, but one of them is simply that the devil had the legal right. Remember, we've already looked at what transpired with Adam & Eve in the Garden. When Adam & Eve obeyed the devil over God, they subjugated themselves and their authority to the devil – this is when the devil became "the god of this world" (2 Cor. 4:4). Now Jesus has dealt with this (we'll explore this more later), but at the time of Job (and just FYI: Job is considered to be the oldest book in the Bible by age) there is simply a case to be made that the devil was seeking to enforce his legal rights. There is evidence (albeit a bit debatable) that Job was outside of any covenants with God and thus from a pure legality standpoint, the devil had the right and God allowed him to exercise it (though not Himself wanting it). I realize that may not be a very satisfying answer, but it may well be true. Or there could be other reasons. The truth is we aren't given a whole lot to go on to fully know for sure. One thing though that is very clear from the book of Job is that God didn't afflict Job and God didn't want the devil to afflict Job. It was the devil that hurt Job, not God.

When I think of the book of Job, I am reminded of a quote from Pastor Chuck Smith I heard several years ago. He said this: "When I can't understand what's happening and what's going on, then I fall back on what I do understand. I do understand that God is good. I understand God loves me … And I am not going to give up what I understand for what I don't understand. That's a foolish mistake that a lot of people make."[3]

Now, let's move on to the Apostle Paul and his "thorn in the flesh" as recounted in 2 Corinthians 12. The reason this often gets brought up in discussions regarding God's will (particularly in regards to sickness) is because, quite bluntly, this is one Biblical story that's been blatantly taught incorrectly in many pulpits across this land – and I'm going to prove it in just a moment. Before we look at it, is it your understanding that Paul was dealing with a physical sickness/disease that God put on Him, and that Paul begged God for it to be removed, but God told him no? That is the impression that many people have. Many pastors and teachers have taught that Paul had a physical disease of some sort – usually they mention a potential "eye disease" because of a comment Paul makes in a different letter to the Galatians. It's just a guess that people have made; the truth is none of us really know if he had an eye problem or not.

Let's take a look at the "thorn in the flesh" account in 2 Corinthians 12:7–10:

> 7 And lest I should be exalted above measure by the abundance of the revelations, a thorn in the flesh was given to me, a messenger of Satan to buffet me, lest I be exalted above measure. 8 Concerning this thing I pleaded with the Lord three times that it might depart

from me. 9 And He said to me, "My grace is sufficient
for you, for My strength is made perfect in weakness."
Therefore most gladly I will rather boast in my infirmities, that the power of Christ may rest upon me. 10
Therefore I take pleasure in infirmities, in reproaches,
in needs, in persecutions, in distresses, for Christ's
sake. For when I am weak, then I am strong. (NKJV)

This passage follows right after Paul relates his vision of Heaven
and talks about how he he heard things there he can't even repeat.
But right after he relates this experience in verses 1–6, it is then that
he jumps into verse 7 and says that he was given a thorn in the flesh
lest he be exalted above measure because of the incredible revela-
tions he had. People have been arguing for centuries about what the
thorn in the flesh is. Many assume because it mentions that it was
"in the flesh" that it was a bodily ailment. However, the word for
"flesh" there is the Greek word "sarx" (transliterated) which doesn't
necessarily just refer to the physical body itself but our makeup as
humans in this fallen world – in other words it can include our
mind/will/emotions. Notice that nowhere in this passage does it say
God gave Paul a sickness or a disease.

The passage plainly tells us what the thorn in the flesh is, and
you almost have to have help from some well-meaning pastor or
theologian that wants to claim it is a disease in order to miss it. It
says right in the text in verse 7 that the thorn in the flesh was "a
messenger of Satan" that buffeted/harassed Paul. In other words,
Paul was experiencing some serious demonic oppression and harassment. This oppression could have taken a variety of forms, but to
read into this anything relating to sickness or disease is to go beyond what this scripture says. If we take it at face value, it clearly
tells us what the thorn is and that's all we have to go on.

If you've ever really experienced demonic oppression, then you
know that often the form this takes is in your mind – thinking
thoughts or lies originating from the devil. I'm just throwing this out
there, but could it be that given the fact that the whole purpose was
to keep Paul from getting too puffed up after his incredible heavenly vision/experience, that he experienced being constantly reminded

by this demon of all the mistakes he had made in his life (such as when he formerly persecuted Christians)? Just using pure logic, given that we're told what the purpose of the demonic oppression is, that type of thinking makes MUCH more sense than to try to claim there was some sickness or disease involved. If the problem is Paul might get too puffed up in himself because of his incredible experiences, then being reminded of his failures and mistakes to keep him in check makes more logical sense then bringing some disease into the picture. Right?

Paul didn't like this demonic harassment one bit and asked the Lord three times for that oppressing demon to depart from him. Jesus' response was that His grace was sufficient for Paul and that in Paul's weakness, His power is made perfect. The Lord did not tell Paul "no"; He told him that His grace was sufficient – basically that Paul could trust in the Lord's grace for him to be enough. Thus, in verses 9–10, Paul is willing to boast of weaknesses of all types because it is in that place that Christ's power is able to show itself strong on his behalf.

These are true statements when talking about any weakness on our part of any type. It is true that when we are weak in ourselves (regardless of the issue or cause, whether demonic oppression like Paul had or not) that we can look to Jesus and draw on His grace – His strength. This is absolutely true, even *when* dealing with sickness. When we are weak in sickness, we can draw on Christ's strength; we can also receive the healing grace that He has for us (we'll explore this more later).

Also, I don't know about you, but I have asked God for things before that I thought I wanted Him to do and He's given me answers similar to Paul. Rather than telling me that He would do what I wanted, I'll hear Him tell me to just trust Him or to just rest in Him – in essence to find my strength in Him and His grace. God isn't really interested in being a magic genie for us; He's interested in really being in deep relationship and fellowship with us. There are times where what we think we're after isn't really as important as just diving into the fellowship with Him and drawing on His power. As we do that, THEN we often discover the situation is taken care of. Sometimes it's a matter of "first things first."

Getting back to God's sovereignty though, in the "thorn in the flesh" account, we do apparently see God allowing demonic activity in Paul's life; I don't really see a way around that – it says what it says. This brings us to another really important point though that I think many haven't considered. If God allowed this in Paul's life because He knew that with where Paul was at, Paul would get conceited and prideful which would hinder what God wanted to do with Paul (i.e. the plans and purposes God had for Paul), then was God being mean to Paul or good to Paul to allow this oppression in the big picture? The answer, of course, is good. We can get angry at God for allowing something evil that God actually is using in our life to do something good. In saying this, I know that some of the "faith camps" in the Church will get on me for saying this, but it is true. I've already stated (and intend to prove) that God is NOT putting any sickness or disease on Christians. But He DOES allow sickness and disease in the lives of Christians. As already discussed, God usually gets the blame when the originator is the devil and/or us. But God will allow it. Now that doesn't mean it's His will for us. God wants us whole in every respect. But God can use sickness, just as He can use anything else, in our lives to help bring about a greater purpose in fulfillment of His will for us of wholeness in every respect.

A personal example: In my life as a Christian I struggled for years with addiction. I also had a lot of emotional hurts and pain where I was very sick in my soul stemming from things such as rejection in my childhood. I also have had serious struggles with physical sickness. Often I had intense battles in all three of these areas raging at the same time or in the same timeframe. It is my personal testimony that God, while not causing my emotional hurts, addictions, or physical sickness, has at different times used one of those things to bring about a greater good in another. For instance, He has used physical sickness to draw out things (such as fear) that have helped provide healing to me in the emotional realm. He's used the results of the addictions to bring healing in the emotional realm. I can also say that He has used physical sickness to help bring healing in regards to the addictions. The reason I'm saying all of this is that some pastors or teachers teach that God does not use sickness or disease in a person's life. And I'm sorry, but I have to disagree. He can, and He does. That doesn't make Him "bad", it makes Him "good!" He works with us where we are at to bring about the full healing He desires for us. God wants us well in *every* area of our lives!

Sometimes well-meaning people get too myopic in their view, but God is looking at the total picture. He doesn't want us physically sick, He doesn't want us emotionally sick, and He doesn't want us beholden to addictions or sin of any kind, but He will work with us where we are at. Again, I'm NOT saying that God causes any of these things to teach us lessons – this is a key mistake that many pastors and teachers have made in their teaching on this subject. But He will work with us where we are at, which means He can definitely use sickness, just as any number of other things, in fulfillment of His will of wholeness in every area of our being.

But make no mistake about it: God DOES want us well. He is a good God who desires what is best for us – and health and wholeness are what's best for us! The fact that God will work with us where we are at doesn't mean we should just sit back passively and say: "well, God's will be done." No, it means we actively engage with God to take hold of health and wholeness and move forward! THAT is God's will!

God gets an awful bad rap for having caused sicknesses, deaths, disasters, and evil of all types that we see in this world. And the sad thing is that Christians have often times been the ones pointing the fingers. This morning I turned on the radio and heard a sermon from a well-known American pastor. His message was extremely blunt in saying that God causes sickness and disease and that what we need to do is come to a point where we are willing to in a sense, forgive God. No, that was not a typo. He said that God assumes responsibility Himself for every sickness and disease and that what we need to do is come to a place where we "hold God accountable" by realizing His role in causing bad things in our life and then in a sense forgive Him for what we consider are those wrongs that He's committed. This is absolute nonsense of the highest order! He based his view on some wrong interpretations of certain passages of Scripture and failed to consider numerous other passages. Again, this was a

well-known, popular pastor in America that many look to for spiritual direction and insight.[4] This is the kind of stuff that's out there.
Not only does God get blamed for evil, but incredibly some Christian pastors are leading the charge! We need to stop blaming God
for what is the result of our choices (now and going all the way
back to the Garden) as well as the work of satan.

One of the reasons it is so easy for us to blame God is because
our emotions are involved. It HURTS to watch a loved one die of
some disease or get killed in a car crash or whatever the case may
be. It hurts for ourselves to be really sick. There is usually a lot of
pain involved with sickness and death. Friends, I was a caregiver
for both of my parents that had cancer. I KNOW what it feels like to
watch someone you love be in terrible pain. I KNOW what it feels
like to have someone that you are closer to than anyone else on this
planet not be here any more. I KNOW what it feels like to have terrible struggles with your own health. I KNOW what it feels like to
have been rejected and hurt by others for years on end. I know pain;
I know it real well. Perhaps you can identify also.

But you know what else I know? I know that God didn't cause
any of it! People did. And the devil did as people gave place to him.
But God certainly did not! Sickness was never God's will for us.
Death was never God's will for us. Children being hurt was never
God's will for us. And each one of us have to come to a place where
we are able to reconcile this world of hurt and pain and sickness
with a God that the Bible portrays is good and is for us.

It is understandable that people get angry when sickness or death
touches them – after all, it really hurts. It IS terrible. All the sickness and death that we see absolutely IS HORRIBLE! And when we
are forced to come face to face with it, a natural response to our
pain is anger, and usually the one that this anger gets directed at is
God because we know He has the power to have prevented it.

But this is why we have to watch letting our emotions rule the
day. There is a very reasoned and rational explanation according to
the Bible for why things are as they are as I've shown in this chapter. I know that it doesn't take away the pain. But if you let it, it will
help put that pain in its proper context. We have to set aside some
of the emotions so that they don't cloud our vision. If we let emo-

tions overrule, it can be easy to get bitter at God, or even just be subtly distrusting of Him.

God is good. The devil is bad. Do not confuse the two.

Chapter 3 – God Wants Us Well

Simply based on the chapter title alone, I can already hear some people thinking: "Wait a minute! So you're saying emphatically that God wants people well?" Why yes, yes I am.

> Beloved, I wish above all things that thou mayest prosper and be in health, even as thy soul prospereth. (3 John 2 KJV)

Now all cards on the table, this isn't God speaking in this verse. It is the Apostle John writing to a fellow believer. However, if this is John's desire, as a human being, for a fellow believer in the Lord, doesn't it stand to reason then how much more this would be God's desire for us as believers in Jesus? Do we think that John has better desires than God Himself?

God desires us well and to be prospering in every respect. He desires good things for us. Yet, it is amazing that when someone makes a statement like that, many times people immediately start trying to come up with exceptions or reasons why that cannot be. "Well, God doesn't *always* want us healthy." Or, "God doesn't *really* want me to always prosper." Part of the reason we react this way is that many of us have been taught to be wary of the so-called "Health, Wealth, & Prosperity Gospel." And a large part of that is because of the way things have been presented for years by certain people, including some who have been on Christian television. I'm just going to say upfront that I completely understand – I've seen & heard plenty of nonsense and it turns me off just the same as it probably does you.

The other reason why we naturally kind of rebel against a statement that God wants us well and prospering is because of our own experiences and the experiences of those we love. We all have been sick and experienced lack in any number of areas. So if someone comes along and tells us that God desires us well and healthy and prospering, there's a part of us that has trouble reconciling that with the experience that we've had, and so we just tend to naturally dismiss it out-of-hand.

While I certainly understand, I'm going to ask that we just kind of set all of this stuff aside for now. Let's just focus together on Jesus and the Word.

We'll zero in more on the prospering thing in a later chapter, but for now I'd like to spend some time looking at this notion of God wanting us healthy.

God does want us well – and Jesus proves it.

The Book of Hebrews, speaking of Jesus, opens with the following passage:

> Long ago, at many times and in many ways, God spoke to our fathers by the prophets, but in these last days he has spoken to us by his Son, whom he appointed the heir of all things, through whom also he created the world. He is the radiance of the glory of God and the exact imprint of his nature, and he upholds the universe by the word of his power. After making purification for sins, he sat down at the right hand of the Majesty on high, (Hebrews 1:1–3 ESV)

This passage tells us several important things. First it tells us that while prior to Jesus' coming, God primarily spoke to humanity through prophets, now in these days we are living in, Jesus Himself is how He has spoken to us. What Jesus said and what Jesus did – everything about Him is meant to speak to us. Among other things, this passage also tells us that Jesus is the "exact imprint of his nature" – speaking of God the Father. The King James Version says that He is the "express image of his person." Colossians 1:15 refers to Jesus as the "image of the invisible God" and Jesus Himself told us that those that have seen Him, have seen the Father (John 14:9). The point being that when we look at Jesus, we can KNOW what God the Father is like. We can know God by looking at the life of Jesus.

So, for instance, if we want to know what God thinks about sin, we can look to Jesus and see what Jesus said and did in regards to sin. If we want to know whether it is God's will for people to sin, we can look to Jesus and find out. Likewise, if we want to know what God thinks about healing, we can look to Jesus and see what He said and did in regards to healing. And if we want to know whether it is God's will for people to be sick, we can look to Jesus and find out. And it just so happens that Jesus said and did a whole lot on this subject. In fact, quite a bit of the gospels are dedicated to it.

A whole lot of people were healed by Jesus and it obviously was important to God that a number of these healings get recorded. God could have just put a one-liner that said "Jesus healed a whole lot of people." But, He went much farther than that and gave us a bunch of representative examples. Each of them, just as with the rest of the Word, tells us things that are important.

When it comes to Jesus and healing, there is one crucial point. There is no record of anyone, not one person, coming to Jesus for healing and Him turning them away without their receiving their healing. We never read of Jesus telling someone that "It's God's will for you to be sick." We never read of Jesus telling someone "God wants you sick – He's trying to teach you things – just submit to the sickness." We never read that – not once. We don't have any record of anybody coming to Jesus for healing that did not receive their healing. Sometimes Jesus would push them a little bit – usually to draw out and get them exercising their faith, but the end-result we read is that they were healed.

We also never see Jesus asking the Father if it is God's will to heal someone that came to Him. We never see Him praying, as much of the church world does, "Father, if it be Your will, heal." Jesus tells us in John 5:30 that "I can do nothing on my own. As I hear, I judge, and my judgment is just, because I seek not my own will but the will of him who sent me." (ESV). Jesus looked to the will of the Father to do all that He did. And yet, we never see Jesus questioning the Father's will in regards to healing. We never see Him using this "if it be Your will" stuff – no, Jesus *knew* it was the Father's will to heal.

The only time we have record of Jesus being point-blank asked if He was willing to heal, He replied affirmatively:

40 Now a leper came to Him, imploring Him, kneeling down to Him and saying to Him, "If You are willing, You can make me clean."

41 Then Jesus, moved with compassion, stretched out *His* hand and touched him, and said to him, "I am willing; be cleansed." 42 As soon as He had spoken, immediately the leprosy left him, and he was cleansed. (Mark 1:40–42 NKJV)

The leper basically asked Jesus if He was willing and Jesus clearly responded that He was.

Just on the basis of the clear examples in the gospels of Jesus healing people and expressing His will to heal, combined with the fact that Jesus is the "exact imprint" of the nature of the Father, this alone shows us that God wants people healthy; God wants people well. It's part of His nature – His person.

Some believers argue that the reason that Jesus performed so many healings was only because He wanted to prove that He was the Messiah so people would believe in Him so they could have their sins forgiven. In other words, that it wasn't so much about the healings themselves, but about proving who He was so that people, by believing in Him, could have their sins forgiven and go to Heaven someday. Certainly there is some truth in that – a purpose for the healings was to show that Jesus was the Messiah. But that wasn't the *only* purpose. Another purpose is because He just genuinely wanted to see people well and healthy. Notice in the Mark 1 account above, that in verse 41 it says that Jesus was "moved with compassion" when He looked at the leper. It was out of that compassion that Jesus stretched forth His hand and brought physical healing to this man. We see this phrase elsewhere also. In Matthew 14:14 we read, "And Jesus went forth, and saw a great multitude, and was moved with compassion toward them, and he healed their sick." (KJV). People that were sick touched the heart of Jesus. He cared about the fact that they were sick and He wanted them well. There's no doubt that He cared about their eternal souls, but He also clearly cared about their physical bodies. Jesus loved people, and He was willing and desiring to heal them physically.

Acts 10:38, speaking of Jesus, tells us that "...God anointed Jesus of Nazareth with the Holy Ghost and with power: who went about doing good, and healing all that were oppressed of the devil; for God was with him." (Acts 10:38b KJV). Jesus went about doing good and healing people. Notice two important things from this passage: (1) healing is shown to be good, and (2) that it was the devil that had oppressed people in regards to sickness, not God. Jesus wanted people well and healthy. The devil wanted them sick.

In Luke 13:10–17 we read of an account of a woman that was bent over and couldn't straighten herself up for 18 years. After the religious leaders of the day got on His case for healing her on the Sabbath, Jesus said this in verse 16: "And ought not this woman, being a daughter of Abraham, whom Satan hath bound, lo, these eighteen years, be loosed from this bond on the sabbath day?" (KJV). Notice who had done the binding (Satan). And notice who did the loosing in bringing healing (Jesus).

One of Jesus' disciples, John, tells us: "For this purpose the Son of God was manifested, that he might destroy the works of the devil." (1 John 3:8b KJV) Just from the previous two scriptures we can see that sickness is a work of the devil. Jesus came to destroy the works of the devil. Jesus wants people well.

Back to the woman in Luke 13 that was bent over: Notice that part of the rationale Jesus gave for why this woman should receive healing in verse 16 is because she was a "daughter of Abraham." This is a very easy thing to gloss over, but it is very important. He didn't refer to her as a "daughter of Moses" or even a "daughter of Israel"; He referred to her as a "daughter of Abraham." Why? Before we answer that, let's look at another account.

In Matthew 15:21–28 and Mark 7:24–30, we find a Gentile woman seeking healing from Jesus for her daughter. You have to remember that this is prior to Jesus going to the cross. As a Gentile, she was not in a covenant relationship with God and did not have the promises that the Jewish people had. Jesus knew this, and He knew that His ministry at this time was to the people of Israel. Unlike the woman that was bent over that Jesus said should be healed because she was a "daughter of Abraham", with this Gentile woman, Jesus says no such thing. In fact, He says something very different. In Matthew 15:26, Jesus tells the woman, "It is not right to take the children's bread and throw it to the dogs." (Matt. 15:26b ESV). Now, you're probably thinking, "Did Jesus just call this lady a dog?" And although I've heard differing explanations, it clearly says what it says, so yes I believe He basically did. But it wasn't really an attack on her – it is clear that Jesus wasn't being malicious from the way He goes on to interact with her. What He was doing was using an analogy to explain that He was sent first to the Jewish people, who were God's chosen people in a covenant with God, and that you don't take what is theirs and give it to people that don't have that special relationship. Now, even in the face of this, this woman didn't give up and Jesus ends up commending her faith and her daughter was healed.

There's a whole lot that could be said about that, but what I want to focus on is this "children's bread" phrase. In the context, Jesus could have been talking specifically about Himself as the "children's bread." But an equally possible scenario in my opinion is that He was referring (at least partially) to healing as the "children's bread." In other words, that healing is for His children. Either way, given the fact that this was His response to the woman seeking healing, it really doesn't matter much, since the overarching context was one of healing. He essentially told her that healing was for the children of God.

This corroborates what He said when He stated in Luke 13 that one reason the bent-over woman should be healed was because she was a "daughter of Abraham." Jesus was making clear that healing was a right for God's chosen people. Now, in the Old Covenant, while this was a right, it was conditional (see Deuteronomy 7:15, Exodus 23:25, Exodus 15:26) just as a whole lot of other things were conditional. But in the New Covenant, everything is based on Jesus. Jesus was the game changer as rather than everything being based on our performance, it is based on Jesus' performance and our faith in Him. It's based on faith!

We are told the following in Romans 2:28–29:

> 28 For no one is a Jew who is merely one outwardly,
> nor is circumcision outward and physical. 29 But a Jew
> is one inwardly, and circumcision is a matter of the
> heart, by the Spirit, not by the letter. His praise is not
> from man but from God. (ESV)

Being a Jew isn't just about physical things but an inward issue
of the heart. Paul goes on throughout much of the book of Romans
to make the case that the real issue is, and always has been, one of
faith.

In Romans 4, we are told this about Abraham:

> ... that he might be the father of all those who believe,
> though they are uncircumcised, that righteousness
> might be imputed to them also, 12 and the father of cir-
> cumcision to those who not only *are* of the
> circumcision, but who also walk in the steps of the
> faith which our father Abraham *had while still* uncir-
> cumcised. (Romans 4:11b–12 NKJV)

In other words, as Gentile believers in Jesus Christ, though we
may not be physical descendants of Abraham (with the sign of cir-
cumcision), Abraham is still the father of ALL who believe, whether
Jew or Gentile. Paul makes the case in Romans chapter 4 that just
as Abraham was justified by His faith prior to the sign of circumci-
sion, so everyone who is justified by faith now are in essence sons
and daughters of Abraham, who modeled this faith for us. He gets
even more bluntly clear in Galatians 3:7, saying, "Know ye therefore that they which are of faith, the same are the children of
Abraham." (KJV) And Galatians 3:29 which says, "And if you are
Christ's, then you are Abraham's offspring, heirs according to promise." (ESV)

Jesus gave, as a rationale for why the bent-over woman should
be healed, the fact that she was a "daughter of Abraham." Biblically, as believers in Jesus Christ, we also are sons and daughters of
Abraham, which means that the same rationale applies to us.

Likewise, Jesus told the woman seeking healing for her daughter that healing was the "children's bread." As believers in Jesus, while through our faith we in a sense become Abraham's children since He modeled that faith for us, we are also told in the Scriptures that we are actually God's children.

> 15 For you did not receive the spirit of bondage again to fear, but you received the Spirit of adoption by whom we cry out, "Abba, Father." 16 The Spirit Himself bears witness with our spirit that we are children of God, (Romans 8:15–16 NKJV)

If we are the children of God, and healing is the "children's bread", then that means healing is ours! It is for us!

The reason that the Gentile woman's daughter was healed is because, even though she was not a Jew, she appealed to the greater law of faith – the same faith that Abraham exhibited. This is why Jesus ended up commending her faith for being great. By exercising her faith in Jesus, it overcame any obstacle, even the fact that she was not a Jew. Likewise, as believers in Jesus Christ who are not physically Jewish in ethnicity, through our faith in Jesus Christ, we can exercise our faith just as this woman did. But actually we've got something one step further than she had – we've got God's declaration in His Word that as believers in Jesus, we *are* His children! And as His children, healing is ours!

So if you've been sick or dealing with a disease or illness (no matter whether big or small) and thinking that God maybe wants that for you, think again. God does NOT want His children sick or ill in any way. His will on this is clearly expressed in the person of Jesus.

So where does this leave us now? You may be thinking to yourself: "Well, it's nice that Jesus cared about people and touched them and healed them when He was on this earth, but He's not here now! If only He could touch me now, I would be healed, but He's not here." The implication is that we are then "out of luck" since we didn't live when Jesus was here. Nothing could be further from the truth!

[Note: If, as you were reading this chapter, you thought of one or more specific Scriptural instances that might contradict the idea that God wants people well, you can cheat and take a side detour if you would like and read Chapter 15 ("Overcoming Objections") before continuing on. Otherwise, it is MUCH better to wait to read that chapter when you get there and forget I ever brought this up. :)
]

Chapter 4 – Atoned

In the previous chapter we looked at the fact that Jesus healed people while He was on the earth and that He showcased the will of God in regards to healing. But the natural question arises then, "What about us now?" After all, we weren't there when Jesus was doing His healing. Is it just "tough luck" for us?

When Jesus was here on this earth, while He healed people physically, He also forgave people's sins. In Luke 7:48 we find Him telling a woman, "Your sins are forgiven." (NKJV). We are specifically told that it was her faith that brought this about as Jesus tells her in verse 50, "Your faith has saved you." (NKJV). In Mark 2:5, we find Jesus similarly telling a paralytic, "Son, your sins are forgiven you." (NKJV). And again, faith is identified as a reason.

So, while Jesus was physically here on this earth, He forgave people's sins. Let me ask you a question if I may? Since you and I weren't physically around when Jesus was here on this earth, how did we get our sins forgiven? The answer of course is that it is through our faith in Jesus being the Messiah and what He accomplished for us. We are looking back to the finished work of Jesus on the cross and it is through our faith in Him that we receive forgiveness of sins. Forgiveness of sins was available to those while Jesus was here, and it is available to us now. It didn't "pass away" when Jesus died and rose again and then left this earth, but it was actually cemented as being available for all of us still to come through Jesus' death and resurrection. Right?

Likewise, physical healing was available to people while Jesus was here, and I am about to prove that it is available to us now in the exact same way that forgiveness of sins is.

In the Old Testament book of Isaiah, one of the most fascinating chapters is chapter 53, which gives prophecy concerning Jesus. See the following in verses 4–5:

> 4 Surely He has borne our griefs
> And carried our sorrows;
> Yet we esteemed Him stricken,
> Smitten by God, and afflicted.

> 5 But He *was* wounded for our transgressions,
> *He was* bruised for our iniquities;
> The chastisement for our peace *was* upon Him,
> And by His stripes we are healed. (Isaiah 53:4–5
> NKJV)

The chapter goes on to say a bunch more related to Christ's atonement for us – if you haven't read it or haven't read it in awhile, I'd recommend a read-through of the chapter.

For years I had heard people that claimed that physical healing was purchased for us by Jesus, quote these two verses and declare that, "By Jesus' stripes, we are healed." Perhaps you've heard this as well. I never really understood that, and actually thought it a stretch to claim that, because the text mentions "griefs", "sorrows", "transgressions", and "iniquities", but doesn't on the surface seem to refer anything to physical healing. I grew up in parts of the Body that essentially taught that when it says that we are healed by Jesus' stripes (or wounds) that that is referring to a "spiritual healing" – that we are healed by Jesus spiritually. I was taught that it had nothing to do with physical healing.

But then one day that nice little theory that I had heard about how it was only referencing spiritual healing got completely blown up – and by the Bible no less. The Bible actually gives us a commentary on part of what was meant by Isaiah 53:4–5. From the Gospel of Matthew, speaking of Jesus, we read:

> 16 When evening had come, they brought to Him many who were demon-possessed. And He cast out the spirits with a word, and healed all who were sick, 17 that it might be fulfilled which was spoken by Isaiah the prophet, saying:
>
> "He Himself took our infirmities
> And bore *our* sicknesses." (Matthew 8:16–17 NKJV)

The ESV version of the Bible renders verse 17 as:

17 This was to fulfill what was spoken by the prophet Isaiah: "He took our illnesses and bore our diseases." (Matthew 8:17 ESV)

It turns out that the word translated "griefs" in Isaiah 53:4 also can be translated as "sicknesses" or "diseases." In fact, there are a few notable versions of the Bible such as the CSB (HCSB) and YLT that do indeed render Isaiah 53:4 with "sicknesses" in place of griefs. And some other popular translations, such as the ESV, mention this fact in the footnotes. [By the way, just a sidenote, but the same issue with the word "griefs" also occurs in verse 3 where we are told that Jesus was acquainted with sickness].

You might be wondering what the point is. Stay with me, because this is all crucial. Much of the Isaiah 53 chapter describes the atoning work of Jesus. In part of its prophecy it declares that Jesus bore our sicknesses. And Matthew 8:16–17 validates this by telling us that when Jesus was healing people that were sick, it fulfilled what Isaiah had said. The clear implication by this is that when you read Isaiah 53:4–5 where it tells us that Jesus bore our sicknesses and also that "by His stripes we are healed" (Isaiah 53:5b NKJV) that at least given the context of Matthew 8:16–17, that can easily, at least partly, be taken to mean healing in a physical sense. Scripture interprets Scripture – and the Matthew passage directly informs us about Isaiah 53:4, and by extension also Isaiah 53:5, since they both are one clearly linked thought (not to mention that verse divisions didn't exist in the Scriptures when they were written).

After Jesus' death and resurrection, we are given some further insight by the Apostle Peter. Speaking of Jesus, 1 Peter 2:24 says:

who Himself bore our sins in His own body on the tree, that we, having died to sins, might live for righteousness—by whose stripes you were healed. (1 Peter 2:24 NKJV)

In this account, Peter discusses how our sins were borne by Jesus and it is within this context that he makes reference to the Isaiah 53 text by stating that by Jesus' stripes we were healed. So here the context is in reference to sin, not physical healing. So, which is it? It's both! Healing is healing – whether that's in a physical sense or a spiritual sense. Matthew and Peter both reference the same basic portion of Isaiah 53, and one of them applies it physically, and the other spiritually. In fact, I intend to make the case going forward that throughout the Bible there really isn't nearly as much differentiation on this stuff as people like to think. People have drawn these lines and one camp will say that verse X only applies to healing in a spiritual sense and another camp will say that it only applies to healing physically. And I intend to show that throughout the Bible, both camps are usually right (and wrong at the same time) because it isn't an "only" situation. Anyway, we'll get there shortly, but for now, even if you're not yet convinced, humor me if you would by just supposing that I'm right on this.

I have to point out though that the word "healed" that is used in 1 Peter 2:24 is the Greek word "iaómai" (transliterated). This same Greek word is found in 28 other verses in the New Testament and almost always is referencing physical healing. For example, Luke 6:17 tells us of a multitude of people that came to hear Jesus and be healed of their diseases. We are told: "And all the crowd sought to touch him, for power came out from him and healed them all." (Luke 6:19 ESV). The word "healed" in verse 19 is the same Greek word "iaómai" that is used in 1 Peter 2:24 when it tells us "by whose stripes you were healed." (NKJV).

The point of all of this is that in the entire chapter of Isaiah 53, which describes the atonement and surrounding events, we see both sin and sickness mentioned together in its description of the atoning work of Jesus. I also have to mention that verse 4 of Isaiah 53, which is the part clearly dealing with sickness, is started with the word "Surely." In other words, "you can take this to the bank!" It's telling us "Listen up – this is important – SURELY He has borne our sicknesses – you can bank on this being true!" If we believe that every word in the Bible is important, then the placement of that word "Surely" is important too.

There's something else very interesting I'd like to bring out about these three passages we've looked at (Isaiah 53:4–5, Matthew 8:16–

17, and 1 Peter 2:24). This gets a little complicated, but is important.

Isaiah, speaking prophetically of the future and what would be accomplished by Jesus, actually speaks of what Jesus did in the past tense. It says in Isaiah 53:4 that "He HAS borne" (NKJV, emphasis mine) our sicknesses. And that out of what He has DONE, then we ARE healed ("... by His stripes we are healed" Isaiah 53:5b NKJV). I know this is confusing, but in other words, it's a future prophecy describing a present-tense reality of healing that comes out of what Jesus has already done (in the past).

Matthew seeks to show us that as Jesus is healing people, He is fulfilling what Isaiah said about Jesus bearing our sicknesses. In other words, that the present-tense events with Jesus are fulfilling Isaiah's prophecy that uses past-tense verbiage. So, as Jesus IS (present-tense) bearing our sicknesses, then He is also necessarily fulfilling Isaiah's past-tense verbiage.

Peter is writing from a perspective after Jesus' death and resurrection – after the present-tense events that Matthew records (at which Peter was an eye-witness, having been one of the 12 disciples with Jesus). When he refers to Isaiah, he mentions it in the past tense. Notice in 1 Peter 2:24 that it says "... by whose stripes you WERE healed." (1 Peter 2:24b NKJV, emphasis mine). It changed from "are" to "were" because Peter is looking back. In the context of what Peter is talking about in regards to our sins being borne by Jesus, when did that occur? Answer: On the cross, as Peter himself says in that verse. Peter tells us that Jesus "bore our sins in His own body on the tree," (1 Peter 2:24b NKJV).

Now, while Jesus paid the penalty for our sins on the cross, you might recall earlier in this chapter that I gave some examples where Jesus forgave people's sins before He had gone to the cross. Jesus told some people that their sins were forgiven them (through their faith in Him) even though He hadn't yet actually gone to the cross and paid for it. It was almost like what we might think of as "layaway" – they received the benefits now because of the surety of the future payment.

Likewise, we are told in the gospels that Jesus healed people physically while He was here. But when you combine that with the picture of the work of the atonement as portrayed in Isaiah 53, and then you further combine that with 1 Peter 2:24, you are left with the clear picture that healing was paid for by Jesus in the atonement.

Just as we today are looking back to the finished work of Jesus on the cross to receive forgiveness of sins, we also are looking back to the same finished work in order to receive healing. By Jesus' stripes, we WERE – already done – healed. In every respect. It's a done fact. The only issue is one of faith: What are we willing to believe? If a person believes that what's available to them through the cross is only forgiveness of sins, then that is all that they will receive because that's all they've appropriated of Jesus' gift in their life. As awesome as that alone is, there is more available. For those who can accept it, more is to be had... (And actually it goes beyond just forgiveness of sins and healing – as a whole the church has greatly limited and undervalued what Jesus purchased for us across-the-board, and this is a primary reason why we haven't been walking in much victory.)

Forgiveness of sins was available to people while Jesus was here, and it is available to us now. It didn't "pass away" when Jesus died and rose again and then left this earth, but it was actually cemented as being available for all of us that were still to come through Jesus' death and resurrection. Likewise, healing was available to people while Jesus was here, and it is available to us now. It also didn't "pass away." It is still very much available.

If healing is a part of what Jesus has provided for us in the atonement, then that means that it's our right as believers in Jesus. Now there can be all sorts of reasons why Christians don't experience healing, and we'll explore many of them later on in this book. But one of them, without a doubt, is simply that many don't know what is theirs to have! Just as getting "saved" in the sense of receiving forgiveness of sins requires you to understand and agree to that – at least on a basic level – and exercise faith, the same is also true of healing. If one doesn't really believe that healing is something provided by Jesus that's accessible to us by our faith, then it will not profit them. Just as appropriating what Jesus did in regards to forgiving sin requires active participation on our part by exercising our faith and doesn't just come automatically to us, the same is true in regards to healing. It requires an active response as well.

There will be further expounding on all of this later, but hopefully you are now at least partially convinced that it's not only God's will for you to be well, but also that it is your right as a child of God through your faith in Jesus and His sacrifice on your behalf. If not, that is okay – we are just getting started friends.

Chapter 5 – A Fresh Look At Communion

We last left off discussing how Isaiah 53, which describes the atoning work of Jesus for humanity, mentions both sins and sicknesses as a part of what Jesus addressed for us. Once you understand this, all of a sudden a bunch of other things in Scripture start taking on a whole other dimension. One such item is that of communion.

Now, I recognize that different branches of the Body of Christ teach different things regarding communion. To many, communion is an act solely of remembering Christ's work for us. To others, it also involves the elements actually mysteriously becoming the body and blood of Jesus as we partake. And there's some other views as well. I'm not going to get in the middle of that debate right now. However, I would like us to look at a few things. First, let's read through part of the communion-related account as given in 1 Corinthians 11:23–26:

> 23 For I received from the Lord that which I also delivered to you: that the Lord Jesus on the *same* night in which He was betrayed took bread; 24 and when He had given thanks, He broke *it* and said, "Take, eat; this is My body which is broken for you; do this in remembrance of Me." 25 In the same manner *He* also *took* the cup after supper, saying, "This cup is the new covenant in My blood. This do, as often as you drink *it*, in remembrance of Me." 26 For as often as you eat this bread and drink this cup, you proclaim the Lord's death till He comes. (NKJV)

This part of 1 Corinthians 11 is commonly quoted in many churches. However, this actually isn't the end of what it says on the subject. Most churches stop their reading/quoting with verse 25 or 26. However, let's pick up the continuation of what is said in verse 27 and we'll take it through verse 32:

27 Therefore whoever eats this bread or drinks *this* cup of the Lord in an unworthy manner will be guilty of the body and blood of the Lord. 28 But let a man examine himself, and so let him eat of the bread and drink of the cup. 29 For he who eats and drinks in an unworthy manner eats and drinks judgment to himself, not discerning the Lord's body. 30 For this reason many *are* weak and sick among you, and many sleep. 31 For if we would judge ourselves, we would not be judged. 32 But when we are judged, we are chastened by the Lord, that we may not be condemned with the world. (1 Corinthians 11:27–32 NKJV)

You don't often hear these verses quoted, or at least I sure haven't. And yet, there's something obviously extremely vital in this portion. I direct your attention to verses 29–30. It equates taking communion in an "unworthy manner" by not "discerning the Lord's body" as being a reason that many (not some, but "many") believers are sick and have died (when it says "sleep" it is referring to them having died). Wait just a minute! If this is true, this alone should mean that churches should be taking communion MUCH more serious than most do, both in their instruction and in practice. I don't know about your experiences, but in many of my church experiences, communion has often been done in a fairly cavalier fashion – sometimes even almost coming across as an afterthought.

Whether once a week, once every other week, or as is seemingly more common these days, once a month, it often is relegated to this short little blurb where the pastor reads a short line or two (perhaps from 1 Corinthians 11:23–26) and we sing a song or two while people partake (often at their leisure). The whole attitude that's conveyed is usually one that's very laid-back. And yet, these verses paint a whole different picture. Communion is not supposed to be taken nearly as lightly as many churches take it. Somehow the Church has gone from getting together on a regular basis with fellow believers to partake of communion apparently in eating a meal (1 Cor. 17–22 and 33–34) to spending 5–10 minutes once a month at the end of a service while people come forward and (often, individually) partake of a wafer or small piece of bread and a sip of juice or wine. My point isn't in saying that I think we need to go back to doing a full meal (although this was the case when Jesus instituted it and seems to be what the early church did...), but I am just making a general statement that as a whole it seems the Church has gotten away from some of what communion was really intended to be. It's become a formulaic, "thing we do", but is missing the heart and importance of it. It's become just a ritual we Christians do, and one that many haven't put a whole lot of thought into as to exactly why we do it and what it's really about.

If the manner of taking communion can have an effect on my physical health and possibly even lead to me dying, that's kind of a serious thing, don't you think? Again, this passage is directed at Christians – people that say they love Jesus. It's not addressing heathen outside the church! And it tells us that many Christians are weak, sick, and have died because of the way this whole communion thing is handled. That's serious, is it not?

Since none of us want that to be the case in our lives, the question we need to answer is what does it mean to take communion in an "unworthy manner" and to be "not discerning the Lord's body?" Many people have taken this to mean that we need to make sure we confess all our sins. Thus, communion becomes less a time of remembrance of Jesus (which is what Jesus told us it was for) and more a time to "confess everything and get right with God once again." The focus subtly shifts from Jesus and what He has provided for us, to ourselves and what we've done wrong.

Now, this doesn't mean that there's not a place for this to a degree. We are told to examine ourselves (vs. 28) and the whole context of these communion passages is a church where people were not acting right towards one another. 1 Corinthians 11:17–22 showcases that in the Corinthian church there were divisions among the members, where those that had a lot materially and were popular in the sight of people were honored, while those that didn't have anything were shamed. We see a church where people put their own needs and wants above their fellow brothers and sisters. This was the immediate context of the communion passages shared earlier. Thus, this type of behavior would seem to at least partially be what

Paul was referring to when he refers to partaking in an "unworthy manner." The divisions and positioning for prestige in our churches may not get drawn out as much as the Corinthian church in regards to communion because the way we partake it is so different (including often being much more individualistic), but it is still very much there in many churches.

The issue with the Corinthian church wasn't just that they were not acting right towards one another, but that they were missing the whole point of communion. They should have treated it as a holy (set apart) time to get together to corporately remember what Jesus did for them. The focus was to be on Jesus and the cross, and yet they were missing that by all of their fleshly nonsense that was going on. That is why Paul then goes on to remind them exactly what communion is and what it is for.

For us today, while we should be examining ourselves, communion was never intended to be "your one-stop confess all your sins for the week or the month to get in God's good graces" event. The purpose of communion isn't to confess all your sins, but to remember that your Jesus has ALREADY forgiven you of your sins through His work on the cross. In doing this remembering, if there are sins that you know of that come to mind, then absolutely go right ahead and confess them. It is good especially for us to examine ourselves and make sure we are not presently in sin. But then turn that focus right back to Jesus and what He's done for you, thanking Him that those sins are forgiven. Remember Him, thank Him. The focus of communion is to be on the sacrifice of Jesus on our behalf. This is why Paul tells us that when we partake of communion, we are proclaiming the Lord's death (vs. 26). It's all about His sacrifice for us.

When it comes to forgiveness of sins, while Jesus already made payment for all of our sins, this has to be appropriated in our life. In other words, even though Jesus provided forgiveness for us, we need to take hold of it. When we first come to Christ, we acknowledge that we are sinners and we acknowledge that Jesus paid for those sins – thus we exercise our faith in Jesus and become "born again" and made new. Correct? But it's not like we just exercise faith one time to come to Christ and then we never exercise faith again. We are meant to walk in an abiding relationship with Jesus (John 15) where we are continually staying in this resting place of faith (Hebrews 4) where we are trusting in Christ's sacrifice to pay for all of our sins. Communion is a part of this abiding and resting process. In regards to forgiveness of sins, it is a time where we specifically remember what Jesus has done for us. In essence, we are re-affirming our present faith and trust – staying in a place of practically appropriating Christ's sacrifice on our behalf. Communion is not just a show we put on or some crazy tradition that the church has just for the sake of it, but rather it was instituted by Jesus for a specific reason: for us to stay in a place of remembrance of His work for us. It helps us keep our focus on Christ and His provision for us – where we are exercising our faith in Jesus.

Now, we need to probe a little deeper because we specifically need to address what the connection is between partaking of communion unworthily and sickness and death. If communion is all about remembering the sacrifice of Jesus, and Jesus' sacrifice only provided forgiveness of sins, then quite bluntly it seems quite a stretch for Paul to make such a strong correlation between partaking of communion unworthily and many people being weak and sick and dying. On the other hand, if the sacrifice of Jesus also provided healing for our physical bodies, then it makes a whole lot more sense why Paul would say this.

Paul mentions in verse 29 that a person who is partaking unworthily is not "discerning the Lord's body" and he then directly goes on to say that it is for this reason that many are weak and sick and have died. There are some translations which omit the word "Lord's" so that it just says "discerning the body", however the context is clearly of the Lord's body just as it is the Lord's body and the Lord's blood in verse 27. Thus it is not, as I've heard claimed, referring to the Body of Christ in the sense of all believers. That perhaps could be a secondary application, but the context clearly is referencing Christ's actual body and His actual blood (note that I'm not offering commentary one way or the other on the elements themselves actually being or becoming Christ's body and blood).

It is interesting that Paul mentions both the body and the blood in verse 27, and mentions eating and drinking (body and blood) in verse 29, yet only mentions a failure to discern the body as the reason for them being sick. He doesn't specifically call out not discerning the blood, but only the body, in relation to his immediate point regarding a reason for why they are sick. He says that a person partaking of both the Lord's body and the blood unworthily produces self-inflicted judgment on themselves, but then only mentions the lack of discerning the body. Why?

In the communion account of the Last Supper in Matthew 26, Jesus says this regarding the blood:

> Then He took the cup, and gave thanks, and gave *it* to them, saying, "Drink from it, all of you. For this is My blood of the new covenant, which is shed for many for the remission of sins. (Matthew 26:27–28 NKJV)

Jesus tells us that the cup we partake of is the blood that is shed for the forgiveness of our sins. The blood is specifically mentioned in regards to forgiveness of sins. The body, as mentioned in 1 Corinthians 11, references Christ's body that was broken for us.

Going back to Isaiah 53 that we discussed in the last chapter, where it talks in verse 4 of Jesus bearing our sicknesses, it says in the very same verse that "we did esteem him stricken, smitten of God, and afflicted." (Is. 53:4b KJV). Where was He stricken? Where was He smitten? Where was He afflicted? The seeming answer to this would be in His body. His body was broken for us.

It does seem that one could scripturally make a case that while the blood references forgiveness of sins, the body, at least partially, is what references physical healing. Now, let me ask this: If a person does not believe that physical healing was provided by Jesus in the atonement, and it really IS provided in the atonement, then is that person correctly "discerning the Lord's body" in relation to Christ's sacrifice?

We discussed a little bit ago that when it comes to forgiveness of sins, when we partake of communion, we are remembering Christ's work on our behalf to forgive us of our sins. Jesus specifically references the blood in this regards. As we partake of communion, we are in essence once again acknowledging our trust in Christ's sacri-

fice for the forgiveness of our sins, correct? What if Christ's sacrifice also includes healing for our bodies? If, when we partake of
communion, we do not recognize this fact, then we certainly are not
going to be acknowledging our trust in Christ's sacrifice for physical healing, are we?

Is it possible that one reason why many of our churches are filled
with people that are weak and sick (much like the Corinthian
church) is because many of those in our churches do not believe
healing was purchased for them? And is it possible that when it
comes to communion, which is about remembering Jesus' sacrifice
for us, that many are only remembering PART of the sacrifice?
Could this be at least part of what Paul meant when he talks of taking communion in an "unworthy manner" in not "discerning the
body?" I'm just asking...

Chapter 6 – The Full Package

One of the bedrock scriptures of our faith that most believers are familiar with is this one:

> For by grace you have been saved through faith, and that not of yourselves; *it is* the gift of God, not of works, lest anyone should boast. (Ephesians 2:8–9 NKJV)

There's a whole lot of theology packed into this little baby. It is used as a key verse when talking about how it is that we are saved or "born again" – that it is based on God's grace apprehended through faith and not what we do. There's something you might not know though. The Greek word for "saved" in this verse is the word "sozo" (that's how it's transliterated from the Greek into English) and it appears a total of 118 times in the New Testament. You might be wondering why this matters. Let me share another scripture:

> 20 And, behold, a woman, which was diseased with an issue of blood twelve years, came behind him, and touched the hem of his garment: 21 For she said within herself, If I may but touch his garment, I shall be whole. 22 … when he saw her, he said, Daughter, be of good comfort; thy faith hath made thee whole. And the woman was made whole from that hour. (Matthew 9:20–21,22b KJV)

Guess what? In this passage, the word translated "whole" all three times in regards to the woman being physically healed is none other than that same Greek word "sozo." Or how about this one:

> 22 And behold, one of the rulers of the synagogue came, Jairus by name. And when he saw Him, he fell at His feet 23 and begged Him earnestly, saying, "My little daughter lies at the point of death. Come and lay

Your hands on her, that she may be healed, and she will
live." (Mark 5:22–23 NKJV)

Where it says "healed" in verse 23, yep – you guessed it, that's
also the Greek word "sozo." The well-known and trusted Strong's
Exhaustive Concordance lists the following uses for "sozo"
(G4982): "heal, preserve, save (self), do well, be (make) whole."

In John 3:17, the verse right after the famous John 3:16 that people quote in sharing the Good News, we read: "For God did not
send his Son into the world to condemn the world, but in order that
the world might be saved through him." (ESV). Here, many people
would say this is only referring to salvation in a spiritual sense. The
word "saved" here is the same Greek "sozo" as it was in the previous two scriptures where it referenced physical healing.

In Acts 4, when the Apostle Peter and John were being ques-
tioned by the rulers regarding a physical healing of a cripple, we
find this exchange:

8 Then Peter, filled with the Holy Spirit, said to them,
"Rulers of the people and elders, 9 if we are being examined today concerning a good deed done to a
crippled man, by what means this man has been healed,
10 let it be known to all of you and to all the people of
Israel that by the name of Jesus Christ of Nazareth,
whom you crucified, whom God raised from the
dead—by him this man is standing before you well.
11 This Jesus is the stone that was rejected by you, the
builders, which has become the cornerstone. 12 And
there is salvation in no one else, for there is no other
name under heaven given among men by which we
must be saved." (Acts 4:8–12 ESV)

The last part of this – verse 12 – is a commonly quoted verse in
sharing the Gospel in regards to getting one's sins forgiven. But actually the context as can be clearly seen is in regards to physical
healing. Both the word "well" in verse 10 regarding the man being
physically made well and the word "saved" in verse 12, I suppose

you won't be surprised by now to learn are both our good friend "sozo." Peter tells the leaders that the crippled man was made well through the name of Jesus and that indeed there is no other name by which we must also be saved.

The point is that the word that is used for "save" in the New Testament is also the same word that is used numerous times in reference to physical healing. And I think that's really interesting. It's a popular word (used 118 times) that seems to be about communicating a health and wholeness in every respect. Perhaps our thinking where we've split up healing and forgiveness of sins into two distinct categories isn't correct. Perhaps our definition of what salvation actually is has been a bit narrow.

We've already looked at Isaiah 53 and the issue of communion and showed that the Bible links both sins and sickness together in regards to Jesus' atoning work for us. Another interesting item along these lines concerns an Old Testament type (picture) of the sacrifice of Jesus. In Numbers 21, we find a story of the children of Israel being bitten by deadly snakes.

> And the LORD said to Moses, "Make a fiery serpent and set it on a pole, and everyone who is bitten, when he sees it, shall live." (Numbers 21:8 ESV)

Jesus later referenced this event in regards to Himself:

> "And as Moses lifted up the serpent in the wilderness, even so must the Son of Man be lifted up, that whoever believes in Him should not perish but have eternal life." (John 3:14–15 NKJV)

In this passage, as well as in the famous next verse – John 3:16 – Jesus says that those that believe in Him will have "eternal life" (or "everlasting life" depending on your translation). Many people, when they hear the phrase "eternal life", think that means Heaven. But, actually, that isn't correct. Jesus, Himself, defines eternal life: "And this is eternal life, that they know you the only true God, and Jesus Christ whom you have sent." (John 17:3 ESV). Getting to live in Heaven is merely a byproduct of eternal life. Jesus says that knowing Himself and God (context is the Father) is eternal life. This isn't just a passive "knowing" either. In Bible terms, the word "know" is used to denote an extremely personal, intimate relationship. When Jesus says that those that believe in Him have eternal life, He's not talking about some future thing – He's talking right now. Right now we have eternal life. Yes, it is eternal and a byproduct of our knowing God is getting to live in Heaven, but it is a "state of being" right now. Right now we *know* God – we *know* Jesus – we *know* life.

The children of Israel were experiencing physical problems (notably death) as a result of the snakes that were biting them. But when they looked at the serpent that Moses had put on the pole, they were physically healed and lived. Jesus referenced that same story in regards to Himself. While historically much of the Church has assumed that Jesus was only referencing it in a spiritual sense in regards to Himself, what if that isn't necessarily true? What if He never intended to strip the physical typology from this Old Testament example? What if part of experiencing eternal life is physical healing? If I asked you if sickness was related to death or life, you would likely correctly say "death" (this was covered in Chapter 2). If I asked you if health and healing was related to death or life, then you would presumably correctly say "life." If true life on the deepest level is the "eternal life" we receive through truly knowing Jesus and God, then health and healing should be in this same package, right?

God has always been both a forgiving and healing God, and you see these two things grouped together throughout the Bible. One great example is in Psalm 103:

> 1 Bless the LORD, O my soul,
>   and all that is within me,
>   bless his holy name!
> 2 Bless the LORD, O my soul,
>   and forget not all his benefits,
> 3 who forgives all your iniquity,
>   who heals all your diseases,

4 who redeems your life from the pit,
  who crowns you with steadfast love and mercy,
5 who satisfies you with good
  so that your youth is renewed like the eagle's. (Psalm
103:1–5 ESV)

Here in verses 2–3, we are told that being in relationship with God has benefits and the first two specific benefits mentioned are forgiveness of sin and healing of physical diseases. This was in the Old Testament, where forgiveness of sin was "piecemeal" because Jesus hadn't come yet. Jesus, as the final sacrifice that fully paid for our sins, hadn't yet come. So while God did forgive (and heal) in the Old Testament just as the author of this Psalm (David) experienced, it often seemed a more "piecemeal" type approach – we read of constant sacrifices, etc. But since Jesus, as the sacrificial Lamb of God, completely paid for our sin, this forgiveness is ours in Christ, right? Why would we think that one of God's benefits, forgiveness, is ours in Christ, but that another of His benefits, healing, is not? Do we have less than what people in the Old Testament living under the Old Covenant had? No, the truth is that in Jesus, we can truly rejoice and Bless the Lord because ALL of His benefits are OURS!

During Jesus' ministry, when He went to His hometown of Nazareth, He went to the synagogue and read the following passage: "The Spirit of the Lord is upon me, because he has anointed me to proclaim good news to the poor. He has sent me to proclaim liberty to the captives and recovering of sight to the blind, to set at liberty those who are oppressed, to proclaim the year of the Lord's favor." (Luke 4:18–19 ESV). He then went on to tell the people that this scripture was fulfilled in Him.

When you read this scripture of the work of Jesus, do you just see an emphasis on forgiveness of sins and getting to live in Heaven? I don't. I see a scripture that Jesus Himself used to describe His work that shows us that He's all about wellness in every area of our lives. I see a God that cares about the poor, those that are in bondage, those that are sick, those that are oppressed. I see a picture of a

God that cares about people in all respects, and that there's an answer for people in Jesus.

Friends, Jesus proclaimed the "year of the Lord's favor." I'm pretty sure Jesus didn't get out His pocket calendar and think: "Well, I was born x number of years ago and according to my calculations that means that this specific year – and only this year – is the year of My favor." No, He wasn't talking about a specific year, but a season of time. That "year" is still ongoing since we can still come to Jesus. Are you going to tell me that Jesus cared about the blind when He was here physically but doesn't care about them now? Or that He cared that people were in bondage then, but not now? Jesus didn't revoke His favor after His resurrection, but He instead sent us as His followers to go out and proclaim His favor! We are still in the same period where we can receive this favor through the work of Jesus and then we have the privilege to proclaim that favor to others.

The Church as a whole has defined salvation along the lines of "receiving forgiveness of sins by believing in Jesus – being 'born again'." What if this definition is actually lacking? What if "salvation" or "being saved" was never meant to only reference forgiveness of sins, but a total picture of well-being in spirit as well as body and soul? In other words to include the "spiritual" component of being forgiven and having a new nature, but also include a "physical" component of health and wholeness?

To take it one step further, what if when the Bible talks about salvation and Jesus saving us, it's really not so much referring to a specific thing (e.g. having sins forgiven) but about a total package work addressing *everything* that man lost in the Fall back in the Garden of Eden?

Chapter 7 – Back to Eden

When Adam and Eve sinned in the Garden of Eden, everything about their world – and thus our world – changed. Prior to that, things were very different. Inside all of us, whether we are consciously aware of it or not, there is this deep-down knowledge that something very important was once lost...it literally is in the fabric of our being. We innately know that this experience of life that we now know is but a faint echo of what once was and what was supposed to always be.

I've obtained a time machine so please step inside and join me for a moment as we take a journey back to the Garden of Eden prior to the Fall.

WHOA, what a rush! Okay, we're here!

Step outside and let the beauty envelope you. Let the perfect air fill your lungs, fueled by the very breath of God. There's no shame here, nor guilt, nor backbiting, nor hatred, nor people tearing you down. There's no sickness or disease. There's no poverty or people dying of hunger. There's no murder or rape or muggings or carjackings or kids being abused. There's no depression or hopelessness or fear or anxiety or lack of peace or feeling like a failure. There's no pain or lies or broken hearts. You can't even remember what these things are.

There's just you and your God. You start running amidst the trees in reckless abandon, laughing with glee and relishing the freedom. You're naked but you don't even realize it because there's no such thing as embarrassment or shame here. There's nothing to hide. There's nothing to cover up. There's innocence and purity through every part of your being.

It's just you and your Maker together. Your heart is beating with His heart; you are entwined together – The Creator and The Created. You are enveloped in love in all its fullness and you feel no lack or rejection. There's just pure love here and you know through every fiber of your being that you are wanted and were made with deliberate purpose. Your Creator is holding your hand and whispering His love for you. He's more than just your closest friend, He is your absolute Everything.

God's glory shines all around and indeed you yourself having been made in His very image are radiating the glory of God in incredible brilliance! You...are FULLY ALIVE!

Okay, I hate to do this to you, but that time machine is a rental and I've got to get it back by the weekend... :)

Seriously though, although it is difficult for us to truly comprehend what life must have been like prior to the Fall because we exist in a world that's enmeshed in sin and that's all we've ever known, doesn't that experience portray what we all really deep-down want? There is a part of us that in the pit of who we are, whether we consciously realize it or not, knows something of incredible importance was lost...and mankind has been trying to find ever since.

Some years back I wrote a song along these lines and here's a few brief portions of it:

> Echoes of a world lost,
> Man's fellowship with You.
> I see it clearly in my soul;
> I was made to be with You. ...
>
> I cry out with all of creation,
> I cry out for restoration,
> I cry out for no more limitations.
> Now I see that it's found in You.
> Yes I want this life that's only in You.[1]

Men and women to this day run to all sorts of things to try to satiate their soul's cry for fulfillment – a cry that ultimately was started back when Adam & Eve sinned in the Garden of Eden and fellowship with God was broken by their sin.

Most of the problems that we get ourselves into are a direct result of trying to find this core-level fulfillment in everything but the one thing where it is found. We try to find it in relationships with other people, and then when they let us down (as they must, for they are every bit as broken as we are), things go downhill fast. We try to find it in fame and success, only to discover – perhaps years later –

that this never satisfied our soul's deep-down cry. How many stories of famous and wealthy people that are revered to the world, yet are clearly lonely and unfulfilled (which sometimes manifests in very public "train wrecks") do we need to see?

We try to find it in just "living it up" (which is really "living it down"). There's the whole party lifestyle of drinking and drugs. It's pretty much expected in our culture that people get drunk on a regular basis (e.g. Friday night). And for those that aren't getting drunk on alcohol, we've got a great alternative: you can escape reality through mind-altering drugs. While it used to be relegated to a specific segment of society, it has become increasingly "cool" for the masses to use drugs such as marijuana – and even in some circles, "harder" drugs such as crack cocaine.

We try to find it in pleasure. Currently our culture is really trying to find it in every form of sexual activity known to man. Sexual behavior itself is often what people are looking to and attaching their identity to in order to try to find fulfillment and dull the deep-down gnawing they sense within. Everywhere we look, we see sexuality on very public display, and all sorts of things that the Bible says are wrong being trumpeted up as things that are good. And people, in their (often subconscious) quest to find their fulfillment, may find it subconsciously attractive to identify with such things. Across-the-board, much of the confusion we see around us in the realm of gender and sexuality goes to a deeper issue than gender or sexuality.

We all, deep-down, want to genuinely feel loved and wanted. We want to feel that we truly belong, that we are safe and secure, and that all is right. This deep inner need goes all the way back to the Garden of Eden. Unfortunately, most people attempt to meet that need outside of the only One that can truly fulfill that need. Most people don't find their identity in God, but in all sorts of other things. Most people identify who they are based on their behavior. They even will argue that their behavior IS their identity – they see them as one and the same – that "what I do" is "who I am."

This gets into something very important. I know for myself that for far too many years I didn't understand a key concept that once I finally "got", made a world of difference in how I saw myself and how I related to a lot of Scripture. This concerns the very nature of humanity – what it is that makes us up as human beings.

Most of us when we look at another person and we see their body, we think we are looking at them. But that's actually not the case – we are only seeing the outer physical part of them. The actual core of who we are is not our body, it is our spirit. We are spirit beings who have a soul and who live in a body. We cannot see the spirit, but it is very much there. Our core nature is as a spirit being. We also have a soul, which is our mind/will/emotions. The soul can operate in the spiritual realm or in the physical/fleshly realm – it's kind of a bridge between the spirit and the body. We don't see the soul itself either, but it is what people often tend to collectively refer to as our "personality."

This is why the Bible tells us that "the body without the spirit is dead" (James 2:26) and that when when our physical earthly bodies are no longer functioning and we as believers in Jesus "die" here, that to be absent from the body is to be present with the Lord (2 Corinthians 5:8). At death, our spirit and soul separate from the body and go to the Lord.

When God created Adam & Eve, they were created fully alive – their spirit was in full communion and connection with God. When they sinned, they lost their unbroken spirit connection with God and became "dead in trespasses and sins" (Ephesians 2:1). The first thing they did – literally it is the next verse in the Bible after we are told that they ate of the forbidden fruit – was to try to do things their way by covering themselves with fig leaves and then to try to hide from God (Genesis 3:7–8).

Some things haven't changed very much. Most of the things that us silly people do to try to find fulfillment and dull the inner knowledge that something "isn't right" are really nothing more than attempts to hide from God and to try to do things our own way. It really is selfish pride when you get down to it – it's an "I don't need God, I can take care of myself and find my full worth in myself" attitude. Adam & Eve immediately went into hiding. And humanity has been trying to hide from God ever since. Us humans today really aren't any different than Adam & Eve; we're still singing the same old tune.

Now, since this book is geared towards Christians, I am assuming that most people reading this right now believe in Jesus. When a person by faith trusts in Jesus, what happens is they actually get a new spirit. As God says in Ezekiel 36:26, "... a new spirit will I put within you ..." In John chapter 3, Jesus is conversing with Nicodemus:

> 3 Jesus answered and said to him, "Most assuredly, I say to you, unless one is born again, he cannot see the kingdom of God."
>
> 4 Nicodemus said to Him, "How can a man be born when he is old? Can he enter a second time into his mother's womb and be born?"
>
> 5 Jesus answered, "Most assuredly, I say to you, unless one is born of water and the Spirit, he cannot enter the kingdom of God. 6 That which is born of the flesh is flesh, and that which is born of the Spirit is spirit. 7 Do not marvel that I said to you, 'You must be born again.' (John 3:3–7 NKJV)

Jesus tells us right here in verses 5–6 that we must be born of the Spirit of God. When we are "born again", we are not born of the flesh (we were born of the flesh the first time we were born), but we are born of the Spirit. A new spirit is put within us, born by the Holy Spirit. This occurs through our faith in Jesus, as Jesus goes on to tell Nicodemus in the famous John 3:16 passage.

When we come to a saving faith in Jesus, we don't just change a little bit. The incredible news is that we get a new spirit and we actually become a new species of being.

> "Therefore, if anyone is in Christ, he is a new creation.
> The old has passed away; behold, the new has come."
> (2 Corinthians 5:17 ESV)

We become a new creation, or as the King James translation puts it, a "new creature." No matter how you slice it, something radical changes in the core of who we are. We actually become a new creation – not merely figuratively, but literally. We literally change at the moment of conversion to be a whole new creation! This is HUGE!

What was once dead, becomes alive! We become alive spiritually!

> "And you *He made alive,* who were dead in trespasses and sins, in which you once walked according to the course of this world, according to the prince of the power of the air, the spirit who now works in the sons of disobedience, among whom also we all once conducted ourselves in the lusts of our flesh, fulfilling the desires of the flesh and of the mind, and were by nature children of wrath, just as the others." (Ephesians 2:1–3 NKJV)

While we were alive physically in our bodies, we were dead in our spirit man – lacking life. In a sense, we really were the "walking dead." Our nature was one that we lived according to the flesh, fulfilling the desires of the flesh. We were not living by the Spirit, but by the flesh, in accordance with the devil (the "prince of the power of the air"). But when we came to Jesus by faith, we were made alive. A change in our very nature took place. The Bible tells us that "Everyone who believes that Jesus is the Christ has been born of God … " (1 John 5:1a ESV) We became spiritually alive and became a new creation that was born of God Himself!

You might be wondering why in the world I am bothering to go through all of this. I realize that this is all basic Christian theology. The problem is that many Christians don't understand it. The sad reality is that even many Christians don't really understand who they are – what their real identity is. It is my own personal testimony that even as a Christian that believed in Jesus, I for far too long didn't understand about what happened at my conversion.

Society is constantly trying to sell us on the notion that our identity is to be found in how we feel or our looks or our behavior. Earlier I mentioned that we humans try to find our fulfillment in all sorts of places but the one place it is really found. You might have thought I was just talking about the unsaved heathen outside the church. But no, I'm talking about you and me too.

Why is is that we find plenty of people within the church dealing with the same kinds of sin we see outside of the church? If you recall the statistic from the first chapter of this book, why is it that 43% of **pastors** are viewing porn? Why is it that there often seems to be just as many alcoholics, over-eaters, workaholics, divorces, sexual sin, and more, within the church as there is outside of the church? Why is there so little victory for many Christians when it comes to sin?

Sin comes from living by the flesh and not by the Spirit. Perhaps one reason why we in the church are doing a lot of fleshly living is because we haven't really understood who we are in the spirit. We haven't understood our new identity that is ours in Jesus Christ. If we don't truly identify our core nature as being completely new in Jesus, we will continue living out of the old identity – our old nature – that we knew before Christ. Now, having our lives reflect the truth of who we are is a process – the theological term for it is "sanctification." But a vital part of this process is identifying who we now are in reality – understanding that we are truly a new creation. This isn't just a nice saying – we really *are* a new creation born of God. We need to start seeing ourselves that way and move beyond just seeing it as a nice slogan to say. When we start really viewing ourselves correctly, we will find ourselves more and more living up to the reality of who we now are.

> "Or do you not know that the unrighteous will not inherit the kingdom of God? Do not be deceived: neither the sexually immoral, nor idolaters, nor adulterers, nor men who practice homosexuality, nor thieves, nor the greedy, nor drunkards, nor revilers, nor swindlers will inherit the kingdom of God. AND SUCH WERE SOME OF YOU. But you were washed, you were sanc-

tified, you were justified in the name of the Lord Jesus
Christ and by the Spirit of our God." (1 Corinthians
6:9–11 ESV, emphasis mine)

The Bible is clear in the passage above that those that are "unrighteous" will not inherit the kingdom of God and it then goes on
to list some specific identities of unrighteous people that will not
inherit the kingdom of God. But then it tells us that "such were
some of you" in verse 11. Note the word "were" – it's past tense.
Your identity before placing faith in Christ may have been as one
that was a drunkard, but in Jesus, your identity is not as a drunkard
(even if you have still struggled some with excess drinking). Your
identity is as one that has been washed and sanctified and justified
by God. Your whole identity has changed. You are no longer defined by sin, but by Jesus. You are no longer in the category
"unrighteous sinner", but "righteous saint" because in Jesus you
become the righteousness of God. "For our sake he made him to be
sin who knew no sin, so that in him we might become the righteousness of God." (2 Corinthians 5:21 ESV).

Regardless of labels or identities you or others may have put on
yourself, when you became "born again" through your faith in Jesus, your identity completely changed. It's important that you see
yourself as this new identity and do not keep seeing yourself
through the pre-Jesus lens as one that's just a "rotten sinner saved
by grace." No, you WERE a rotten sinner, but Hallelujah – you've
been saved by grace! Your identity has changed. You might still
struggle with some of the same sins you were committing before
you believed in Jesus, but your core identity has changed and you
need to see yourself in line with this truth. If you see yourself as a
rotten sinner, chances are pretty good that you are going to be living
as though you are. You will live up or down to how you see yourself
and who you really believe you are. Step one in living the way God
wants is seeing yourself correctly by acknowledging your true identity.

Before we believed in Jesus, our spirit was not alive, and all we
could do was live for the flesh (carnal, ungodly way of living). We
could do nothing BUT live for the flesh. We weren't "struggling

with sin" – we were freely giving ourselves to it. Through our faith in Jesus, we got a new spirit born of the Holy Spirit, and we now have the choice to either live by the spirit or to live by the flesh. The spirit part of you is not your problem. If you are a believer in Jesus Christ, you are 100% perfect in your spirit and this does not change. Your spirit has been born of God and is perfect. Your spirit isn't your problem. Your soul and your body are the problem, not your spirit.

The soul, which contains our mind/will/emotions, is where we choose whether to go with our new nature (spirit) or to go with our old nature (flesh) in any given situation. This is why the Bible tells us in Romans 12:2 to renew our minds. The process of sanctification for the believer is getting our soul, which had years of practice living solely in accordance with the flesh, in alignment with our new spirit (which was born of the Holy Spirit). The choosing to either live out of our "spirit man" or go with the flesh, takes place in our soul.

Outside of Christ, we all perfected living by the flesh as an art form. Now, however, in some sense we are in essence restored to a similar position as Adam & Eve were before the Fall in that they also had the choice to live by the spirit or to go against God's word (live by the flesh). The devil tempted them to go with the latter, and they did. Just as Adam & Eve could have eaten from the tree of life or from the forbidden tree of the knowledge of good and evil, so also today we can in essence choose to eat from the tree of life (Jesus) or from the tree of the knowledge of good and evil (representing our flesh/trying to do things by ourselves/disobeying God).

When you became "born again" through your faith in Jesus and received this new spirit, if you had a missing arm just prior to that, you still likely had a missing arm after that experience. If you were a glutton or used bad language before that, you likely still (at least initially) struggled with being a glutton or using bad language after that. Just looking around proves that the part of us that got changed when we got born again wasn't our body or our soul, it was our spirit. Now some people do experience an alignment of certain things in their souls or bodies with their new spirit right away. For instance, I've heard testimonies of people that were drug addicts that never had a desire to do drugs again as soon as they came to Jesus. Or someone that had a physical problem in their body that got healed of that as soon as they received Jesus. A lot of whether those things happen or not can depend on what a person is expecting based on what they are believing for. But even in those situations, the reality is that none of us become fully perfect in our bodies or in our behavior as soon as we become "born again." It's a process – the process of sanctification.

Historically, much of the church world has associated this process of sanctification only with our soul – getting our soul in alignment with our new "spirit man." The way that we "renew our mind" – get our soul in alignment with our spirit – is through studying the Word and focusing on our fellowship with God. As we give time to this and change our thinking to the new reality of us being a new creation in Jesus and all that entails, we will find over time that we are less and less apt to live by the flesh. This is one area where there's been a big disconnect because many people don't really know who they are in Christ and don't really spend the effort or time to dwell on the things of God as opposed to the things of the flesh (and there are certainly plenty of "things of the flesh" in our culture!).

The Apostle Paul tells us in 1 Thessalonians 5:23, "Now may the God of peace himself sanctify you completely, and may your whole spirit and soul and body be kept blameless at the coming of our Lord Jesus Christ." (ESV)

Paul understood that the work of sanctification was to be a complete work affecting every part of us. Between the three parts of our being that Paul mentions (spirit, soul, and body), only one of those three is already wholly perfect: our spirit. The work of sanctification is to be a complete work bringing all parts of our being into congruence with one another and with our new nature. This isn't to just include our soul, but our body as well. Just as with our soul, a key part of this process involves acknowledging this and renewing our mind to the truths in God's Word.

The same work of Jesus that made it possible for our soul to be sanctified (our mind to be renewed and our actions to reflect what

God wants, etc.) is the same work that made it possible for our body to be sanctified (made well and allowing us to walk in health).

Some of you may be familiar with well-known Bible teacher Joyce Meyer. Her television program is available in much of the world and on a daily basis she ministers to untold millions. But she started out in life in a terrible family situation: being sexually abused by her father for many years and having a mother that knew of the abuse but did not intervene to stop it. The results of the abuse impacted her greatly; she was full of bitterness, anger, and distrust. It left a terrible mark on her soul and set her up for failure in life. What's incredible though is that many years later, she actually ended up taking care of her parents in their latter years and was even used by God to bring her father – the same father that had wounded her so badly – to the Lord. How does that happen? How does one go from being terribly hurt and emotionally sick due to abuse to becoming a prominent voice in the Body of Christ to help millions and even end up helping the very people that caused her abuse? There's only one explanation for that – and is the explanation she herself gives. She received healing from God in her soul. And she describes that it was a process over many, many years. But she kept pressing forward to renew her mind and receive all that God had for her – receiving healing in her soul.

Joyce details her story and what the Lord did in & through her in an excellent book called "Beauty for Ashes" – I highly recommend the revised edition of it for anyone that needs emotional healing or had a rough childhood. Joyce's story shows that God is able to take ashes in your life and make something beautiful out of it.

Most of the church world has no theological problem accepting that God can heal people in their soul – in the emotional realm. At the same time, even that tends to be fairly downplayed in many circles, where when it is even acknowledged, it only goes so far. For instance, it is becoming increasingly common to talk about people that have mental illness/depression/emotional disorders solely in terms of just being comforting and understanding with them and making sure they have appropriate medication, rather than discussing that God's love and joy and peace can bring healing in replacing the pain and hurt that is in their life if they will be open to that and fight for that.

I am not trivializing emotional issues (as some have wrongly done) – I don't believe all such issues necessarily have "quick fixes" and I also recognize that mental illness and depression can have physical components as well. But that brings me to my next point: We generally accept that God cares about the emotional realm and that God can bring healing to us there. But let me ask this: Why would God be concerned about your soul and not have any concern about your body? Why would God care about limitations of soul, but not care about limitations of body? Why would God be for healing in your soul, but not for healing in your body?

The very same work of Jesus that gave you a new spirit and the very same work of Jesus that provided a way for wholeness in your soul (in your emotions/mind), is the very same work of Jesus that provided a way for wholeness in your body. There is one work of Jesus and that work is a complete work that provided for everything that men and women could need. Jesus didn't just die for us so we could be well in our spirit. And He didn't just die for us so we could be well in our soul. He died for us so that every part of us could be well! The salvation work of Jesus was never meant to only affect part of our being, but to affect every part of us – spirit, soul, and body.

Healing is healing, and wholeness is wholeness, and salvation is salvation! We need to stop parsing these out to only applying to certain things or areas, when the Bible itself – as already shown in the previous chapter – applies these much more broadly. Jesus made the way for you to be well in every part of your being – spirit, soul, and body.

Everything that mankind lost as a result of the Fall in the Garden of Eden is restored to us through Jesus Christ.

Now, listen, we can all look around and see that this ain't no Garden of Eden! Romans 8:22–23 says this:

> 22 For we know that the whole creation groans and labors with birth pangs together until now. 23 Not only *that,* but we also who have the firstfruits of the Spirit,

even we ourselves groan within ourselves, eagerly waiting for the adoption, the redemption of our body. (NKJV)

While everything lost in Eden is restored to us through Jesus, this doesn't all just happen instantaneously in the physical. Sin is still in our world and still affects everything in our world.

I was at a local park the other day, sitting on a bench in front of the lake, enjoying the incredible beauty and peace, when all of a sudden some kids that were off to the side of me started shouting that some ducks were trying to kill another duck. I got up and walked over to them, and sure enough, they were right. There were three ducks on top of another duck in the water seemingly trying with all their might to drown it. They were sitting on its head and biting at it; basically they were doing everything they could to kill their fellow duck. I've never seen such a sight in my life. Who knew that there were evil, murderous duck gangs out there? As several people came over, the ducks relented and let the victimized duck go. But this was just such a clear picture; here I was enjoying the beauty of God's creation, but then I was presented with the full reality that all is not as it was intended to be. Sin has marred every corner of our creation. [update: I've since learned that duck mating practices can appear as I described – in either case though, it's a picture of a marred creation.]

The entire creation itself, according to this scripture, is groaning and waiting for its liberation. There will be a day when that happens. And there will be a day when our physical body will completely experience this liberation in its fullness as well.

As already noted, at salvation, our spirit was changed (this is re-iterated in this verse where it says that we *have* the firstfruits of the Spirit), but our soul and body are still in need of sanctification. However, the same work of Jesus that provided salvation in our spirit provides for salvation in our soul and body. It is true that every genuine "born again" believer in Jesus will eventually get a new body and won't have to worry about any sickness in their body or in their soul. That's guaranteed; that will happen in the future. But we also can appropriate Christ's work on our behalf to receive the benefits He provided for us in the here-and-now. This is how Joyce Meyer was changed and received healing in her soul. She looked to the Word and took God at face-value and kept renewing her mind to what was available to her in Christ. And she saw great emotional healing take place! And you and I can do the same. The same is also true for our physical body. As we take hold of the Word and appropriate what Christ provided for us, we can see health manifest in our physical body as well. We won't 100% get it right and walk in the fullness of victory while we are here – we won't experience the victory won for us in its fullest sense until we get to Heaven. But we can experience a whole lot more victory here than what many of us have been taught or thought was available!

The church world by and large has placed the majority of its emphasis on Heaven and basically adopted an attitude of "we're all just trying to get by until we get to Heaven." The clear picture that's been presented is that we all are just meant to suffer through life here and then when we get to Heaven all will be righted. It is true that we will go through things here because we are still living in a fallen world. And it is true that we will not fully experience the fullness of everything that Jesus purchased for us until we go to be with the Lord. But we also can walk in a whole lot more victory in the here-and-now than what the church world has been living. We can walk in victory over sin NOW, we can walk in victory in our emotional / soulish realm NOW, we can walk in victory in health NOW. It may not be the fullness of victory that we will experience when we don't have to have the battle anymore living in this evil, fallen world. But we can walk in victory nonetheless. Or at least a whole lot more than we've been living.

A chief reason why many Christians haven't been walking in much victory in any area of their lives is that they haven't really realized it was available – they've been living with a defeatist attitude just looking towards their hope being off in the future. Again, I'm not diminishing our future hope. But Jesus didn't just die so that we could be well *some day*; He died so we could also be well *now*.

When Adam, the first human, was created by God, the Bible tells us that "the LORD God formed man *of* the dust of the ground, and breathed into his nostrils the breath of life; and man became a living being." (Genesis 2:7b NKJV). The word "life" where it says that God breathed into him the "breath of life" is the Greek word "zoe" (transliterated). *(Sidenote: The Old Testament was written in Hebrew, but in the Greek Septuagint translation of the OT which was in use in Jesus' day, it uses this word. I'm referring to the Greek because the NT was written in Greek and I'm going to be making a point shortly...)* The word "zoe" is used a couple of different ways in the Bible, but one of the chief ones is in referring to the absolute fullness of life that comes from God, as in this example of God breathing life into Adam.

When Adam later sinned, we are told in Romans 5:17 that "death reigned" through him. Where Adam had previously enjoyed life in the truest and fullest sense of that word, without any trace of sickness or disease or malady of any kind, he subsequently experienced death and its effects. And we've been experiencing the same ever since.

In the same Romans 5:17 verse though, we are told that even though this is a true fact because of Adam's sin, that "much more will those who receive the abundance of grace and the free gift of righteousness reign in life through the one man Jesus Christ. Therefore, as one trespass led to condemnation for all men, so one act of righteousness leads to justification and life for all men." (Romans 5:17b–18 ESV)

The word "life" used both times in this passage is the same Greek word "zoe." It's also the same word used in John 10:10 where Jesus tells us: "... I am come that they might have life, and that they might have it more abundantly." (KJV)

In Jesus, we are positionally restored to fullness of life – life in its abundance – the same type of life that Adam had prior to his sin. As it says in the Romans passage above, what Jesus did for us, leads to "justification and life for all men." Though this is a reality, it is appropriated in our own lives by faith. While the whole world has been justified by Jesus and God is not counting our sins against us (2 Cor. 5:19), the way that is practically applied to our own life is in accepting that gift by faith and thus being found "in Christ." It is through faith that we believe in Jesus and receive the gift of justification and reconciliation to God that Jesus purchased for us. If a person doesn't truly believe that they are fully justified by Jesus, then they will walk around feeling guilty and under condemnation (this seemingly describes a fair portion of the Church). But to the degree that we really believe and appropriate Christ's justifying work on our behalf, is the degree that we will practically walk free from condemnation and guilt and shame. Likewise, the degree to which we really believe that abundance of life is truly ours in Jesus and appropriate it is the degree to which we will experience this "zoe", full, abundant, life here in our daily life. The same life that Adam had prior to the Fall, the same life that was free of all sickness and disease, is the same type of fullness of life that we can experience now through Jesus.

In Christ, we in a sense go back to Eden.

You may recall from the previous chapter that when we are told in the Bible that those that believe in Jesus have eternal (or everlasting) life, that isn't talking about some future state that starts when we get to Heaven. You may also recall that the definition of eternal life, as given by Jesus Himself, is all about truly, intimately knowing God – knowing Jesus. Prior to the Fall, Adam & Eve truly knew God – their spirits were alive and they were in full fellowship and communion with Him. The eternal life that Adam & Eve had prior to the Fall is the same eternal life that the Bible says is ours through our faith in Jesus. This has taken place in our spirit. Our spirit is in full communion with God. We have been restored to full fellowship with the God that made us. The challenge is in renewing our mind to this reality.

For many people this can be a hard concept because many believers don't really feel like they are in communion and fellowship with God on the kind of level that we know Adam & Eve possessed. The reason we often don't feel it is because feelings are a part of our soul – the emotional realm. And this change took place in our spirit, not our soul. Our soul has had all sorts of negative junk fed into it from this sinful world from the day we were born. That's something Adam & Eve didn't have to contend with. But I just have to say that as a personal testimony that once I got ahold of these truths I am sharing in this book – when I really spent time renewing my mind to these things – I started finding it much easier to hear God and "feel Him" than what used to be my experience. I spent years in confusion where it was more often than not hard for me to discern God's voice as opposed to the devil's or my own. The moments where I felt like I was really fellowshipping with God were noticeably separated by often large chunks of time (days or more). These days I much more often am living in the awareness of God on a continual basis – I "feel" God a lot more. I'm not saying I've got it perfect (I don't), but my point is that over time as I've renewed my mind, I've let the change that took place in my spirit affect my mind (soul realm) and I've experienced more of the emotional "knowing" of what was already true in my spirit. The same can be the case for any believer. The eternal, abundant life that we have in our spirit is able to flow out of our spirit and into our soul and body.

We are called, as the Romans 5 passage mentioned above says, to "reign in life through the one man Jesus Christ." We are able to reign in this life – to be victorious. We don't have to live sorry, defeated lives. We don't have to walk around beaten by sin, beaten by sickness, beaten by our emotions. We don't have to be depressed, discouraged and in despair (the "Three D's" as I call them). There's hope for us – and it's not just hope off in the distance. There's hope for us now because of what Jesus has already provided for us. The way we experience victory here in this life – in every part of our being – is through accepting what is ours in Jesus and applying it in our lives. We reign *through* Jesus. It comes in identifying ourselves solely with Jesus – finding our identity in Him – and renewing our mind to the truth of the Word of all that is ours. Everything about our being is meant to spring out of our identity in Jesus.

Chapter 8 – In Christ

There is a major mindset shift that is ultra-important to how we walk out our Christianity that I believe has by-and-large been missing in our churches.

For the most part, the majority of Christians are looking towards the future for their answers, rather than the past. "When I get to Heaven, then I'll be healed." "If I beg God enough, then He will hear me." "If I do all the right things, then God will answer me and bless me." "If I pray enough or have enough people praying for me, then God will maybe heal me."

Most Christians are looking for God to DO something in their lives. They are trying to GET free from sin, rather than understanding that they have ALREADY been freed from sin. They are trying to GET healed, rather than understanding that they've ALREADY been healed.

This is why most Christians aren't walking in victory. People will plead with God to heal them or set them free from some besetting sin, not understanding that the provision has ALREADY been made – that it's already been done. I'm telling you, that if you grasp this, this will revolutionize your entire life! It's a total shift in how we relate to God!

It's a shift from an attitude that we are nothing and have nothing and just are begging God to help us, to realizing what God has already provided for us through Christ and approaching God on that basis.

Much like the last chapter, I'm going to step through some things now that might seem like basic Christian theology but having a correct understanding on these things is vitally important. I'm going to be talking about several concepts at once and eventually providing the big picture that integrates them together, so stay with me. This is one chapter that, while longer, I would especially encourage you to try and read all at one time if you are able.

I'm sure you won't be surprised by now, but we're going back to the Garden of Eden again. :)

After God created Adam & Eve, we read this:

And God blessed them. And God said to them, "Be fruitful and multiply and fill the earth and subdue it, and have dominion over the fish of the sea and over the birds of the heavens and over every living thing that moves on the earth." (Genesis 1:28 ESV)

God gave Adam & Eve authority over this earth. Adam & Eve exercised authority in fellowship with God. Then the devil comes and tempts them to disobey God and they give in. By exercising the free choice that they were given by God and choosing to obey the devil over God, they subjugated themselves and their authority to the devil. This is why the Bible now refers to the devil as "the god of this world" (2 Corinthians 4:4), the "prince of the power of the air" (Ephesians 2:2), and the "ruler of this world" (John 12:31). The devil wasn't the ruler of this world when Adam & Eve were created – that role was given to Adam & Eve by God. When they listened to the devil over God, they subjugated their God-given authority to the devil. Even though this happened, God never took away mankind's authority in their own life to choose God or the devil. God never went back on the gift of choice that He gave to mankind. He honored Adam & Eve's choice and He still honors our choices today. We'll come back to this whole authority thing later, but for now let's set it aside for a bit.

Have you ever wondered why it was that after Adam & Eve sinned that God didn't just immediately send Jesus to pay the penalty for their sin? Why did God wait thousands of years before Jesus came? Let me throw this out for thought: Had Jesus come right after Adam & Eve sinned, would we have known that we needed Jesus? I don't think so; I think we would have thought we could handle things ourselves. Remember: Adam & Eve didn't run to God after their sin; rather they tried to handle things themselves, and it was God that went looking for them. A look through the subsequent human history recorded from the Fall to the end of the Old Testament book of Malachi shows that we human beings constantly thought we could do things ourselves without God. In essence, I believe God needed to show us, through letting things play out, that we need Him and absolutely cannot save ourselves. That's part of why He gave us the law (which He didn't even do for a few thousand years) – it was all a part of this process of showing us God's standards and how we can't keep them – that we can't save ourselves and that left to ourselves we will implode. Let's pause for a moment and just remember some key things from the history of mankind up to the time of Jesus: the Flood (where mankind was incredibly wicked and only one man, Noah, and family survived) –> Sodom/Gomorrah –> Abraham/Isaac/Jacob/Joseph –> Bondage in Egypt –> Wandering in Wilderness (Wanting to do it their way without God/Grumbling/Complaining) –> Giving of the law –> Judges –> Kings (because they didn't want to be under God but to be like the other nations that looked to MAN) –> Captivity –> Silent years/continual bondage –> Roman occupation...

Once we humans sinned, God could judge us and bring wrath because we had wronged Him, but He couldn't SAVE us without our cooperation since He gave us that authority (choice). But as a whole we didn't want Him! So, I believe it took as long as it needed to take to give us a solid history of what life lived apart from God looks like/brings, so there would be those that would be open to receiving the Good News of grace offered in Jesus. This is why the Apostle Paul, Stephen, Peter, and others recounted Jewish history when talking to their fellow Jews about Jesus (e.g. Stephen's defense in Acts 7).

Part of the history involved the giving of the law. When the people of Israel came out of Egypt as led by Moses, God made a covenant with them that involved them committing to keep God's statutes and live righteously – basically to do everything right. The people told God "All that the LORD has spoken we will do." (Exodus 19:8 ESV). I'm sure they really thought that they could and that they would. But they couldn't and they wouldn't.

God gave the people His standards. They, in prideful arrogance, basically said "No problem! We can do that!" And of course they were wrong. There's something very appealing to men and women about doing things to justify ourselves to "be right with God." It basically comes back to pride; we don't want to admit that we are helpless on our own and that we need a Savior because that would mean that we actually need God, are unable to perfectly keep His standards, and are weak apart from Him. Of course, that is the reality. But men and women don't like to admit it. We like to think, as an old 90's expression used to say, that "we're all that, and a bag of chips!"

The Bible tells us in Galatians 3:23 that "the law was our schoolmaster to bring us unto Christ, that we might be justified by faith." (Ga 3:23b KJV). Other translations use the word "tutor" or "guardian" in place of "schoolmaster." Regardless, the idea is clear in that the law's purpose is wrapped up in showing us that we need a Savior and that, while we can't perfectly keep the law, we can still be justified before God through our faith in this Savior that DID perfectly keep the law on our behalf.

When most people think of the law, they just think of the "Big Ten" – the Ten Commandments. But actually there's a whole lot more that are given as well. But even just the Ten Commandments show the folly in trying to justify ourselves by the law. If you've ever lied, put anything ahead of God, coveted, stolen something, taken the name of God in vain, etc. then you've broken the law. And James 2:10 says, "For whoever keeps the whole law but fails in one point has become guilty of all of it." (ESV). You can keep the law 99% perfectly, but if you fail in one item, you aren't good enough. And we've all failed in much more than just one item.

Not only does the law tell us what not to do, but at the same time, it arguably also commands us what TO do – it's got a dual nature. So, for instance, when we are told not to murder, the implication within that is that we are to care about others in such a way that we would never even think about murdering them. So then not only would we have to not do the forbidden things, but then we also have to perfectly do the things we are supposed to do. If that weren't enough, when something is forbidden, it is very broad in scope and application. For instance, Jesus made clear in Matthew chapter 5 that merely looking at another woman with lust or being angry with someone is the same as committing adultery or murdering them as far as the law is concerned. So how do you and I stack up? Not so well, huh?

When people truly understand the law and its demands, they should be absolutely running to Jesus and the finished work of the cross. The law was given for this very purpose.

When people refer to the Old Covenant, they are referring to this law-based covenant with God which is based on us and our behavior. The New Covenant, by contrast, is not based on us or our ability to be righteous at all. Rather it is based on God Himself doing what we could not do and our faith in Him. Jesus came to this earth, and while fully God, He also lived fully as a man here. And He lived perfectly, upholding God's righteous standards. He was unjustly put to death, but death could not hold Him because He had fulfilled everything that needed to be fulfilled. He arose from the dead and now is seated at the right hand of the Father in Heaven.

Most of the New Testament books of Hebrews and Galatians (as well as major portions of several other epistles) deal with the differences between the Old and New Covenant and seek to make the case of how much better the New Covenant is. We are told that Jesus "is the mediator of a better covenant, which was established upon better promises." (Hebrews 8:6b KJV). It's a better covenant than the old one because it is not based on us, but on Jesus. While Jesus died for the sins of the whole world (1 John 2:2), we still have the element of choice. God gave us choice when He created humanity and He has never taken that back. The way we apply what Jesus did to our own lives is by faith. We make a conscious choice to believe and look to Jesus' righteousness to be in right standing with God, instead of banking on our own righteousness. Thus, the New Covenant is a covenant based on faith.

21 Is the law then contrary to the promises of God? Certainly not! For if a law had been given that could give life, then righteousness would indeed be by the law. 22 But the Scripture imprisoned everything under sin, so that the promise by faith in Jesus Christ might be given to those who believe.

23 Now before faith came, we were held captive under the law, imprisoned until the coming faith would be re-

vealed. 24 So then, the law was our guardian until Christ came, in order that we might be justified by faith. 25 But now that faith has come, we are no longer under a guardian, 26 for in Christ Jesus you are all sons of God, through faith. (Galatians 3:21–26 ESV)

We are justified before God through our faith in Jesus. Romans 3:21–22 tells us: "But now the righteousness of God has been manifested apart from the law, although the Law and the Prophets bear witness to it – the righteousness of God through faith in Jesus Christ for all who believe. (ESV). The incredible thing is through our faith in Jesus we actually BECOME righteous because Jesus' righteousness gets imputed (or transferred) to us. "For our sake he made him to be sin who knew no sin, so that in him we might become the righteousness of God." (2 Corinthians 5:21 ESV). This tells us that in Jesus we become the righteousness of God. When the Father looks at us, He sees the righteousness of Jesus. That's huge!

One of the biggest mistakes that the Church has made historically is in portraying the act of faith as a one-time event. In other words, we come to a place where we "accept Jesus" and believe and become "born again" – and that is our point of faith in Jesus. And certainly it *is* a point of faith. But it's not supposed to end there.

As you therefore have received Christ Jesus the Lord, so walk in Him, rooted and built up in Him and established in the faith, as you have been taught, abounding in it with thanksgiving. (Colossians 2:6–7 NKJV)

How did you receive Jesus? Through faith. That's how we're supposed to continue walking day-by-day: through faith, becoming more and more built up and established. "For we walk by faith, not by sight." (2 Corinthians 5:7 NKJV). We're supposed to walk each day by faith. The same way that we receive Jesus for salvation is the same way we are supposed to walk – taking God at His Word over what our natural eyes can see. Our faith in Jesus is not just a one time event, but a lifelong, continual state we are to stay in. It's a place of abiding in Jesus. As Jesus tells us in John 15: "Abide in me, and I in you. As the branch cannot bear fruit by itself, unless it abides in the vine, neither can you, unless you abide in me." (John 15:4 ESV).

Our faith in Jesus is not an event. Our faith is not just a noun, it's also a verb – an action word. We become "born again" by putting our faith in Jesus. But what does that mean? It means that we are admitting that we need Him – that we need His righteousness that He purchased for us at the cross. It means that we are banking our hope on Jesus and not on ourselves. When we do this, we are resting in Jesus (entering into rest, as described in Hebrews 4). We've put all our chips on Jesus and that's where we are resting. But this resting comes as a result of our faith. As we continue to exercise our faith, we continue to stay in that place of resting in the finished work of Jesus – abiding in Jesus.

The danger comes in when people make a one-time act of a profession of faith but then do not continue to appropriate their faith on a continual basis. That to me is a dangerous place to be. We are supposed to continue in and live in a state of faith in Jesus. The fact that twenty years ago someone professed to believe in Jesus doesn't matter nearly as much to me as what they are believing in right now, as to where they are putting their present trust and hope. There are plenty of people who identify as Christians who really aren't trusting solely in Jesus, but rather a mix of Jesus and their own works. People in this category are ones who the Apostle Paul called "foolish" (Galatians 3). Mixing Jesus and the law just doesn't work. Either you are fully banking on Jesus for your salvation or you aren't.

The Bible continually refers to those that are believers in Jesus as being "in Christ" (e.g. Romans 8:1) – our identity is meant to be found in Jesus. Through our faith in Jesus, we are placed in Him. The church world has tended to really minimize the fullness of what this actually means, so I'd like to elaborate a bit. In Christ, we are not some poor beggars trying to beg God to get free from sin or help us with the devil. We have far more in Christ than many realize.

As part of the Old Covenant (the law), God prescribed blessings if the people kept their part of the deal and obeyed, and curses if they did not. You can read these in Deuteronomy chapter 28. I just want to highlight that the blessings and curses affected every part of their lives: physical, financial, protection from enemies, etc. If they were righteous and perfectly obeyed God, they would be blessed in every possible area. This was the covenant God had made with them.

In the New Covenant, God sees us as perfectly righteous because of Jesus. We have already seen that the New Covenant is declared to be a much better covenant than the old one. If it's much better and we're seen as righteous, shouldn't God at the very least be wanting to bless us as much and in the same ways as He declared in Deuteronomy 28 under the Old Covenant? Indeed the blessings we have in Jesus are innumerable and affect every area of our lives. However, what we don't know in ignorance can hurt us. We only will walk in the blessings to the degree that we believe they are ours and appropriate them by faith.

We have been restored to a position of authority. We discussed at the start of this chapter that the devil became the "god of this world" – the "ruler of this world" – when Adam & Eve obeyed him and subjugated their authority to the devil. While the devil still exists here, as a believer in Jesus, you don't need to cower to him or be afraid of him one iota because you have authority over him.

> In Him [Jesus] you were … buried with Him in baptism, in which you also were raised with *Him* through faith in the working of God, who raised Him from the dead. And you, being dead in your trespasses and the uncircumcision of your flesh, He has made alive together with Him, having forgiven you all trespasses, having wiped out the handwriting of requirements that was against us, which was contrary to us. And He has taken it out of the way, having nailed it to the cross. Having disarmed principalities and powers, He made a public spectacle of them, triumphing over them in it. (Colossians 2:11a,12–15 NKJV, bracketed text mine)

This passage tells us that Jesus disarmed the devil and made a spectacle of him and triumphed over him (and his demon cohorts) through the cross. Many people see God and the devil as being in this huge struggle, almost like an intense arm-wrestling match, but that eventually God will win. No, the truth is that God has *already* won! He's already defeated the devil – He's gutted the devil of his power through the cross so that those that are in Christ are not subject to the devil. While we can still choose to give the devil power in our lives, we don't have to. The truth is that as believers in Jesus Christ, the devil only has as much power in our lives as we allow him to have. He has no claim to us. Those that are outside of Christ are still under the devil's power – God did not remove the devil from our world (that will indeed come later) and other people under the devil's power can certainly affect us. But God made a way through Jesus and His sacrifice for us to walk free of the devil. In Christ, the devil is not a concern – he has been disarmed by Jesus.

This passage from Colossians also tells us that just as Jesus has been raised from the dead, so we also have been raised with Him and made alive with Him through our faith.

The apostle Paul prayed this for the Ephesians and I believe he would pray the same for you and me:

> I do not cease to give thanks for you, remembering you in my prayers, that the God of our Lord Jesus Christ, the Father of glory, may give you the Spirit of wisdom and of revelation in the knowledge of him, having the eyes of your hearts enlightened, that you may know what is the hope to which he has called you, what are the riches of his glorious inheritance in the saints, and what is the immeasurable greatness of his power toward us who believe, according to the working of his great might that he worked in Christ when he raised him from the dead and seated him at his right hand in the heavenly places, far above all rule and authority and power and dominion, and above every name that is named, not only in this age but also in the one to come.

> And he put all things under his feet and gave him as
> head over all things to the church, which is his body,
> the fullness of him who fills all in all. (Ephesians 1:16–
> 23 ESV)

This tells us that Jesus right now is seated at the right hand of the
Father, has full authority over all, that all things have been put under his feet, and He is the head over the church. Paul prayed that the
Ephesians (and I'll add "you and me") would understand the glori-
ous inheritance that we have in Jesus and the "immeasurable
greatness of his power" that's available to us.

Through our faith in Jesus, we died with Christ and were also
raised with Him. We're told in Ephesians 2:6 that God "raised us up
together, and made us sit together in heavenly places in Christ Jesus." Notice this is past tense: we died, we were raised up, we were
made to sit in Heaven. It's already been done! The incredible truth is
that there's a part of us right now that is seated with Jesus at the
right hand of the Father in Heaven!

> If then you were raised with Christ, seek those things
> which are above, where Christ is, sitting at the right
> hand of God. Set your mind on things above, not on
> things on the earth. For you died, and your life is hid-
> den with Christ in God. (Colossians 3:1–3 NKJV)

The spirit part of us is united with Christ, and since Christ is in
Heaven, so are we! We need to renew our mind to this truth! Christ
is in us and we are in Him – we are one unit together. 1 Corinthians
6:17 tells us that we have been joined to the Lord ("But he that is
joined unto the Lord is one spirit.") We've already discussed in earlier chapters that Romans 5:17 talks about reigning in life through
Jesus Christ. Reigning implies that we are in a position to reign.
And indeed we are!

We know that Christ defeated the devil through the cross and
resurrection. He triumphed over them. He broke the power of the
devil over us. We are in Christ and seated with Him in His victorious state at the right hand of the Father. We are with Him in His

position of authority. We know that Jesus has authority. He said in Matthew 28:18 "All Power is given unto me in heaven and in earth." He then goes on to delegate that authority to the church. And we are in Christ. We have authority in Him. All the authority that was given to Christ belongs to us through Him and we can exercise it.

When Jesus was here, He sent out seventy of his disciples and told them that they had power to "tread on serpents and scorpions, and over ALL the power of the enemy: and nothing shall by any means hurt you." (Luke 10:19, emphasis mine). Does the Church today after the victory Jesus won at the cross have LESS authority than Jesus gave to the seventy before He died and rose again? NO!

Colossians 1:13 tells us that we've already been delivered "from the power of darkness" and have been transferred "into the kingdom of His dear Son" – that we've switched kingdoms. The devil has no authority over us anymore. We are in the kingdom that has authority over the devil. We are in Christ.

We are told in James 4:7 to submit to God and resist the devil and he will flee from us. We're told in Ephesians 4:27 "Neither give place to the devil." We have to have authority over the devil or the Bible wouldn't tell us to do something about him. We can resist him and cause him to flee. The power that is in us is greater than the devil's power in the world (1 John 4:4).

We are described in the Bible as the "body of Christ." In the Ephesians 1 passage we looked at a moment ago, we saw that Christ is described as being the "head of the body." We also saw that it said that all things are under Christ's feet. We are Christ's body. That means all things are under OUR feet! Christ uses us as the body to exercise authority over the devil here – a body is where the ACTION takes place. Christ is no longer physically here on this planet in His physical body, but before He left this earth, He gave His people authority and called us His body. We as His people are His body on this earth. In the examples we see in Scripture of Jesus delegating authority, He tells us to DO things and take authority over the devil and things that might harm us (e.g. Luke 10, Mark 16). God intends for His Church, the Body of Christ, to be exercising its authority. The Church has much more authority than we've realized. For instance, this is why Jesus told us we can bind or loose things here and they will be bound or loosed in heaven (Matthew 18:18). We have tremendous authority through Christ and God's intention is for us to exercise that authority. We are to be His hands and feet – His Body here – putting the authority we have in Him into action here in this world.

We've been restored through Jesus to a position of authority. One of the devil's most successful strategies against the Church is to convince us that we basically are nothing and have no power. And while in ourselves, that is a largely true statement, we aren't in ourselves – we are in Christ. Jesus told us that apart from Him we "can do nothing" (John 15:5), but praise God that we aren't apart from Him, but rather in Him! The authority that we have springs out of the authority of Jesus and we are in Him. This popular notion that's out there of a weak and wimpy Church that just can't do anything until Jesus comes back is absolute nonsense!

Now some churches have recognized that the Church does have some authority and have gotten all gung-ho on "spiritual warfare." Unfortunately there are churches that have done so while forgetting that the authority that they have is not meant to be exercised apart from Jesus and that it is only in Jesus that they even have that authority. For some, the focus has shifted from Jesus to man. For others, the focus has shifted from Jesus to the devil, where the devil has been given WAY too much credit. They make it seem like the devil is this giant monster where we've got to have 300 believers fasting and praying and pleading the blood to get him to leave or back-off. The devil loves it when he gets elevated among Christians as having lots of power, when the reality is that he has ALREADY been disarmed at the cross by Jesus! I'm not saying there isn't power in believers coming together (because there is), but you yourself right now solely as a child of God that's seated at the Father's right hand ALREADY have authority over the devil because of Jesus.

This notion that we just need to limp along in life and try to keep our head above water as best we can and "hang on" until Heaven is straight from the pit of hell! The last thing the devil wants is Christians actually realizing what's really ours and taking our place of authority and reigning as the royalty that we are. The devil wants to keep us miserable and living weak, powerless lives – full of sin, sickness, discouragement, poverty. He wants us living defeated. We are not supposed to be UNDER anything: not the devil, not sin, not sickness, NOTHING! All things are under OUR feet in Christ and it's high time we start exercising the authority that is ours.

We are already blessed in Jesus! In Jesus, there's no curses, only blessings! In Jesus, we aren't subject to the curses that were pronounced for failing to live up to the old laws and regulations.

> Christ redeemed us from the curse of the law by becoming a curse for us – for it is written, "Cursed is everyone who is hanged on a tree" – so that in Christ Jesus the blessing of Abraham might come to the Gentiles, so that we might receive the promised Spirit through faith. (Galatians 3:13–14 ESV)

This verse is a pivotal one because it shows that in Jesus, there are no curses for us, only blessings. It specifically mentions Abraham. Abraham was also justified before God by faith (Hebrews 11) and he was blessed. This verse tells us that in the same way that Abraham was blessed, so are we.

You want to know something else that's almost too incredible to believe? Remember how sin and death began back in the Garden of Eden with Adam & Eve and have touched all of us since then? It's been a law – there's sin and sin leads to death and it is in the fabric of our world. Guess what? You're free of that too in Jesus.

> For the law of the Spirit of life has set you free in Christ Jesus from the law of sin and death. (Romans 8:2 ESV)

In Jesus, we are subject to a new law: the law of the Spirit of life. As already discussed in the last chapter, we've got a new spirit born of the Holy Spirit which is full of the "zoe" life of God. In Jesus, we are free from the law of sin and death. This is huge and I don't think there's that many Christians out there that really get this. Sin and death have no power over us! I know it seems like they do, but that's because we haven't realized what is ours. You can't walk in something you don't know is yours. Remember that whole renewing the mind thing from last chapter? This is where it comes into play. Just as if we don't realize we have authority over the devil, we will constantly be prey for his schemes and live defeated, if we don't realize that we have ALREADY been set free from the law of sin and death, we won't truly walk in that reality.

Now just because we've been set free from sin, does that mean we can't sin? Of course not – you and I both know that's not the case. But we don't HAVE to sin. People say, "Well of course we have to sin – we are sinners!" No, in Christ, we are no longer sinners, we are saints (1 Corinthians 1:2). John tells us "My little children, I am writing these things to you so that you may not sin. But if anyone does sin, we have an advocate with the Father, Jesus Christ the righteous." (1 John 2:1 ESV). The assumption is not that we just have to keep on sinning, but that we have been freed from sin (though with the knowledge that if we do sin, Jesus and His righteousness is our defense). The Apostle Paul bluntly tells us in Romans 6:15–18 that we are no longer "slaves to sin" and that we've been "set free from sin." It is true that we have ALREADY been freed from sin. But we also have to choose to walk in that (that's what a lot of Romans 6, 7, and 8 are about). As we talked about last chapter, we still have the flesh part of us. We still have to renew our minds – the process of sanctification is ongoing in us. So our experience might be that we still sin (though this should be increasingly less over time if we continue renewing our mind) but that doesn't mean that in actuality we haven't been freed from sin. Just because we aren't walking in the fullness of the reality doesn't mean it's any less true.

When it comes to death, we've been freed from that too. While in our society we refer to Christians as having "died" the same as we do for the atheist down the street, the experience of "death" for the believer isn't really death at all! It is truly death for the unbeliever. But for the believer, it's actually entering into the fullness of life in its ultimate sense. Believers do not actually "die!" Just as the grave couldn't hold Jesus, it can't hold us as we're in Jesus! This is why the writer of Hebrews could tell us:

> Since therefore the children share in flesh and blood, he
> [Jesus] himself likewise partook of the same things,
> that through death he might destroy the one who has
> the power of death, that is, the devil, and deliver all
> those who through fear of death were subject to life-
> long slavery. (Hebrews 2:14–15 ESV, bracketed text
> added)

We have no need to fear death – it's a non-issue for us – death is swallowed up in victory (see 1 Corinthians 15:54). In Christ we are set free from having to be a slave to fear of death (as those outside of Christ are – which usually they deal with by just forcing themselves to avoid thinking about at all costs). Jesus, who calls Himself our "Good Shepherd" (John 10:11) that takes care of His sheep (those that have believed in Him), will take our hand and walk with us "through the valley of the shadow of death" (Psalm 23:4b) – it's just a shadow for us, not the substance – and deliver us safely where we shall "dwell in the house of the LORD for ever." (Psalm 23:6b). There's nothing for us to fear. Now that doesn't mean that we should be anxious to go; we want to fulfill all that God has for us to do. We were "created in Christ Jesus for good works, which God prepared beforehand, that we should walk in them." (Ephesians 2:10b ESV).

As Christians, there is a certain "balancing act" because part of us really longs to be fully at home with the Lord. Sometimes our feelings about our present circumstances sway us emotionally more one way or the other. When things are seemingly going great and we've got lots of people (i.e. friends/loved ones) around us here, we might be more prone to not be in a rush to go home to Heaven. But in those dark times when we are hurting and all alone, all of a sudden the pull gets much stronger.

I'm reminded of the Apostle Paul talking about how he desired to depart and go home to be with the Lord (which he rightfully recognized as far better than this life on earth), and yet, he also understood that the Lord had a present work for him to complete on the earth. (Philippians 1:23–24). Just as Paul finished his race and completed what God had for Him, may we also strive to fulfill all that God has for us, with all our being. And then "depart in peace" (Luke 2:29) and run into the arms of our Jesus that loves us so very much.

But we don't want to "give up" before our time! Particularly people that are struggling with sickness or depression – especially if it's been going on for awhile – really have to guard against this. The devil would love to take you and me out so we don't fully fulfill the call on our lives and do all that God has for us to do. As I've struggled with sickness in the past, the devil has definitely whispered plenty of lies to me in this area, and my guess is some of you can identify. He's also not above whispering some truth, telling you about how much better Heaven will be to try to get you to put all your focus on Heaven and give up the fight here so you don't fully fulfill your purpose and affect others here by drawing them closer to Jesus. I can remember one very poignant example back in 2009 where I was in so much pain physically and emotionally that the devil really worked overtime to get me to "give up and go Home." If I had done so, I would have missed out on all sorts of things God had and still has for me to do and missed affecting people with the love and truth of Jesus – changing lives for all eternity!

Getting back to death itself though, we have been freed from it – there's nothing to fear. But just as with the issue of sin, the degree to which we renew our mind to this truth will affect the degree to which we actually are free from death on a practical level in our own life – the degree to which we are free of the fear of death.

Do you know what else results from the law of sin and death in this world? Sickness. Sin brought forth sickness and disease and death. If you've been set free from the law of sin and death, then you've also by definition been set free from sickness. All sin for all time was paid for by Jesus on the cross, right? The sin problem that started back in the Garden was dealt with by Jesus; He paid for it. Sickness is a fruit, or result, of sin that was introduced in the Garden. The root problem was sin. If you deal with the root, you also take care of the fruit. Jesus dealt with the root problem of sin, and thus also dealt with the fruit of sin, including sickness. Sin, Sickness, Death – you are FREE of these in Jesus Christ! As we've already talked about in regards to sin and death though, that doesn't mean we can't ever be sick. Again, just because we aren't walking in the fullness of the reality doesn't mean it's any less true.

The reality is that because of Jesus' work on the cross, we have already been freed from sin, we've already been freed from death, and we've already been freed from sickness. It's already been done. As a whole, we as a church have greatly underestimated what really happened at Calvary. When Jesus said, "it is finished", He really meant that it was finished! We've already seen in earlier chapters that healing was provided for in the atonement the same as for-giveness of sins. The work that paid for your well-being in every respect has already been accomplished. You've ALREADY been brought into relationship with God, you've ALREADY been forgiv-en of your sins, you've ALREADY been freed from the power of sin, you've ALREADY been made righteous, you've ALREADY been restored to a place of authority over the devil, you've ALREADY been freed from the power of death, you've ALREADY been healed, you've ALREADY been freed from the power of sick-ness, you've ALREADY been made a victor, and I can go on and on. The work has already been done! All these things are yours in Christ.

The mistake that people make is because we can look at our-selves and look at others and see that we still have sin issues or are still sick or are still fearful of death, or whatever, that that means that we need to still GET something from God. So, many will try to earn God's approval through their actions. Even though most Chris-tians intellectually recognize that salvation is by God's grace and that works flow out of that, in practice, many still try to do things in order to get things from God. Many still operate on a law-based mentality, rather than a grace-based one. It's an "If I do X and I'm worthy enough, then God will do Y" way of thinking. When we get into a situation where we feel like what we're doing isn't worthy enough/not working such as still being in bondage to a sin (addic-tion) despite our best efforts, then we will beg God for freedom and to set us free. Or if we're sick, we'll beg and plead with God to heal us or cry out for "Heaven to come down" and touch us. Most of the church world is looking for God to do something in their lives that He's already done! You may remember that this is how I opened this chapter. Many people approach God in this way. It's all an attitude of "God, I am nothing and I have nothing, and I've got this problem and I need you to do something about it."

It's a total shift when we begin to realize that God has ALREADY done something about it and that what we REALLY need to do is renew our minds to these things and get in agreement with God about who we are in Christ and what's already been provided for us in Him. It's a difference of approaching God in begging mode, or approaching God in victor mode because of Jesus and appropriating by faith the things that God has already provided for us.

If we see ourselves, as most Christians do, as those that just are powerless and helpless in this world unless God in His sovereignty does some miracle, we will continue going around and around the same mountains over and over again. God does sovereignly do miracles (praise God!), but if He does so, we'll only be good to go until the next time we need His miraculous intervention. This is a major reason why there's so little victory in the lives of many people. They are relying solely on God's sovereign miracle intervention instead of relying on what He has already provided for them. God's plan for us is to realize what He's already given and for us to walk in those blessings.

People think it's being presumptuous or not being humble to step beyond the "Poor Me" mentality, but it's not true! People sing songs about how small and insignificant we are, but how Great and Mighty God is, and they quote select Old Testament scriptures that back up this worldview. It is true that outside of Christ, we are nothing. But as Christians, we are not outside of Christ! We are "hidden with Christ in God" (Col. 3:3 ESV) – we are in Christ. Jesus is not nothing or insignificant and we are joined to Him. It sounds good on the surface for us to say that we are nothing and that God is everything and we just need His help to intervene in our lives – it sounds very religious. But it's not in line with what the Bible says is ours and that mentality keeps people in bondage! It's not being humble to not take hold of what God has provided for us; rather it's just being ignorant or stupid (pardon my bluntness). For most people (including myself for far too long), it's just ignorance – we were not taught correctly.

When we grasp hold of our true identity as royalty: that we are a son or daughter of the Most High God that's seated at His right hand in Jesus, party to all of God's blessings and favor and everything we could ever need, and are already in a place of victory – when we really grasp that, it changes everything about how we relate to ourselves and relate to God.

If we don't know who we really are and what's been provided for us, it doesn't really matter much if it's been done or provided for us, because it won't profit us. The first step in practically walking in victory here is knowing what has already been provided for us. Jesus said "If you abide in my word, you are truly my disciples, and you will know the truth, and the truth will set you free." (John 8:31b–32 ESV). Notice Jesus didn't just say that the truth will set you free; He first said that you will *know* the truth. It is out of knowing the truth that it will set you free. What you don't know can hurt you. As we abide in Jesus and His word (this is basically the "renewing the mind" part), we will know the truth and then the truth will set us free. If you don't know the truth, it won't have a whole lot of practical effect for you.

You know why there's lots of Christians in bondage to sin? A major reason is because while we've acknowledged that Jesus has forgiven us, we haven't realized He also has freed us! Many keep trying to free themselves by doing this or doing that, and that's not much different than a dog chasing their own tail. The ultimate answer to the sin problem is to realize that God has *already* provided the ultimate answer to the sin problem. Many approach God continually begging Him for forgiveness as if He might say "no" – not realizing that forgiveness has already been fully paid for and provided. They don't realize that because of the shed blood of Jesus, they are already righteous in God's eyes. People will live up (or down) to how they see themselves. If they see themselves as a rotten sinner, they will most likely live in line with that. If they see themselves as a righteous royal saint that's deeply loved and is already seated with Christ in a position of authority, they will be more apt to live in line with that. Behavior follows our beliefs.

You know why there's just as many sick Christians as unbelievers? A major reason is because most Christians haven't expected anything different! We've thought that all we got out of this whole Jesus thing was forgiveness of our sins and a good future in Heaven when we die.

We need to start elevating our view of who we are and what's been provided for us.

> His divine power has granted to us all things that pertain to life and godliness, through the knowledge of him who called us to his own glory and excellence, by which he has granted to us his precious and very great promises, so that through them you may become partakers of the divine nature, having escaped from the corruption that is in the world because of sinful desire. (2 Peter 1:3–4 ESV)

God has already granted to us all things that we need for life and godliness, and this comes through our knowledge of Jesus and who He is and what we have in Him. We have incredibly precious and great promises, and through these promises we are actually able to partake of God's divine nature. Just a quick sidebar, but I have to point out that God isn't sick or diseased in his nature. God's divine nature is full of life and health. Through Jesus, we are able to partake of God's divine nature – this is almost too good to be true news. Colossians 2:9–10 says "For in him [Jesus] the whole fullness of deity dwells bodily, and you have been filled in him, who is the head of all rule and authority." (ESV, bracketed text added for clarity). Jesus has the fullness of deity and we are in Jesus – through Him we partake of God's divine nature. This might sound almost blasphemous if it wasn't for the fact that it is what the Bible says!

We are God's children that He dearly loves and we are actually His heirs. And heirs get stuff from their parents. God is our father and we have an incredible inheritance!

> The Spirit Himself bears witness with our spirit that we are children of God, and if children, then heirs—heirs of God and joint heirs with Christ, if indeed we suffer

with *Him,* that we may also be glorified together. (Romans 8:16–17 NKJV)

Notice that it doesn't just say that we are heirs, but joint heirs with Christ. As a co-heir with Jesus, that means everything Jesus gets, we get because we are co-heirs with Him. From an inheritance standpoint, everything that Jesus gets from the Father is also ours. This is off-the-charts incredible!

Now the naysayers against all this good news of all that we have in Jesus tend to skip right over the part that tells us that we're children of God and "heirs of God, and joint-heirs with Christ" and instead hone in on the part of this verse talking about suffering. They'll say: "See – it says right here that we're supposed to suffer here in this life!" There are some people that really want to defend their view that this life here is supposed to be miserable. And it's hard to blame them, because there's been a lot of erroneous teaching out there that's put that forth. In regards to this specific passage, in light of what Paul has been talking about in Romans 6–8, he has been talking about the fact that as believers we already were baptized into Jesus' death and we need to live in such a way that we practically die to ourselves and walk in the life we have in the Spirit. In other words, to identify ourselves with Christ's suffering on the cross and then identify with His resurrection. This could fit with what Paul says here.

But I want to address the bigger point because as soon as you start talking about all the good things that we have in Jesus and how we can live a victorious life here, some people start throwing scriptures around that talk about suffering. Most people when they see the word "suffering" think of all the sickness and pain and sin and so forth we see around us. The problem is that most of the scriptures that talk about suffering in the New Testament are within the context of suffering for our faith as can be easily seen by reading the surrounding texts! The early believers suffered much persecution and they wrote along those lines encouraging people to endure it, hang on, etc. Many people just apply the word "suffer" or "suffering" much more broadly than I believe was likely intended. For instance, Paul in the first chapter of 2 Corinthians talks quite a bit about suffering and things that he and his companions endured. But in talking about this suffering, he says this: "For as we share abundantly in Christ's sufferings, so through Christ we share abundantly in comfort too." (2 Cor. 1:5 ESV). He's equating his suffering as sharing in Christ's sufferings. How did Christ suffer? Was Christ walking around sick or diseased or depressed? No, he was persecuted which then caused him to suffer in various ways (including in his body). Paul identifies that his suffering is similar.

While I do believe we have victory in Jesus and are blessed in Him, I don't see anything in the Word that tells us that we won't suffer persecution for our faith – in fact, I read the opposite (e.g. 2 Timothy 3:12). If we're doing it right, we will suffer for our faith. It may be relatively minor or it might be major like the early church experienced or believers in some third-world countries today experience, but suffering's pretty much a guarantee. So even if you didn't like my explanation for Romans 8:17 above (which I concede could be wrong), it is still legit for Paul to mention suffering with Christ. Christ suffered persecution and as fellow heirs with Him that are truly following Him, we will too.

In addition to persecution, there just is the simple fact that we are living in a fallen world and even though I believe we can walk victoriously in Christ, this is a process as we renew our mind. So believers do still experience hard things here. In John 16:33, Jesus says, "I have said these things to you, that in me you may have peace. In the world you will have tribulation. But take heart; I have overcome the world." (ESV). This world is indeed full of tribulation and it touches all of us – I don't think anyone would dispute that. But notice that Jesus tells us to take heart (or "be of good cheer" in other translations) because He has overcome the world! If He's overcome the world, and we're in Him, then we've overcome the world too! This is why we can really be of good cheer!

Most of us have been programmed by religion to see God as being in a bad mood all the time and this world as nothing but trouble and heartache that we can't do anything about but passively just experience until we go be with Jesus! I tried to heavily address the part about how we view God way back in Chapter 2, but it's just so ingrained in most of us that it bears a little repeating. We have a good God that is for us! As the Romans passage mentions, we are "children of God" and "heirs of God, and joint-heirs with Christ"! Our Daddy loves to lavish on His kids.

> "Or which one of you, if his son asks him for bread, will give him a stone? Or if he asks for a fish, will give him a serpent? If you then, who are evil, know how to give good gifts to your children, how much more will your Father who is in heaven give good things to those who ask him!" (Matthew 7:9–11 ESV)

Jesus said the above to "unsaved" people, hence the "evil" designation. His point though was that if even men and women outside of Christ love their kids and want to do good things for them, how much more our good Heavenly Father! God enjoys giving us good things! And the truth is that the ultimate lavishing came in the form of Christ Himself and His sacrifice for us. We deserved hell, but God loved us so much that He gave us Jesus to not only pay for our sins, but also to bring us into an abiding relationship with Him in fullness of life where everything He has is ours. Through Jesus, much like the older son in the parable of the Prodigal Son in Luke 15, all that the Father has is already ours (Lk 15:31). In Christ, we get it all! This is the real message of Grace. This is the real Good News.

In Christ, all of God's promises are a resounding "Yes." "For all the promises of God in Him *are* Yes, and in Him Amen, to the glory of God through us." (2 Corinthians 1:20 NKJV). It's never "well, some promises are only for you if you are good enough or do enough things right." It's always "yes" for you in Jesus because Jesus paid the price for that. It's based on Him, not you.

When we really start realizing all that God has given us through Christ, we really start realizing just how incredibly loved we are. You have a Heavenly Father that's crazy in love with you and has never rejected you. He knows you intimately and loves you personally. He knows who He made in you and He knows the plans He has for you. He is on your side and He is with you every step of the way on this journey through this life on into all eternity. He doesn't want you defeated and negative and constantly "under" things, but rather to walk confidently and joyously and victoriously knowing who you are and what you have.

You are in Christ. And that is enough.

Chapter 9 – Faith & Healing

One of the areas that we have spent some time talking about is that of healing and how it is something that is available to us as children of God. This is a major and controversial subject within the Body of Christ, especially when it comes to how faith and healing inter-relate. Faith in the context of healing is something that just tends to make some people very wary. People that are apt to dismiss divine healing or believe that God heals but only as He sovereignly chooses, often dismiss anyone outright that starts talking about having faith for healing – they get dismissed as being "one of those crazy faith people." For some, anyone that believes that there's an interaction between faith and healing is off the deep end. Usually people that feel this way also feel the same about those that speak in tongues or talk about the baptism of the Holy Spirit. I'm not getting into tongues or the baptism of the Holy Spirit right now, except to say that there *are* Biblical references to both and there are reasons why people believe in such things. Unfortunately because some people that believe in healing and tongues and the baptism of the Holy Spirit have also made real spectacles of themselves or have gone to extremes, it has sometimes been somewhat easy for people to dismiss them and what they believe. There's definitely been some "showy" nonsense out there. At the same time, just because there are such people, doesn't mean that everything that they believe is wrong.

One of the challenges when talking about the subject of healing is that we all either ourselves have had, or are having, issues with health, or we have people close to us that have had, or are having, issues with health. And most of us probably have had those close to us die from ill health. Because of this, the natural tendency is often for people to get offended if a teaching in any way seems that it is putting responsibility back on us. Most people just tend to adopt an attitude that everything that happens must be God's will because that is a much more comforting thought. So if a loved one comes down with cancer, well that must be God's will. And while we might pray for healing, often those prayers will reflect this view by saying something along the lines of: "God I ask to you heal so-and-so, if it be Your will." In other words, we just put everything for healing 100% back on God, if He feels like it. This is the position that much of the church world takes. It really requires very little from us.

The problem I have with this is that you can look to the vast majority of individual healing cases recorded for us that Jesus performed and you will find faith in operation on the part of the person needing healing. There is a clear interplay in Scripture between our faith and our receiving healing. I'm not saying that I fully understand that interplay and I'm not convinced that anyone does *completely* understand that interplay, but that one Scripturally exists cannot be denied. Let's look at some examples together, shall we?

> 25 Now a certain woman had a flow of blood for twelve years, 26 and had suffered many things from many physicians. She had spent all that she had and was no better, but rather grew worse. 27 When she heard about Jesus, she came behind *Him* in the crowd and touched His garment. 28 For she said, "If only I may touch His clothes, I shall be made well."
>
> 29 Immediately the fountain of her blood was dried up, and she felt in *her* body that she was healed of the affliction. 30 And Jesus, immediately knowing in Himself that power had gone out of Him, turned around in the crowd and said, "Who touched My clothes?"
>
> 31 But His disciples said to Him, "You see the multitude thronging You, and You say, 'Who touched Me?'"
>
> 32 And He looked around to see her who had done this thing. 33 But the woman, fearing and trembling, knowing what had happened to her, came and fell down before Him and told Him the whole truth. 34 And He said to her, "Daughter, your faith has made you well. Go in peace, and be healed of your affliction." (Mark 5:25–34 NKJV)

Here we have a woman that had a real problem – she had a problem with female bleeding that had been going on for a long time. She went to the doctors and had spent all her money on them. Rather than just being sick, she ended up even more sick AND broke besides (see vs 26). She was in a desperate situation – one that seemed absolutely hopeless.

In those days, the fact that this woman had a continual flow of blood meant that she was considered "unclean" and she couldn't go into a crowd without yelling out "Unclean!" so that others could scurry away from her. If she didn't do so, then she could be stoned to death! This was a very limiting and disabling problem this woman had – one for which she had no hope in the natural. I imagine she was quite weak and exhausted due to this physical problem. But then something changed! She heard about Jesus (vs 27). She heard that He was the Messiah and that He had been healing people. And this caused hope to stir and her faith to well up and she declared with her mouth: "If only I may touch His clothes, I shall be made well." (Mark 5:28b NKJV).

This same story is also reiterated in Luke 8 and Matthew 9 (this fact alone tells us that it's something God must think is important to relate to us since it is in the Bible in three different places!). In Mark's account as related above, it doesn't actually tell us what she did next (though it's obvious from the rest of the text), but she got herself out into the crowd and made her way right behind Jesus. She let her faith propel her into action. Even though she was "unclean" and could have been stoned to death not only for mingling in the crowd without yelling out that she was unclean, but also for touching Jesus, she had such faith that if she could just touch Jesus that she would be well, that she didn't let those facts distract her. She "came from behind and touched the border of His garment. And immediately her flow of blood stopped." (Luke 8:44 NKJV).

In verses 29–30 in the Mark account above, we see that as soon as she touches Jesus' garment, that she knows she has received her healing and that Jesus also knows that healing power has gone out from Him. Jesus turned around in the crowd to see who it was and He asked the crowd who had touched Him (vs 30). Yet this question from Jesus amazed the disciples because pretty much EVERYONE was touching Jesus and they couldn't understand why He would even ask such a question (vs 31). Yet, Jesus's response to them was that "Somebody touched Me, for I perceived power going out from Me." (Luke 8:46b NKJV). While most everyone else in the crowd may have been touching Jesus, only one caused power to flow out of Jesus: this courageous, faith-filled woman.

The woman realizes that she can't stay hidden and she explains everything to Jesus and the crowd. She tells all about her condition, and all about what she believed. And Jesus tells her in verse 34 of Mark 5: "Daughter, your faith has made you well." (NKJV).

Wait just a minute! I thought it was Jesus' power that made her well as it flowed into her? Yet Jesus doesn't say one word about His power. He doesn't say: "Daughter, it's my power that made you well." Jesus point blank told her (and us) that it was her own faith that made her well. It is true that it was His power flowing to her that healed her, but that power was released to her because of her faith! Jesus knew the source of her healing was her faith in Him and that's what He called out.

This woman heard about Jesus, she believed something about Jesus, she spoke something about Jesus, and then she got herself to Jesus! This woman exercised faith and her faith overcame her situation. Her faith made her well.

Let me ask a question if I may? Why didn't all those other people touching Jesus cause power to come out of Him? All these people were touching Him and bumping into Him, and yet only one caused power to flow out of Jesus. What made the difference? Jesus Himself identified the difference for us: faith.

Don't you imagine in a crowd that size with people all thronging around Jesus that there was at least one other sick person or someone with some malady of some kind? Why aren't we told of anyone else causing power to flow out of Jesus and receive their healing besides this woman? Jesus makes clear that despite all the people touching Him, only one caused power to flow from Him. Note also that Jesus didn't actively choose to have that power flow from Him; In fact, the way the text reads, He actually almost seems a bit surprised by it. This woman exercised her faith in Jesus and she received from Jesus without Him consciously seeking her out. Rather, she sought HIM out in faith, and she received her answer.

If this example showcasing an interplay between faith and healing (which as mentioned, is repeated three times in the Bible) was the only one, it would be enough to establish that fact. But alas, this story is NOT the only one – there are many more. For the sake of time, we'll just quickly examine another one – that of the blind man Bartimaeus:

> 46 And they came to Jericho. And as he was leaving Jericho with his disciples and a great crowd, Bartimaeus, a blind beggar, the son of Timaeus, was sitting by the roadside. 47 And when he heard that it was Jesus of Nazareth, he began to cry out and say, "Jesus, Son of David, have mercy on me!" 48 And many rebuked him, telling him to be silent. But he cried out all the more, "Son of David, have mercy on me!" 49 And Jesus stopped and said, "Call him." And they called the blind man, saying to him, "Take heart. Get up; he is calling you." 50 And throwing off his cloak, he sprang up and came to Jesus. 51 And Jesus said to him, "What do you want me to do for you?" And the blind man said to him, "Rabbi, let me recover my sight." 52 And Jesus said to him, "Go your way; your faith has made you well." And immediately he recovered his sight and followed him on the way. (Mark 10:46–52 ESV)

This same event is also recounted in Luke 18:35–43. I want to point out a couple of items if I may. First, we are told in verse 47 that Bartimaeus began to cry out when he heard that Jesus was passing by. He obviously had heard about Jesus previously and he knew and believed that Jesus was the Messiah. How do we know this? He called Jesus the "Son of David." This is a Messianic title referring to the Messiah being in the line of David (see Isaiah 9:7), which was well known to be the case by the people (e.g. Matt. 12:23). By calling Jesus the "Son of David", he in essence was saying: "Jesus,

I believe you are the Messiah, have mercy on me!" He was exhibiting faith in Jesus by vocalizing the belief that was in his heart.

The response of the people to his crying out was to rebuke him and tell him to be quiet. Many people might have given up at this juncture. When everyone around you comes against you, it can be hard to stand alone, and the temptation is to just shrink back. But not this man; his faith propelled him further. They told him to be quiet, but not only did he not do that, he did the opposite – he got louder! He "cried out all the more" to Jesus, declaring Him to be the Messiah and seeking His help. And you know what? Jesus stopped and called him. I find it interesting that Jesus didn't go to him, but rather called Bartimaeus to come to Him. Remember, Bartimaeus is blind! We are told that Bartimaeus was sitting by the roadside begging. I imagine that this was common for him and that all the people (including Jesus) knew who he was and why he was there.

When reading many of the healing accounts in the gospels, you find that it was common for Jesus to in some way provide an opportunity for the person in question to speak forth and exercise their faith. In this case, not only does Jesus call the blind man to come to Him, but then He asks him to vocalize what he desires of Jesus. Upon hearing that Jesus called him, we are told in verse 50 that Bartimaeus threw off his cloak and sprang up and went to Jesus. His faith propelled him up and to Jesus! It's no accident that the Bible tells us that he sprang up. This man acted in very clear terms on his faith in Jesus!

Jesus asks Bartimaeus what he wants Jesus to do for him and he responds that he wants to see. Jesus's response in verse 52 to him is: "Go your way; your faith has made you well." (ESV) Like the woman with the issue of blood, while the healing comes from Jesus, Jesus Himself credits the healing as due to the man's faith.

Let me ask a rather uncomfortable question if I may. What if Bartimaeus had just sat by the side of the road feeling sorry for himself and just passively saying: "Jesus, I wish you'd heal me if you can, or if it be your will." Or what if when the people told him to be quiet, he did so? Would Jesus have stopped and called him? Would Bartimaeus have received his sight? Jesus credited this man's faith and we see his faith in action. Had he not exhibited that faith and put his faith into action, would he have received the same result? It's worth considering this.

In addition to Bartimaeus and the woman with the issue of blood, faith is showcased to be a major issue in numerous other situations. With the two blind men in Matthew 9:29, Jesus says "According to your faith be it unto you." He told one of the ten lepers, "Rise and go your way; your faith has made you well." (Luke 17:19b ESV) He told the Canaanite woman, "O woman, great is your faith! Be it done for you as you desire." (Matthew 15:28b ESV). With the paralytic, we are told that Jesus responded when He saw the faith of he and his friends as showcased in Luke 5:20, Mark 2:5, and Matthew 9:2 [the text is taken by some to just refer to the faith of the friends, but the paralytic himself surely had to have some faith operating also to even let his friends lower him down!] Jesus told the Centurion, "Go your way; and as you have believed, *so* let it be done for you." (Matthew 8:13b NKJV). He also commended the Centurion's faith saying, "I tell you, not even in Israel have I found such faith." (Luke 7:9b ESV). When Jairus was told that his daughter had died, Jesus said to him, "Do not fear; only believe, and she will be well." (Luke 8:50b ESV). Even though his daughter had just died and the people told him not to bother Jesus any more, Jesus highlighted the importance of faith for Jairus – He told him not to fear, but rather to believe.

Friends, I could go on and on. Even where faith is not explicitly called out in the text, the actions and words frequently showcase faith in operation to some degree. Often Jesus actually had to push a little bit to get people exercising their faith, but that was the end result.

This whole "faith thing" wasn't only just for when Jesus was here physically, but it's also for us today in the church. After Jesus had ascended into Heaven, there's a story of a lame man healed in Acts 3. Peter gives this explanation for the healing: "And his name – by faith in his name – has made this man strong whom you see and know, and the faith that is through Jesus has given the man this perfect health in the presence of you all." (Acts 3:16 ESV). Notice, Peter didn't say it was special anointing that he or John had because they were Apostles that brought healing to the man, but rather it was faith that brought about the healing.

This actually is somewhat important because one of the arguments against divine healing that sometimes gets touted is that it passed away with the Apostles. In other words that the Apostles had special healing anointing that nobody else could have. This used to be a fairly common argument, though you don't hear it as much these days. I know I grew up with this sort of assumption – that there were things that the Apostles could do because they were "special" that you and I can't do. The problem with this view is that the Bible completely rejects that! All of the book of Acts and all of the epistles/most of the rest of the New Testament are all about showing us and teaching us what we have in Christ and showing us how we as a church should operate, not telling us stories of what the early church did but we could never expect to see. There is zero indication that any of the spiritual gifts have passed away with the Apostles. There is zero indication that people receiving healing has passed away with the Apostles. The age that began when Jesus ascended and left His followers here as His body on the earth (the church) is still ongoing. We are still in that same period of time. What was available to the early believers is available to us now.

In Acts 3, when the lame man was healed, people were apt to do the same thing they do today when someone receives some blessing through the means of another believer: assume that the other believer must be "super special" and that it was all their doing. Peter put a stop to this. He told the crowd: "Men of Israel, why do you wonder at this, or why do you stare at us, as though by our own power or piety we have made him walk?" (Acts 3:12b ESV). He then went on to share, as quoted earlier, that it was Jesus and specifically faith in and through Jesus that brought about the healing. Peter specifically debunked the view that it was because he had special power or that it was because of his own works, but he made quite clear that the issue was one of faith.

In Acts 14, we are told of a crippled man that Paul came across.

8 Now at Lystra there was a man sitting who could not use his feet. He was crippled from birth and had never

walked. 9 He listened to Paul speaking. And Paul, looking intently at him and seeing that he had faith to be
made well, 10 said in a loud voice, "Stand upright on
your feet." And he sprang up and began walking. (Acts
14:8–10 ESV)

Notice that the man had been listening to Paul speaking about
Jesus. Something about what Paul was saying must have caused
faith to rise up in the man to believe God for healing (which tends
to suggest that Paul was speaking about the healing available
through faith in Jesus). Paul perceived this faith (vs. 9) and told the
man to take a faith action by standing up – which was something he
couldn't do. We are explicitly told upfront that the man could not
use his feet and hadn't ever walked. And yet, Paul told him to stand
up on his feet! The man could have said, "But I CAN'T!" But he
didn't do that. His faith propelled him into action and he stood up –
actually he SPRANG up – and began walking. Paul sensed in his
spirit (the King James uses the word "perceiving") that this man
had faith to be made well and indeed he did. The man's faith
brought him healing. Paul did not heal this man, just as Peter and
John didn't heal the lame man in Acts 3. In both cases, faith was the
identified issue.

If the reason that people were healed when Jesus was here was
only because Jesus was physically here and touched them and it was
all up to Jesus, and if the reason that people were healed in the early
church was only because the Apostles had special anointing and it
was all up to the Apostles, then I could understand the argument
that says that healing isn't available today. But that isn't what the
Bible shows us. The Bible showcases the central issue, not only in
regards to healing, but everything (going all the way back to the
book of Genesis) is one of faith. Faith was a central issue in people
receiving healing when Jesus was here. Faith was a central issue for
the early church receiving healing. And faith is a central issue for
you and me. Faith has not passed away. Just as the early church
looked back to the sacrifice of Jesus and through faith received
healing (this is what Peter specifically calls out as the reason for the

lame man's healing in Acts 3), so also today we can receive in the same way.

None of these people that I've mentioned were passive. They didn't adopt a "maybe Jesus will heal me if He feels like it" attitude. No, they were very active in their faith. You see the blind guys crying out for Jesus. You see the woman with the issue of blood, who spent all her money on doctors and continued to grow worse, push through the crowd (despite the fact that she could have been stoned to death for doing so since she was unclean) and say to herself that if she could just reach Jesus she would be made whole – and you see Jesus commend her faith telling her point-blank that it was her faith that made her whole. You see guys lowering their friend (and him allowing them to lower him) through the roof to get to Jesus. You see the Centurion who's servant was sick believing Jesus so much that He knew that even Jesus' Word would make His servant well and you see Jesus commending His faith. You see Jesus telling the father of the little girl that died to just believe. After Jesus had already ascended into Heaven, you see the lame man in Acts 3 and the crippled man in Acts 14 both leaping / springing up and putting their faith in Jesus for their healing into action. And on and on...

The point is with most all of the individual healings recorded, you see some degree of faith in action on the part of the individual, not some passive, "if it be your will" kind of talk. In fact, the one time that we have record of Jesus being asked if He willed to heal someone, He replied affirmatively (Matthew 8:2). So I just can't get around the fact that there is an interplay between our faith and healing. In other words, I can't just 100% put it all over on God. I've got a part to play too.

There is an interaction between our faith and healing, and I think many people just ignore this because it's less painful that way. It's much easier (on our emotions) to just put it all 100% over on God. We lower our theology to match our pain. This bears repeating, because it is what I believe much of the church world has done: We've lowered our theology to match our pain.

If we can just say that whether someone gets healed or not is solely 100% up to whether or not God wants to heal them, then it removes any responsibility from us. We can just say, "what will be, will be" and talk about how God is sovereign and knows what He is doing. So we talk about God "taking someone" when they die because God must have wanted them, and how when someone dies that "it must have just been their time." We never allow for the possibility, that when it comes to our own healing, that any of our own actions or beliefs could enter into the equation – it all gets put on God. It's "no-fault Christianity." Whatever happens, it's NOT my fault.

I realize that some of what I've been saying could be stirring feelings of guilt or anger. There is a balance to be struck with this stuff and some people take this faith stuff to an extreme that is not helpful in my opinion. I believe that there can be variables involved with healing beyond just this one. However, we do need to come to a place of acknowledging that there is a clear showcase in Scripture that our faith (or lack thereof) can interact with whether or not we receive healing. Anyone honestly looking at the Scriptures that isn't blinded by their own pain or experiences, has to come to that conclusion.

While the fact that such an interplay between our faith and receiving healing exists cannot be denied, as I said, I don't think that is necessarily the end of the story. There can be other things to consider as well. I also don't claim to fully understand everything related to faith as it relates to healing, but there are some things that I do know.

I do know that "faith *comes* by hearing, and hearing by the word of God." (Romans 10:17b NKJV). So part of us really having faith means that we are really hearing the word of God. This means that we are being taught appropriately. It's going to be hard for me to really have faith for healing (with no unbelief) if I'm being taught that maybe God will heal or maybe He won't depending on how He's feeling, etc. So the type of teaching that's been going around on this subject can be affecting our faith level for healing. If I'm only taught that the only thing I use my faith for is to become "born again", but I'm not taught that I can also exercise faith for healing (whether physical or emotional), then I'm not going to be having much faith for healing, am I?

Faith as a whole is a subject that I think many people do not really understand, and I also think is a subject that people get tripped up on. Biblical faith at its core is really about trusting God – it's about taking God at His Word, even if that contradicts what we might see or feel. Faith is not about having proof that we can see or feel in the natural, but about choosing to trust in what God tells us. This is why the Bible definition of faith tells us that "faith is the substance of things hoped for, the evidence of things not seen." (Hebrews 11:1 KJV). Faith has substance – it literally, as some other translations put it, is the assurance of things hoped for, and faith itself is evidence of things that we cannot see. Faith isn't about what we physically see, but about trusting in what God says is ours in His Word. It's about trusting God.

When you got "born again", isn't this what you did? Hebrews 4:2 tells us: "For unto us was the gospel preached, as well as unto them: but the word preached did not profit them, not being mixed with faith in them that heard it." (KJV). Many people hear the Gospel message but they don't become "born again" because they don't mix their faith with what they hear. But you heard the Word preached about how Jesus came and died for you and rose again and paid for all of your sins. You may have heard a Bible verse like John 3:16 that told you that if you believed in Jesus you would have eternal life. And at some point (perhaps even as a child where you don't really remember), you made a choice – you made a decision to believe in what God told you in His Word. You exercised your faith and put your faith in Jesus to have your sins forgiven and receive eternal life. You mixed your faith with what you heard. When you did that, you chose to believe in what you couldn't physically see, but you chose to believe it based on the Word of God (which God confirmed to your heart). In doing that, even though Jesus had already paid for the sins of the whole world, it became applicable to you because you exercised your choice in your own life to want Jesus' payment for your sins. You became a "born again" new creation. The method you used to do so was faith.

Faith for healing (be it physical or emotional) works exactly the same way. As I've already shown in previous chapters, salvation was never meant to be parsed out to only being for forgiveness of sins or only being for physical healing, but was rather a package deal encompassing wholeness in every respect. But the problem is that most people haven't been taught that. Most people have only been taught that Jesus came to forgive them of their sins. Since we've already mentioned that faith comes by hearing the Word of God (Romans 10:17), since that's the only part of the Word they've been taught, faith has only come for them to receive forgiveness of sins. They've believed in Jesus for part of His benefits, but not all. They've received part of salvation, but haven't fully realized all that is available to them in the salvation package. Once a person realizes though that health is also rightfully theirs as a blood-bought child of God and that they can exercise their faith for healing, then they are in a position to mix their faith with what they've heard and to receive.

On this side of the cross, we aren't trying to get healed, but as we discussed in the previous chapter, we are looking back to the finished work of Jesus whereby healing has already been provided for us. The faith that we exercise isn't in trying to get healed. The faith that we exercise is in believing what we already have in Jesus – that healing is ALREADY ours right NOW and must showcase in our bodies because it was purchased for us and is rightfully ours. God through His grace has provided for us, and we access and apply that provision to our lives through faith.

One of the chief arguments that come from people that don't understand healing and the topic of faith as it relates to healing is the "hospital argument." They'll claim, "Well, if all this faith stuff is true, why don't you just go to a hospital and heal everyone there by believing hard enough?" Sometimes a variation of this is used depending on what's being discussed. For instance, another method of receiving healing can be through the laying on of hands. We'll discuss this later. But in this case, the question gets modified to being one of "Why can't you just go clear out a hospital by laying hands on everyone?"

The answer in both cases is the same and is ultra simple. You can't do this for the same reason you can't go to a hospital (or a drug dealer's house) and get everyone "born again!" While our faith can have an impact on other people, those people have their own wills and they choose for themselves what they want to believe and what they want to receive. We each have authority over our own life. People don't become "born again" just because you believe for them; they have to believe in Jesus for themselves. (Sidenote: I do believe that children are 'covered' by their parents until they reach their own personal age of accountability). Likewise, just because I believe in healing, I can't go to a hospital and heal everyone there through what I believe any more than I can get them born again through what I believe. They have to participate. Now when it comes to healing, I can pray for them in faith and believe God and if they are receptive to that, then that can make a difference. But I'm not able to go clear out a hospital based on what I believe or just because I lay hands on someone. Laying hands on someone still requires the person to be receptive and exercise at least a degree of faith themselves in order to receive. I've been in several hospitals and I can tell you that there are plenty of people in them that are not even remotely exercising faith for healing. Some people even seem to almost enjoy being negative about their ailments.

In the western world, there's a certain wonder in some circles why there seem to be more evidences of the supernatural in "less civilized", third-world countries as opposed to places like America. I'm just throwing out that perhaps part of the reason for that is that people in those countries maybe haven't been polluted with as much of our unbelief – they have a more simple, child-like expectation than perhaps some of us more "learned" people have. Many of us have been taught to be very skeptical of the supernatural evidences. We've been taught that divine healing is a bunch of nonsense or only happens when God feels like it or if we beg Him hard enough. In being taught this, we haven't been having much faith for healing.

We've expected little, and we've gotten little.

There is a better way. It is time to elevate our expectations and believe God.

Chapter 10 – The Role of Faith

While many Christians are content going through their lives expecting little (and thus getting little), the Bible is constantly seeking to try and elevate our view and stir us up towards really believing and trusting God.

> But without faith it is impossible to please him: for he that cometh to God must believe that he is, and that he is a rewarder of them that diligently seek him. (Hebrews 11:6 KJV)

In this verse from Hebrews, we are told that having faith is a necessary component of pleasing God. We are told that those who come to God must believe that He is. I don't think that just means to believe that He exists, but also that He is indeed God and all that the Bible says He is, and thus all that we really need. When we believe that He "is", we are believing that He is everything that the Bible says He is. We are acknowledging that God "himself gives to all mankind life and breath and everything" (Acts 17:25b ESV) and "in him we live, and move, and have our being." (Acts 17:28a KJV). Our very life and all we need comes from God. He is our source and the appropriate object of our faith.

The Hebrews verse could have stopped there, but it goes out of its way to tell us that we also need to be believing that God really wants to reward us – telling us that God is a rewarder and that faith that pleases God believes this. We've already talked previously about how God is a good God who desires to do good for us. God's desire is not to hurt you, but to help you. His desire is for you to look to Him in faith and trust Him and believe that as you do that – as you genuinely look to Him and seek Him and trust Him – that He will reward you. God is for you, not against you.

Faith as a concept is first introduced to us in the first book of the Bible and it continues as a central theme all the way until the end. The 11th chapter of the book of Hebrews is known as the "faith chapter" because it shows the importance of faith and various ways that faith played a pivotal role in the history up to that point. We are told in verse 3 that "By faith we understand that the universe was created by the word of God, so that what is seen was not made out of things that are visible." (Hebrews 11:3 ESV). In other words, believing that the universe was created by God through His word requires faith. If you recall from the Genesis account, God spoke things into existence, and it is by faith that we believe the Bible account and choose to believe God. Believing in God and believing that God made our universe requires faith.

Hebrews 11 goes on to talk about the faith of Abel, Enoch, Noah, Abraham, Sarah, Isaac, Jacob, Joseph, Moses, and even the prostitute Rahab, highlighting some actions that they took that showcased faith in action. It then switches to make this generalized statement in verses 32–35:

> And what more shall I say? For time would fail me to tell of Gideon, Barak, Samson, Jephthah, of David and Samuel and the prophets – who through faith conquered kingdoms, enforced justice, obtained promises, stopped the mouths of lions, quenched the power of fire, escaped the edge of the sword, were made strong out of weakness, became mighty in war, put foreign armies to flight. Women received back their dead by resurrection. (Hebrews 11:32–35a ESV)

Notice that all of these things were accomplished through faith. This included people obtaining promises, kingdoms being conquered, protection from various enemies, people being made strong, and even resurrections from the dead. The chapter then goes on to relate that even how some people dealt with persecution (including death) also showcased faith.

The reason I am pointing all of this out is that faith is consistently portrayed in the Bible as a way that we are supposed to live, regardless of our circumstances or experiences. Our entire life is supposed to be a life of faith – trusting God and His Word above our natural circumstances. Whatever our need, faith is a vehicle by which we can see those needs met. Whether we need to be made strong, stop the mouth of a lion that's about to eat us, put enemies to flight, or even see someone raised from the dead, this passage clearly shows that these things can be done through faith. Faith is a very powerful thing. It is much more powerful than many of us have given it credit.

This Hebrews 11 chapter talking about faith and giving examples of faith uses examples from the Old Testament, prior to the time of Jesus. Faith has ALWAYS been a really important thing. It has ALWAYS been a mechanism to receive from God. It was in the Old Testament, and as was already proved in the last chapter, it was both in Jesus' day and in the life of the early church as well. The whole Bible from beginning to end showcases that faith is an important thing.

In Hebrews 11:40, in referencing examples of peoples' faith in the Old Testament, it tells us that they didn't see the fullness of their faith realized and that God "provided something better for us" (ESV) as the Church under the New Covenant. Their faith wasn't fully realized because Jesus the Messiah had not come, who is the ultimate object of faith. But we, living under the New Covenant, do have that benefit. Jesus is the "something better" referenced. Our faith centers around Jesus and all that is available to us because of, and through, Him. Jesus is our flashpoint of faith! This is why, if you recall from the story of the lame man healed in Acts chapter 3, that it was declared that it was faith in and through Jesus that brought about the healing to that man. As New Covenant believers, Jesus is our focal point. Faith itself is actually all about Jesus because our entire salvation – our entire entrance into "eternal life" – our entire everything that we need comes to us because of Jesus! In the Old Testament, they were looking forward to the fulfillment of the promise of the Messiah, but they did not have Him and His sacrificial work in actuality as Jesus was still to come to this world and be our atoning sacrifice. But we, with Jesus having come and performed His atoning work for us, do have this! Our faith hinges upon Jesus and all that we have available through Him.

Everything has always been about faith. The only way that people have ever actually been justified before God has been by faith, including in the Old Testament. I don't want to get too far sidetracked, but there's a righteousness that comes from yourself trying to do things right – it's based on you performing perfectly. As was discussed in a previous chapter, this is what the law was about. Many people throughout history have banked on their own righteousness and many people today are banking on their own righteousness. That righteousness always has, and always will, come up short. But there also is a righteousness that is by faith. And this righteousness has always been available. Several people such as Abraham and Noah exhibited this faith. We are told that Noah "became heir of the righteousness which is by faith" in Hebrews 11:7. Those in the Old Testament period such as Abraham and Noah, by exercising faith in God, actually were in a sense looking forward to the Messiah whereby God provided everything that we need, including righteousness.

Simply by reading Hebrews 11 alone, we find out that through faith, we can receive righteousness, healing, resurrection from the dead, provision, protection, and more, and that actual scriptural examples are given to back these up. Faith has always been a primary methodology to receive from God, whatever the need. Given this, it is extremely sad when you realize that what's happened in many Christian circles is that while it is accepted that faith is required to receive righteousness from God (i.e. through believing in Jesus' sacrifice on our behalf for forgiveness of sins), it has largely been limited to only that. The role of faith when it comes to anything else is largely downplayed, even though the Bible is FULL of examples of such things.

I believe a primary reason for this is that people are afraid to get their hopes up. What ends up happening is people actually get angry when you start offering teaching like this and they start countering with all their reasons for why we CAN'T believe God and trust Him and elevate our view of God and what's available to us. It amazes me just how far people will go to keep a very small and narrow view of what is available for us and how much God has provided for us. People will fight to the death to defend their view that we just have to accept everything that happens to us as a part of "God's Sovereign Plan for us." People are afraid to believe that there might actually be a part that we can play in our own story.

The fact of the matter is that all things are possible with God. Jesus told us "The things which are impossible with men are possible with God." (Luke 18:27b KJV). He also told us "with God all things are possible." (Mark 10:27b KJV) and when praying to the Father in the Garden of Gesthemene, He prayed: "Abba, Father, all things are possible for you." (Mark 14:26b ESV).

I don't care if a doctor looks you right in the eye and tells you that you only have twenty-four hours to live! You've got God – the Creator of the Universe – and all things are possible with Him. But here's the thing: Most Christians do, at least to a degree, believe this. It's just that they also believe that it's solely up to God whether something happens for you based on His will for you. They discount that we also could have a part to play.

In Mark chapter 9, there is a story of a man whose son has serious convulsions/seizures, which is identified by the story to be caused by a demonic spirit. The father relates all about the situation to Jesus and then says to him: "But if you can do anything, have compassion on us and help us." (Mark 9:22 ESV). The way the father talked to Jesus is the way that many people talk to God today: "Well God, if you can do something and you want to, would you please help me?" They might even take it a step further and declare that they know that He CAN do something, but they still question whether He will. With this father, Jesus does not respond to him and say, "Well of course I can do something – I'm the Son of God – it's all up to me and I choose by my will to heal him." Jesus doesn't do that. Instead, He turns it right back on the father and challenges him by saying to him, "'If you can'! All things are possible for one who believes." (Mark 9:23 ESV). The man asks Jesus that if He can do something, to please do it, and Jesus turns it right back on the man and almost asks it back to him like an exclamatory question as in: "If you can?!" [there was no punctuation in the original text so the punctuation is a guess]. Other translations such as the KJV also have the word "believe" as in "If you can believe." In any event, Jesus put it back on the father by in essence telling him: "Of course I can do it – that's not the issue. The issue is whether you can believe for it! All things are possible if you can believe!" The man, upon hearing this from Jesus, did exactly the right thing: "Immediately the father of the child cried out and said with tears, 'Lord, I believe; help my unbelief!'" (Mark 9:24 NKJV). Jesus had confronted the man with the reality that he could affect the outcome through his faith, and the man had a choice to make. He mustered up whatever faith he could and chose to believe Jesus and take Him at His Word. At the same time, he was honest in admitting that there was still part of him that was having trouble believing. Long story short, Jesus rebuked the spirit and even after the boy appeared to be dead, Jesus took him by the hand and he rose up and was fine.

The reality is that whether we like it or not, what we believe matters and can affect things, either positively or negatively. There is a fascinating story in Mark chapter 11, where Jesus offered some very clear (albeit hard to accept) teaching related to this. There was a fig tree that Jesus and company passed by that didn't have any figs on it and Jesus cursed it by speaking to the tree, "May no one ever eat fruit from you again." (Mark 11:14b ESV). The next day they passed by the same tree and that's where I want to pick up the story:

> 20 Now in the morning, as they passed by, they saw the fig tree dried up from the roots. 21 And Peter, remembering, said to Him, "Rabbi, look! The fig tree which You cursed has withered away."

> 22 So Jesus answered and said to them, "Have faith in God. 23 For assuredly, I say to you, whoever says to this mountain, 'Be removed and be cast into the sea,' and does not doubt in his heart, but believes that those things he says will be done, he will have whatever he says. 24 Therefore I say to you, whatever things you ask when you pray, believe that you receive *them,* and you will have *them.* (Mark 11:20–24 NKJV)

The disciples seemed surprised that the tree that Jesus had cursed the day before had dried up. Jesus did NOT respond to their surprise by saying: "Well of course it did because I'm the Son of God and I have all power and when I speak to something it must obey me!" Instead, He turned it back on the disciples and used it as a teaching moment for them so they could see that they also could have done the exact same thing. Jesus' first words to them (and thus us as His disciples today) were "Have faith in God." (vs 22). He identified faith as the central issue that was in operation and gave an explicit instruction to them. He then goes on to give a rather profound faith lesson.

I don't deny that this can be some hard teaching to swallow. Jesus seems to be saying that if we have enough faith in God, and do not doubt, that we can speak to things and they have to obey – whether that's a mountain or a fig tree or really accomplishing whatever we need to accomplish or receiving whatever we need. Now you can go read any number of theologians if you want that will, I'm sure, explain to you why what Jesus plainly said isn't what He really meant. But on face value, this teaching is actually very clear and simple. It's just that it's hard for us to accept.

In verse 24, Jesus tells us that when we pray that we are to believe that we receive what we've prayed for, and we will have it. That's pretty clear. It's just hard to accept, and it's hard for us to actually do. Most of us want to see what we pray for and then we'll believe, but Jesus switches it up and tells us that the believing comes first before the "having." Notice the key opposing force that Jesus identifies in verses 23 and 24 is that of doubt or unbelief. The reality is that we all have doubt and unbelief that is countering our faith. The reason why we don't often see results is because we aren't really believing in faith, and when we do, we're also full of doubt or unbelief that's counteracting that faith. Just a sidenote, but a lot of that doubt and unbelief that we have is because we've been taught wrong – we've been taught to have doubt and unbelief and not fully trust God.

Now, before some of you go jumping up and down in anger wondering just what kind of theology I am promoting, just hang tight a minute. This situation is not the only time that Jesus offered "hard" teaching along these lines. Let's look at a few more portions of Scripture. In John 15:16, we read, "You did not choose me, but I chose you and appointed you that you should go and bear fruit and that your fruit should abide, so that whatever you ask the Father in my name, he may give it to you." (ESV).

In John 14:12–14, Jesus tells us, "Truly, truly, I say to you, whoever believes in me will also do the works that I do; and greater works than these will he do, because I am going to the Father. Whatever you ask in my name, this I will do, that the Father may be glorified in the Son. If you ask me anything in my name, I will do it." (ESV).

In John 16:23–24, speaking of the time after He rises from the dead, Jesus says, "In that day you will ask nothing of me. Truly, truly, I say to you, whatever you ask of the Father in my name, he will give it to you. Until now you have asked nothing in my name. Ask, and you will receive, that your joy may be full." (ESV).

When you read the words "truly, truly" as it is shown twice in the above passages from John, that means it's ultra important. In other words, Jesus is saying: "What I'm about to tell you is important and most definitely true – pay attention." He did this specifically with two things in the above passages . First, He told us that those that believe in Him would not only do the works that He did, but also greater works. That's a mind-blowing statement on its own because Jesus did some pretty incredible works (such as raising people from the dead!). But He also used this phrase when telling us in John 16:23 that what we ask of the Father in Jesus' name, He will give to us! That's a rather significant promise and Jesus went out of His way to emphasize it.

Some of you are probably a bit uneasy with where I am going with this because these and other verses have been abused by some to mean that we can have anything we want. So if we want a billion dollars and ten cars and three private jets and a harem of women, well, we just believe it's ours and proclaim it and it will be so. This is how the "name it and claim it" moniker came about – it was largely developed to describe people that have adopted this kind of approach. Such people do have a basis in truth; it's just that they've neglected a few key things.

We get a little further clarification on all of this from John (the same John who wrote down Jesus' words to us in the Gospel of John text quoted above) in his first epistle: "Now this is the confidence that we have in Him, that if we ask anything according to His will, He hears us. And if we know that He hears us, whatever we ask, we know that we have the petitions that we have asked of Him." (1 John 5:14–15 NKJV).

This puts a very important qualifier: that what we ask is according to God's will. Also, when Jesus told us those things in the book of John, they were surrounded by His words to us about abiding in Him (John 15). If we are truly living and abiding in Jesus, we won't be asking for stupid things that we don't need, to fulfill our own lusts and desires. We'll be asking for things that are in line with Jesus' will for us. We'll be asking for things that are good for us and helpful for us in line with His will for us. In that case, the Bible is very clear: We should believe that we receive what we ask!

So, no, you can't use these scriptures to just selfishly get anything you want. That is an abuse of Scripture and it is unfortunate that some people have put forth such a view. The Bible bluntly tells us: "You do not have, because you do not ask. You ask and do not receive, because you ask wrongly, to spend it on your passions." (James 4:2b–3 ESV). God is not the slightest bit interested in giving you things just to fulfill your own selfish desires. He cares a whole lot about motivations on things. And I will just say that it is always a good idea to check our motives on whatever we are praying for.

But when it comes to believing God for things that are His will and you are in alignment with Him, then yes, you can absolutely bank on the truth of these scriptures. And what is God for? What is His will for you? God is for things that are truly helpful for you! God wants you well and healthy and prosperous in every sense. He is for you, not against you. He has no interest in you being a sick, poor, beggar and it's time to let go of that mentality.

When it comes to healing, we have already proven that healing is God's will (if you need a refresher, go re-visit chapter 3). If healing is God's will for us (and it is) and if we are abiding in Jesus (I'll be talking more about this in a moment), then we absolutely should be elevating our view and EXPECTING what we pray regarding health in our bodies to come to pass.

By and large, we have expected little and we have gotten it. But the Word teaches that we should instead be really believing God and expecting results. When it comes to health problems, we should be "speaking to our mountain" and speaking to our body – commanding it to come in line with the truth of God's Word that healing is already ours because of Jesus' sacrifice. We should be speaking to organs or cells or whatever the problem is, commanding them to be healthy and in line with the life of God that is in us. If there's an infection in our body, we can speak to that infection and curse it. Per Jesus' teaching in Mark 11:23, if we believe and do not doubt in our heart, we will have what we say! We should be praying and asking God in alignment with these truths, trusting God to bring about the health in our body that He has provided for us! It's time to stop being passive, but to be active in our faith!

The word "faith" is very interesting because Biblically it is showcased to be both a noun and a verb, and the clear implication in Scripture is that it is always supposed to be both at the same time. Every time faith is spoken of in what we would consider a noun form, such as in a person "having faith", the implication is also that that faith is active. Bible faith, by definition, is both a noun and a verb. It is NEVER supposed to be only a noun, though this is how it is sometimes treated by people. To "have faith in Jesus" implies not that you have had a one time experience of putting faith in Jesus, but that you possess an ongoing, continual faith in Jesus; that your faith in Jesus is an active and alive thing. Faith, as revealed in the Bible, is always shown in this manner.

This is what abiding in Christ is all about. When we are abiding in Christ (described by Jesus in John 15), we are staying in a place of practically appropriating our faith in Jesus and His sacrifice for us. We recognize that we absolutely need Jesus on a moment by moment basis – that He is our very life – that He is the vine giving life to us, the branches (John 15:5). We are acknowledging that we continue to put our full trust in Jesus and His sacrifice for our righteousness before God. This abiding place is also a place of resting (Hebrews 4) – we are resting in Christ's finished work on our behalf and have ceased from our own strivings to please God on our own merits (Hebrews 4:10). As we abide in Christ, we are also continuing to acknowledge that all that Christ purchased for us (including health) is ours.

We're supposed to stay each day in this place of faith. We exercised faith to come to Jesus and we exercise faith to live each day. This is why we are told that we "walk by faith, not by sight" (2 Corinthians 5:7b) and that the "just shall live by faith." (Galatians 3:11b). We are the "just" since we've been justified before God by Jesus, and faith is how we are supposed to walk out our life every day – it is how we are to live. This means that we continually take God at His Word over what our natural eyes and physical senses can see and feel. It doesn't matter what a situation looks like; it could look like the most hopeless of situations. But we don't walk by sight, but by faith in God and His Word. If God calls you healed in His Word, then you are healed, whether it looks like it in the natural or not. And you can take your authority in Jesus and speak to your body and command it to come in line with God's Word. You can pray, believing God for the healing power that is available for you to flow through your body in the natural, bringing your body into alignment with what's already yours in the spirit.

Romans 8:11 gives us some great news: "But if the Spirit of him that raised up Jesus from the dead dwell in you, he that raised up Christ from the dead shall also quicken your mortal bodies by his Spirit that dwelleth in you." (KJV). In other words, you have the same "raising from the dead" power living on the inside of you that raised Jesus up from the dead, and that power can "quicken" (or "bring life to") your physical body! That's a scripture you can claim, friends! You can put your faith in alignment with God's Word and believe that His power is bringing life to your body, even if it doesn't seem like it. As you exercise your faith, you are putting yourself in a place to experience and receive what God has for you. Faith opens the conduit.

In the Book of Galatians, Paul tells us: "I have been crucified with Christ, and I no longer live, but Christ lives in me. The life I now live in the body, I live by faith in the Son of God, who loved me and gave Himself for me." (Galatians 2:20 CSB)

Paul recognized that everything about his life (including his body) was wrapped up with the life of Christ through his faith in Him. *[Sidenote: I almost didn't share this verse because it requires me explaining something or some will undoubtedly be upset with me. Some believers in certain camps get way too hung up on whether Paul said/meant that he lived by faith IN, or by the faith OF, Jesus, as different translations render it differently. The reason there is such confusion is because the original Greek text doesn't actually say "in" OR "of" – there's no preposition there at all, so it's a guess as to what Paul meant and some translations pick one and some pick another. Even the NKJV uses "in" while the KJV uses "of." I tend towards the "in" side as I think that squares better with other portions of Scripture, but Jesus is "the author and finisher of our faith" (Hebrews 12:2) so it is Biblically true that, though there is a bit of a mystery to it, even our ability to believe comes from Jesus. Paul's context is also in talking about Jesus living in us, which could support an "of" rendering. However, while I'm fine with that, the problem I have is some people use the "of" rendering to create this out-of-balance doctrine that pretty much negates our responsibility for believing and instead puts it all on Jesus and His faith. I don't care which rendering you want to use as long as you recognize that you have a part to play in exercising your faith too.]*

Paul made a choice to see himself – every part of his life – wrapped up with Jesus through faith. He declared that Christ lived within Him. If Jesus lives within us through faith, then that means that all that is true of Jesus can affect every part of us as well. Most Christians see healing as trying to get something from outside of us. When Jesus was here on this earth, this was the case. But now, He actually dwells within us through the Spirit. We already have healing power dwelling within us. The same power that raised Jesus from the dead is within us. The issue then is releasing that power that dwells in our spirit into our soul and body. Faith is the force that releases that power.

Romans 4 gives us some powerful faith insights through the experience of Abraham:

> [Abraham believed] God, who gives life to the dead and calls those things which do not exist as though they did; 18 who, contrary to hope, in hope believed, so that he became the father of many nations, according to

what was spoken, "So shall your descendants be." 19
And not being weak in faith, he did not consider his
own body, already dead (since he was about a hundred
years old), and the deadness of Sarah's womb. 20 He
did not waver at the promise of God through unbelief,
but was strengthened in faith, giving glory to God, 21
and being fully convinced that what He had promised
He was also able to perform. 22 And therefore "it was
accounted to him for righteousness." (Romans 4:17b–
22 NKJV, bracketed text mine)

God had previously told Abraham about 25 years earlier (when
he was 75) that he and his wife Sarah would have a child and that
through that child, he would be a father to many. I don't know about
you, but I think 25 years is quite a long time to wait for a promise to
be fulfilled! We know from the account in the book of Genesis that
Abraham made a rather serious error in thinking at one point during
those years in thinking that maybe God wanted him to do something to help out. On the advice of Sarah (who could not bear
children), Abraham slept with Sarah's servant, Hagar, and bore a
child named "Ishmael", which was not the child God had planned
for them. Ishmael, as a "child of the flesh" (see Rom. 9:8), is a picture of what happens when we do things our own way instead of
God's. A raft of trouble ensued from that, and actually, just as a
sidenote, we are still affected today from this bad decision as the
whole Arab/Israeli conflict goes back to this! Abraham and Sarah
made a mistake in thinking they needed to help God, but apparently
even in that mistake, Abraham never wavered at God's actual promise (vs. 20).

Setting aside that (albeit large) mistake, Abraham believed God.
Over those 25 years of waiting, it was clear that Abraham and Sarah
were old and Sarah was past child-bearing age, and at some point
after Ishmael was born, Abraham's body "became dead" sexually as
well. It became a situation where it was absolutely hopeless in the
natural for God's promise to come to pass. Abraham had a choice:
He could believe what all the natural data was telling him, or He
could believe God even though doing so might seem crazy or illog-

ical because there was no data to back that up except for God's Word. We are told in verse 18 that Abraham believed in God even though the situation looked hopeless ("contrary to hope"). Abraham chose to trust God even though his body was shouting to him that it was impossible. He "did not consider his own body" (vs. 19 NKJV) – he didn't listen to his body or his mind, but rather he listened to God. We are told in verse 20 that he did not waver through unbelief but rather believed God in faith. Just in case you don't know what happened, Abraham and Sarah did supernaturally give birth to a son named Isaac.

I need to point out that this Romans 4 passage starts in the end of verse 17 by telling us that God "gives life to the dead and calls those things which do not exist as though they did." (NKJV). Don't miss this – this is huge! When God made His promise to Abraham, to God it was already a done deal – even though the fruit of that promise was not showcased in actuality here for around 25 years! This is a powerful faith principle. Faith involves seeing with your spiritual eyes over what your physical eyes can see. It involves standing on the Word of God and seeing your answer as already existing, even though it hasn't shown itself in the natural here yet. While we need to be realistic about symptoms and situations that are existing in the natural, we also want to be keeping ourselves in a place, through our words and thoughts and actions, where we are seeing our answer as already done and that it will be showing itself! Remember what Jesus said in Mark 11:24? He told us that "whatever things you ask when you pray, believe that you receive them, and you will have them." (Mark 11:24b ESV). It doesn't say to believe that *some day* that you will receive your answer, but that you are to believe you receive it *now*. The word "receive" there in the Greek also can be translated "to take" – it is an active action. By faith, there is a sense in which we are to take what Jesus has provided for us. We pray in faith and we take our healing (or anything else we need that Jesus has provided) now.

How long will you have to wait to see in the natural what you are believing? I don't know. In the case of the fig tree, it was the next day before what Jesus had spoken and believed became visible for all to see (though it began working the moment Jesus spoke to it). For Abraham and Sarah, it was 25 years. I'm not saying it will take that long for you and me, but I do know that regardless of how long it takes, we need to stand firm on God's Word because God's Word will NOT fail! We need to follow the example of Abraham in not wavering in unbelief concerning God's Word. The principle of faith is that we need to see our answer with our spiritual eyes before we see it with our natural eyes.

When it comes to sickness and disease, this is a big deal because we have all been trained to look at our symptoms to determine whether we are well or sick. When we come to a place where we truly believe and confess God's Word that healing is ours irrespective of our symptoms is when we know we are standing in a place of faith. Having faith does not mean denying the reality of the symptoms! That is a mistake that many a person trying to stand in faith has made. I've personally run into such people and honestly they just come across as loony. We don't live in la-la land and deny the reality of symptoms. The symptoms may be real. It's just that God's Word is MORE REAL. The natural must submit to the supernatural. The symptoms may be real, but we don't need to put our focus there. We can choose instead to look past the symptoms and keep our eyes fixed on Jesus and His Word. We look past the symptoms to the sacrifice of Jesus which already paid the price for us to be well and healthy and that is where we choose to stand – believing that the Life that Jesus purchased for us is flowing in our body and bringing it into line and that those symptoms have to get lost.

We need to put the focus on what is ALREADY true in the spirit realm – that we are well and healthy, and speak that forth. Again, it's not a denial of the symptoms, but looking past the symptoms to the greater reality. Based on this greater reality, we then reckon (count it true) in ourselves that we are ALREADY well and healthy in the natural. In doing this, we are exercising our faith to join with God in calling those things that be not as though they were (because they actually ARE in the unseen realm). And though I realize that can initially seem counter-intuitive or a bit weird, that is a solid place to stand. It is a place of believing God's Word above our symptoms. You've got to see yourself well in the spirit before you see it in the natural!

When you use your faith to see that because of Jesus, you are already healed right now and you truly on a heart level believe in line with that and see yourself well and whole, that is where things that might have seemed to "be not" (or "not exist") in the natural can be primed to showcase. Because the truth is that we aren't just calling something (health) that isn't. Health and wholeness exist in the unseen realm where Jesus resides in our spirit. It does exist – it just may not be working within our physical body or soul. The conduit from the spirit to the body and soul is activated by faith. When through faith we truly see and reckon that we are already well and healthy and declare that truth over our body and soul, we in essence are opening up the pipeline for what is already true in our spirit in the unseen realm to be drawn into the seen realm. I know this can be hard-to-understand or accept teaching (and is easy fodder for skeptics to criticize), but I believe grasping this concept is a really huge deal. Just because you don't see something with your physical eyes doesn't mean it doesn't exist. Again I remind you that Jesus taught in Mark 11 that the believing comes before the seeing.

I've got to mention something else related to all of this stuff, because my guess is that some of you, like me, have been taught to stay away from something called "Word of Faith" teaching / teachers. Some of these warnings have elements of validity because there have been people that have perverted teachings related to faith (as I've already mentioned). However, like many things, what has happened is that far too broad a brush has been used so that even clearly Biblical teaching like I've shared is warned against as being heretical by people that are well-meaning, but are ignorant to many of the faith concepts that I've highlighted from Scripture.

What you might not know is that the Apostle Paul was a "Word of Faith" teacher in a manner of speaking. And I'm not just saying that based on my opinion – he himself said it:

> 8 But what does it say? "The word is near you, in your mouth and in your heart" (that is, the word of faith that we proclaim); 9 because, if you confess with your mouth that Jesus is Lord and believe in your heart that God raised him from the dead, you will be saved. 10

> For with the heart one believes and is justified, and with the mouth one confesses and is saved. 11 For the Scripture says, "Everyone who believes in him will not be put to shame." (Romans 10:8–11 ESV)

Please take note that Paul in verse 8 says that he proclaims the "word of faith." And what at its core is "word of faith" teaching? This is it right here! It's confessing with your mouth and believing in your heart! In verse 9, we are told that we are "saved" by in essence confessing with our mouth the truth that we believe in our heart about Jesus (that Jesus is Lord / God raised Jesus from the dead). As verse 10 highlights, the believing takes place in our heart and with our mouth we declare our belief as a "line in the sand" so to speak. In this, all (including angels and demons) will hear and clearly know our decision. Confessing with our mouth is putting our faith into action. What we declare with our mouth showcases what we believe in our heart. This is unperverted "word of faith" teaching right here. It lines up with the type of teaching I shared earlier from Mark 11 where Jesus told us that we can speak to mountains and can have what we say.

When it comes to salvation, we can have that by what we say (as per verses 9–10 above). If you remember the teaching from earlier chapters, you probably won't be surprised to learn that the word for "saved" in verse 9 is the Greek word "sozo" – which as previously mentioned is a word that is used throughout the New Testament to denote wholeness in every respect, including in regards to physical health. The same way we receive forgiveness of sins is the same way we receive health. We confess with our mouth what we believe in our heart.

In all cases, it all goes back to Jesus and His sacrifice for us. Regardless of our need, our faith ultimately is to be in Jesus and what He has provided for us through His death on the cross and resurrection from the dead. He has provided salvation for us in all its fullness. Let's get a hold of that, truly believe it, confess it, and never let go!

It's time to lift our heads, elevate our view, quit the negative whining, and stand in faith based on what the Word says is ours, regardless of our physical circumstances. It is time to walk by faith and not by sight! (2 Cor. 5:7).

Chapter 11 – Healing Today

You may be wondering why I have been spending so much of this book talking about healing. The simple reason is that sickness and disease is pretty much a universal issue that seems to be about as common among believers as unbelievers. It is a major preventer of us living the abundant life we were meant to live and is an area that I think much of the church world has been confused about.

If you recall from way back in chapter 2, the ultimate cause of the sickness and disease we see today is traced back to Adam & Eve's sin in the Garden of Eden. Biblically, there are several things that can be the cause of sickness and disease in our lives:

(1) Simply existing in this fallen world that is tainted by sin and has sickness and disease in it. You don't have to be doing anything wrong whatsoever to be affected by sickness/disease. However, as Christians, we have already discussed how we also can exercise our faith to walk in the health that Jesus has purchased for us and trust Him for divine protection – even from the so-called "naturally occurring" sicknesses/diseases going around in the world. For instance, just because most other people get a cold or the flu every year doesn't mean that *we* have to.

(2) Actively caused by God/angelic forces. As was mentioned back in Chapter 2, the Bible does have examples of God causing sickness or disease (whether caused directly or through angelic intermediaries). However, also as previously mentioned, you won't find any examples of New Covenant believers in Jesus being afflicted by God (unless someone tries to make what I would consider a fairly flimsy case relating to Ananias and Saphira). The Bible is very clear that God is for health, not for sickness. When God did afflict people, it was as a result of their sin and usually after very long, prolonged periods of God having extended mercy time and again that went unheeded. As believers, Jesus paid the price for our health and wholeness and God is NOT punishing us or afflicting us with sickness as believers. Jesus paid the price for our sin and it would be "double jeopardy" for God to punish you through sickness when Jesus already paid the price for your wellbeing. God loves you and is for you. God is NOT the cause of your sickness or dis-

ease! *Note: I do have to put a slight asterisk to this because there is more to say on this as there is another variable related to this that we will be exploring in a later chapter, but for now, this will suffice.

(3) Actively caused by the devil/demonic forces.

(4) Your own personal sin.

These last two causes are the areas I would like to dig into a little bit deeper. First let's discuss demonic involvement.

The devil is able to inflict sickness and disease – and he loves to do it. As believers, we have already discussed how we have authority over the devil. While unbelievers are still under his authority, we as believers have switched kingdoms and he has no legal claim to us and we can take our authority over him. If we allow him access to our life, he will surely take it. But we don't have to allow it.

When Jesus was ministering to people, on many occasions, demons were shown to be directly involved in afflicting the person. This includes a mute man in Matthew 9:32–33, a blind and mute man in Matthew 12:22, an epileptic boy in Matthew 17:14–20, a mentally-ill man in Mark 5:1–20, a Canaanite woman's daughter in Matthew 15:21–28, a guy who was speaking under the power of a demon in Luke 4:31–36, Mary Magdalene in Mark 16:9, and many others.

In Luke 4, we read this summary statement regarding a group of people healed by Jesus: "Now when the sun was setting, all those who had any who were sick with various diseases brought them to him, and he laid his hands on every one of them and healed them. And demons also came out of many, crying, 'You are the Son of God!'" (Luke 4:40–41a ESV). While I suppose the two could theoretically be completely unrelated, the implication seems to be that demons in many cases were involved in the people's physical infirmities.

In Matthew 9, we find this account of a guy that couldn't speak: "As they went out, behold, they brought to Him a man, mute and demon-possessed. And when the demon was cast out, the mute spoke." (Matthew 9:32–33a NKJV). Jesus dealt with demons by casting them out; He seemed to cast out demons left and right. For instance, we read verses like this: "And he went throughout all Galilee, preaching in their synagogues and casting out demons." (Mark

1:39 ESV). And "That evening they brought to him many who were oppressed by demons, and he cast out the spirits with a word and healed all who were sick. " (Matthew 8:16 ESV). It wasn't just Jesus doing this either. His disciples did also:

> The seventy-two returned with joy, saying, "Lord, even the demons are subject to us in your name!" And he said to them, "I saw Satan fall like lightning from heaven. Behold, I have given you authority to tread on serpents and scorpions, and over all the power of the enemy, and nothing shall hurt you. Nevertheless, do not rejoice in this, that the spirits are subject to you, but rejoice that your names are written in heaven." (Luke 10:17–20 ESV)

Now, Jesus made sure they didn't lose their focus on what the most important thing was, but He gave them power over the devil. (e.g. Mark 6:7). In the book of Acts, we also find the early church casting out demons: "For unclean spirits, crying out with a loud voice, came out of many who had them, and many who were paralyzed or lame were healed. " (Acts 8:7 ESV).

This is something you hardly ever hear anything about today when it comes to sickness. Yet, it seemed to be fairly prevalent in Jesus' day and in the time of the early church. The devil hasn't stopped working in our world. Demons still affect people today. It's not that there's any less demonic involvement now; it's that we don't recognize it and call it out as such. We see things only on a natural plane. We just assume that a person has a "chemical imbalance" or that a migraine headache is just from stress, when it really could be a demonic issue. It could also certainly just be from stress or a person could just have imbalances that have nothing to do with demon activity. But it's something to at least consider.

It may not be politically correct to say, but the devil is very involved in our world and in people's lives. I personally believe that at least a fair amount of mental illness has its roots in demon activity in a person's life. Then what people do is medicate themselves and try to deal with some symptoms, rather than take care of the root problem. (Note that I am not saying that there aren't potentially legitimate uses for medication). For unbelievers, lots of mental issues and sicknesses can come as a direct or indirect result of their lack of peace with God – the devil just has a field day with them – messing with their minds and bodies. For believers, the same can actually be true because many believers *let* the devil have a field day with them.

Some Christians get hung up in playing word games – oppressed vs. possessed. They'll say Christians can't be possessed by the devil, though they can be oppressed. That's true in the sense that if you are truly born again, the devil can't reside in your spirit; God lives there. But you still have an unrenewed soul (i.e. mind) and body and the devil can very much affect those things, even as a Christian. The devil can affect your mind and your body. The difference is that as a Christian, you don't have to let him affect you – you have authority over him. You can renew your mind to the truth of what is yours in Christ and exercise your authority. We've previously talked about that authority. Most Christians don't realize they have that authority and so they don't use it. They just passively let the devil walk all over them and often don't even realize it's the devil doing it.

Because of some popular movies and crazy antics in some churches, the whole topic of "exorcism" has gotten a "scary" and "crazy", "fringe" connotation for a lot of believers. But it's nothing to be afraid of at all. If you are in Jesus, you are stronger than the devil (1 Jn 4:4). It is very possible that there could be physical manifestations when you cast out a demon (e.g. Mark 9:26) but there's been some nonsense out there in this arena where people assume that a person that has a demon cast out needs to throw up and so forth to get the demon out. I'm going to say this nicely: that's just stupid... Some people have made this stuff way too complicated and way too "weird" – just take your authority that you have in the name of Jesus and command any and all demons to pack their bags and move on.

When it comes to demonic involvement, my advice is whether you think there might be or not, is just to exercise your authority in Jesus and cast out all demonic spirits from your life. Cast out any spirits of infirmity or disease, cast out any spirits of doubt and discouragement and fear, cast out any evil spirits of any kind. The only spirit you want is the Holy Spirit. All others are trespassers on God's property. Enforce that by determining that you will not allow any demons to hang around, and command them to go. As you keep yourself submitted to God and resist the devil, he will have to flee (James 4:7).

Now let us shift to discuss everybody's favorite topic (I'm being facetious): the role of our own personal sin in regards to sickness and disease.

The reality is that sin does still bring forth death (in all its forms). Remember that "law of sin and death" we talked about in an earlier chapter? It still exists. When we disobey God, we are opening the door for sickness. Probably one of the clearest examples from Jesus' healing ministry where sin was an identified cause is the man healed at the pool of Bethesda as told to us in John 5. After Jesus got the man to let go of his excuses and take a step of faith (John 5:6–8), Jesus healed the man. Jesus then told him, "See, you have been made well. Sin no more, lest a worse thing come upon you." (John 5:14b NKJV). There are other linkages in Scripture between sin and sickness. When I'm talking about sin, I'm not just talking about the types of things people usually think of such as lust, jealousy, lying, adultery, etc. There's certainly plenty of those kinds of sins going on even among Christians. But I'm also talking about things like fear and worry. Fear itself is sin because it is in essence putting faith in natural things to do you harm instead of putting faith in God; it is elevating circumstances above God.

Fear and anxiety alone can be major doorways to sickness. For instance, one could have a perpetual problem with fear and anxiety, constantly living life in an anxious or fearful state. In that, they might talk negatively and say things like: "I know I'm going to get sick this year just like I always do at this time." Or someone might have had a parent that had cancer or heart-disease and part of them expects that when they reach the age their parent was, they also will probably come down with cancer or heart-disease. These types of things can open doors through fear and fearful words, for the devil, who can can then take advantage of that to afflict with sickness.

Fear is really faith in the devil! We aren't supposed to be fearful of any sickness or disease – even cancer – but rather as believers in Jesus to stand in faith, realizing that ALL things, including cancer and other diseases, are under the feet of Jesus (see Eph. 1:21–22).

As believers, we have discussed previously how we have been set free from the law of sin and death and are now subject to another law: that of the Spirit of Life (Romans 8:2). I do believe it is possible as a believer to get ahold of this truth and exercise your faith and not have your own sin open doors for sickness. In other words, I believe it is possible to live above the "law of sin and death" through the greater "law of the Spirit of Life" that we access by faith. However, we also need to be honest and realize that many of us have spent years being "sin conscious" and by disobeying God, it can just make it extra hard to stand in faith for healing/health if you also have to deal with feelings of guilt/shame/unworthiness and so forth that often comes as a result of sin (even if repented of quickly). It just makes it so much harder on yourself. This assumes you even recognize and repent of the sin. For the person living in unrepentant sin, then they really aren't even staying in an abiding place of faith in Jesus anyway and they will already have flung the door to sickness wide open.

Sin can produce natural results that negatively affect our bodies. Not taking care of God's temple (our bodies – see 1 Cor. 6:19–20) can be sin and affect us negatively. For instance, if a person makes a habit of getting themselves drunk, in the natural they can probably expect to start having liver trouble at some point. If a person abuses their body by constantly overeating and they end up very overweight, there might be some natural health effects from that in parts of their body. Even things like fear and anxiety themselves, if practiced on a continual basis, will probably at some point showcase as detrimental effects in a person's health.

Our bodies are incredible machines designed by God, but we can affect those bodies through our choices. For instance, the Bible explicitly declares that the "sexually immoral person sins against his own body." (1 Cor. 6:18b ESV). In our culture today, including in our Christian culture, there is rampant sexual immorality. The Bible explicitly declares that when we sin sexually we are actually sinning against our own body – we our hurting our own body. I'm certainly not saying that just because a person is sick that means they have been sexually immoral. But I am saying that what the Bible indicates is that sexual sin affects our bodies in a negative way. And given that our body is also the place where sickness manifests, that doesn't seem to be a very smart thing to do.

The truth is that a person's own sin can be a factor in them being ill, and when you realize that sin includes things such as fear and bitterness, it probably is even a likely factor (at least part of the picture). One of my frustrations, though, is when I see someone that's dealing with sickness or disease and some "well meaning" believer tries to diagnose them and tell them definitively why they are sick! Throughout church history, some people have really gone out of their way to tell people that they are sick because they are in sin and have largely just ended up making people feel hopeless and condemned. At the same time, some churches and movements that believe in healing have responded to that extreme by going to the other extreme in teaching people never to mention that someone's sickness could be caused by sin. Both extremes are wrong.

I do believe God could use a person to reveal to someone (who might not even realize it) that sin might be an issue, but by and large, I think that it is not my place to tell a specific person why they are sick, because I just plain don't know. I've got enough trouble trying to figure out my own life; I have no business telling someone else why they are having problems. Unless I can see a very clear and blatant sin issue (i.e. an ongoing or unrepentant issue) or God's given me some special revelation, I generally need to avoid making any judgment calls at all along these lines and should not be ascribing blame to a person. Even if I do feel I maybe should share something, I need to tread lightly and it needs to be completely bathed in love, realizing that ALL of us have at points in our lives opened doors to sickness and disease through sin. We're all learning how to walk out this Christian life.

Regardless of whether a person's personal sin enters into the equation or not, whatever the cause is, the answer is the same: Jesus. We have already talked about the importance of exercising our own personal faith in Jesus and receiving the healing that He has already provided for us through our own faith. In addition to that, God has also given us other brothers and sisters to be a help to us when it comes to getting well. God has built into His Body (the Church) mechanisms for dealing with sickness.

James, the half-brother of Jesus, laid out specific instructions to churches as to how to deal with people who are sick.

> 14 Is anyone among you sick? Let him call for the elders of the church, and let them pray over him, anointing him with oil in the name of the Lord. 15 And the prayer of faith will save the sick, and the Lord will raise him up. And if he has committed sins, he will be forgiven. 16 Confess *your* trespasses to one another, and pray for one another, that you may be healed. The effective, fervent prayer of a righteous man avails much. 17 Elijah was a man with a nature like ours, and he prayed earnestly that it would not rain; and it did not rain on the land for three years and six months. 18 And he prayed again, and the heaven gave rain, and the earth produced its fruit. (James 5:14–18 NKJV)

If we are sick, we are supposed to be able to call the elders of our church to have them pray over us and anoint us with oil (the oil is a symbol of the Holy Spirit). It tells us in verse 15 that the "prayer of faith" will save the one who is sick. So, not only does a church need to have elders that are able and willing to pray for people and anoint them with oil, but they also need to be praying in faith. If those elders don't believe that healing is God's will for you – in other words, if they pray prayers like: "God, heal them, if it be your will," then they are NOT going to really be praying a "prayer of faith" – they will be praying a prayer laced with doubt and unbelief (at least in their heart, even if not spoken).

You would think given the clarity of James' instructions here that all churches would be putting this into practice, but I have found that most do not. I live in an area where there are literally hundreds of churches within a very short radius, and I have dealt with much sickness. And I honestly have struggled with finding a church that actually puts this James instruction into practice in a solid way. Some churches don't even have elders or don't have elders or pastors that are accessible! If you even find a church that has elders that do make it a habit to fulfill this responsibility (or at least make themselves available) for healing prayer, finding one that has people that are truly going to be believing God in faith based on what He's revealed is yours in His Word can be a tough challenge. At least that's been my experience. The problem is that much of the church world has been ignorant in this area (this is one of the reasons I have written this book) and so people just don't know what they don't know. I have had pastors and elders pray weak prayers over me ("Oh God, we ask you to heal our brother, if it be your will – we don't understand but we know you can do everything so we just ask you to heal, but teach him what you want to teach him through this...") That's very different from someone praying a bold, faith-filled prayer, based on God's word, declaring you to be well and whole and rebuking sickness and commanding it to leave your body.

Personally, I made a decision quite some time ago that I was done asking people to pray for me unless they are going to pray in faith. If I've got a health problem, I have no interest in weak, wimpy prayers given by people who really aren't standing in faith on God's word for my healing. That's just a waste of all of our time.

We are told that when the prayer of faith is prayed that the Lord WILL raise the person up. We are told in verse 16 that effective and fervent prayer from a righteous man avails much. Who is righteous? None in ourselves, but all of us in Jesus. In the context here it is implied that it is one that KNOWS they are righteous because of Jesus' righteousness. How does one pray an "effective prayer?" By believing God's Word and praying in faith, that's how! There are effective prayers and ineffective prayers out there. An effective prayer is one that is prayed in faith based on the truth of God's Word! It also mentions prayer being "fervent" and goes on in verses 17–18 to talk of Elijah (who is described as a man like us) and how he "prayed earnestly" and got miraculous results. Perhaps saying a quick 30-second prayer might not cut it. Perhaps the elders will need to be willing to truly commit and stand in faith with you to fully see your answer come about. That's a rare thing to see in this day and age where we all are so busy. But, perhaps if we got back to doing things the Bible way, we might start getting more Bible results. These instructions seem pretty clear. If the elders are really praying in faith and putting forth effective and fervent prayers, we are told that the Lord WILL raise the sick person up. That sounds like a promise to me. Regardless of how incredible that might sound, we need to bank on that and stand on that in faith as well.

I also want to point out in verse 15, that sickness and sin are mentioned together. While talking about physical healing, this verse mentions that if there's sin issues, those will be forgiven as well. This seems like kind of an odd thing to mention unless, as we've already discussed, one can have to do with the other. Per verse 16, if we know of any sin that might be an issue, we can confess that and receive forgiveness based on the work of Jesus which has already provided that forgiveness for us. The same work of Jesus that provides the forgiveness is the same work that provides the healing.

At first glance, it can seem like all the "faith work" in this passage is on the elders. But actually, the sick person needs to be exercising some faith as well. By the sick person obeying this passage and calling on the elders, that itself is a step of faith. But then they also need to exercise their faith to believe that what God's Word declares here is true: that when they are prayed for by those elders and anointed with oil that they WILL receive their healing. The elders' part is to pray in faith and believe for the sick person's healing without doubt. The sick person's part is to agree in faith with the elders and to receive their healing.

The picture this whole passage paints here is of a church that is supposed to take its authority (given to it by Jesus) and pray faith-filled prayers for one another, ministering God's healing grace. You might recall that we have previously talked about the fact that we as believers are the Body of Christ and that it is the body where the action takes place (Eph. 1:22–23). Jesus intends for His Body to be doing His works!

In addition to this instruction from James, we are also told that some people within the Body can have special gifts of healing. In his teaching on spiritual gifts, Paul outlines several gifts that are available for people:

> 7 But the manifestation of the Spirit is given to each one for the profit *of all:* 8 for to one is given the word of wisdom through the Spirit, to another the word of knowledge through the same Spirit, 9 to another faith by the same Spirit, to another gifts of healings by the same Spirit, 10 to another the working of miracles, to another prophecy, to another discerning of spirits, to another *different* kinds of tongues, to another the interpretation of tongues. 11 But one and the same Spirit works all these things, distributing to each one individually as He wills ... 28 And God has appointed these in the church: first apostles, second prophets, third teachers, after that miracles, then gifts of healings, helps, administrations, varieties of tongues. (1 Corinthians 12:7–11,28 NKJV)

Within the Body of Christ, God through the Spirit has given gifts to people for everyone's common good (for all of our "profit" per vs. 7). There's a number of gifts mentioned, including "gifts of healings" which God has "appointed" (vs. 28) in the church. All of these gifts mentioned are supposed to be in operation within the Body, however the practical reality is that many churches have really downplayed most of these gifts out of fear – including tongues, prophecy, healings, miracles, word of knowledge, and even word of wisdom and discerning of spirits. Out of this list, many churches only really acknowledge or promote the teaching, administration, and helps gifts. Therefore many people are not taught to expect or want anything else and are even taught that these other gifts are no longer for today. I don't know who decided that teaching, administration, and helps are for today and all the others are not, but I'm guessing it was some theologian way back who just couldn't see how God could possibly want to use those other gifts today. People today still do what people have always done: they lower their theology to match their experience. They, in their limited experience, don't see miracles and healings and tongues in their circle and so they just assume that they aren't for today and teach that to those under them, and on and on the cycle goes.

There are people out there right now in the Body – even some prominent people, mind you – that teach that these gifts went away with the Apostles and early Church and that those practicing such gifts today are really "of the devil" – masquerading as light. It's just incredible, really. The Bible is very clear and there is no indication that the experience of the early church as recorded in the book of Acts was supposed to end with them. Jesus commissioned His church in Matthew 28:18–20 and Mark 16:14–20, giving clear instructions – telling us that He had authority and we are to go in that authority doing His works. The last thing He said to His followers before ascending to Heaven was:

> 8 "But you will receive power when the Holy Spirit has come upon you, and you will be my witnesses in Jerusalem and in all Judea and Samaria, and to the end of the earth." 9 And when he had said these things, as they were looking on, he was lifted up, and a cloud took him out of their sight." (Acts 1:8–9 ESV)

We are still in the same season of time doing what Jesus commissioned us to do. And the last thing Jesus told us was that the Holy Spirit would come upon us and help us. Isn't it funny that that seems to be the type of thing Paul described in his mentioning various gifts! Paul specifically mentioned the various gifts as manifestations of the Spirit (1 Cor. 12:7). Some people have been taught to be afraid or be wary of many of these gifts (e.g. tongues, healings, miracles, prophecy) which oddly enough seem to correspond with the gifts that are really specifically demonstrative of God's POWER – the very thing Jesus told us we would get from the Holy Spirit! This wrong teaching that's out there is based out of fear from people that don't understand these gifts and are afraid to admit that they just maybe could still be for today and that their purpose is still to be a help to all of us in the Body. Many pastors fear these gifts being abused or getting out of control in a church setting (which can indeed happen if not controlled as Paul addressed in 1 Corinthians 14) and their point of reference is some wacky nonsense they've seen on television or the internet, and thus they sadly just keep them out of their church completely.

The purpose of the gifts is so that we will have a well-functioning Body that is demonstrating the truth of God's Word to people – it is used as a witness to people. This correlates with Jesus' teaching in Mark 16 where He said: "And these signs will accompany those who believe: in my name they will cast out demons; they will speak in new tongues; they will pick up serpents with their hands; and if they drink any deadly poison, it will not hurt them; they will lay their hands on the sick, and they will recover." (Mark 16:17–18 ESV). I am aware that the reliability of the Mark 16 segment of Scripture is disputed among some, but it still correlates well with the picture we see of what Jesus' followers are to be in the rest of the Bible, such as we see in Luke 10:19 where Jesus said: "Behold, I have given you authority to tread on serpents and scorpions, and over all the power of the enemy, and nothing shall hurt you." (ESV). The Church is supposed to be full of power and demonstrating that power. As a whole, we as the Body of Christ are NOT demonstrating the power of God. We have gotten really good at TALKING! We can preach people silly, but when it comes to signs demonstrating that the message we are preaching is true, we are lacking. We are living far below what's available to us, and a chief reason for that is that we have been taught wrong and haven't expected (or wanted) anything different. God won't force anything on us...

The early church showcased all sorts of God's power to people and it gave them credibility, just as it did for Jesus when He was here. Why would God want that to stop? With the early church, you find them doing things such as showcasing God's healing power on a regular basis. They even raised people from the dead (e.g. Acts 9:36–43, Acts 20:9–10). The signs they showcased confirmed the truth of the Word. Now days we have settled for church just being a place we go to once a week to hear some worship music for 30–45 minutes and then hear a message for 30–45 minutes, and then we go home. We've gutted church of much of the power it is supposed to have and instead just made it a formula and thus many people in our culture just plain dismiss us because we often appear just like any other gathering. We are merely one voice among many competing for attention and we aren't standing out (at least not for the right reasons) in our culture. We should have a compelling message backed up by demonstrations of God's power. We should be appearing to our culture as much more than a weekly social club, but rather a group of people that have been radically transformed and are being transformed by Jesus, giving obvious testimony to God's love and power in our life.

Getting back to gifts of healings though, the point is that there are people that God has given these special gifts to through the Spirit. Again, because many churches downplay these types of gifts and aren't expecting, asking for, or wanting these gifts in their midst, you won't find them around in abundance, but they do exist. Such people, it would seem, do have a special anointing from God to minister healing to people. Paul had such an anointing to the degree that even handkerchiefs or aprons that had touched him and then touched sick people caused healing power to flow into those that were sick. (Acts 19:11–12).

I just want to offer some practical advice though related to all of this. Some people that have been sick have just tried to go from healing meeting to healing meeting looking for a miracle to come through "the special anointed" healing minister. What happens is people begin looking to a man or woman to be their answer, which isn't what God intended. Never forget that your "source" is God, not the vessel that He might work through. There are people out there in the Body that ARE fakes and charlatans where the focus is all about them and not really Jesus. There is weird nonsense out there in some circles and so you do need to be a bit wary.

But even if you manage to find someone with a genuine gift of healings and receive your healing through them, the problem is it might only be temporary in nature if you don't really understand the types of truths that I have laid out in this book. You might get a healing touch based off of *their* faith, but if you don't know yourself how to stand on the truth of God's Word for your healing and to enforce that healing in your body, most likely it will either come back or another sickness will come down the road. You'll then have to keep repeating the process, running from healing minister to healing minister to get a special touch every time you get sick. Honestly, in my opinion, it is much better for people, rather than relying solely on a special gift through someone else, to stand for themselves in faith believing God based on the Word.

One reason why God has given such giftings and why God uses other people to minister healing (whether through one with a special gift or through elders) is because God is all about meeting us where we are at. You can receive your healing completely on your own between just you and God as you exercise your own faith. But many people, especially as they are just learning about all this faith stuff, need some extra help. God knows that, and He's given fellow brothers and sisters in the Body that are operating in faith to be a help. Even if you fully get the truth in the Word of all that's yours and you are standing in faith, it's still a great idea to go to your brothers and sisters and have them pray in agreement with you. We are here for one another to be a support and help for one another.

Elders and those with gifts of healings are assumed to be operating in faith and thus when you go to them as a sick person, what you are doing is really relying some on *their* faith. There's nothing wrong with this. As your brothers and sisters in the Lord, their faith can be a big help to see you through. Jesus told us there is great power in agreement:

> 18 "Truly, I say to you, whatever you bind on earth shall be bound in heaven, and whatever you loose on earth shall be loosed in heaven. 19 Again I say to you, if two of you agree on earth about anything they ask, it will be done for them by my Father in heaven. 20 For where two or three are gathered in my name, there am I among them." (Matthew 18:18–20 ESV)

You have probably heard of the idea or have witnessed "laying hands" on people. Biblically, the concept of "laying hands" isn't some magic "hocus pocus"; it is simply a means of connecting the one doing the praying with the person being prayed over. God's power that resides in the spirit of the person praying, by faith is released by that person and it flows through their physical body to the person being prayed for. There are several examples of this such as Ananias' prayer over Saul (Paul) in Acts 9:17, the imparting of the Holy Spirit to Samarian believers in Acts 8:17, and Paul's healing prayer for a man on the Island of Malta in Acts 28:8. In the context of healing prayer, it can be a really helpful thing.

Personally, when I am praying for someone, when feasible, I often like to actually touch the specific area of the body in question as I am praying and releasing my faith, and as I do that, I am believing and expecting God's power to flow to that body part. Probably the best personal example I have of this comes from May of 2014 where myself and two other prayer ministers prayed for an older woman whose left arm was shorter than her right arm. She stated it had been that way her whole life. We had her stretch forth her arms and there was indeed a clearly noticeable difference. I took an approximate measurement with my fingers and guess it to have been between 1 and 1.5 inches different. I held her hands where they were stretched forth and we spoke for the left arm to grow out and be in perfect unity & congruence with her body. As I was praying over her, I was releasing my faith and could tangibly feel healing power flowing through my hands into hers. Right as I was winding down my prayer, all of a sudden in one very quick moment, the left arm visibly grew to the same length as the other arm – we literally watched it happen before our eyes. We had her stretch her arms out in a couple of different ways and they were noticeably both even. I don't know that lady and haven't seen her since, but I do know that God did a visible miracle that day and that there was a transference of healing power through the "laying on of hands."

It is a great idea if you are dealing with sickness or disease to go seek out fellow believers that will pray over you and stand with you in faith, believing God for the healing that Jesus purchased for you to show forth throughout your entire body. At the same time though that you are looking for others to operate in faith and release their faith on your behalf, just don't forget that you also have a part to play. You also want to be operating in faith as well and not just trying to passively put it all on someone else to meet your need.

In addition to all of this, we also previously in an earlier chapter talked about the role of the sacrament of communion in our health. I'm not going to spell that out again, except to point out that that also is a Jesus-ordained methodology that He's instituted for His Body to deal with sickness.

The point is that God has given us as Christ's Body here on this earth several mechanisms to deal with the sickness and disease that is in our world and can affect us. But they do involve us exercising our faith and believing God. The sad truth is that much of the Body is not experiencing much of these benefits because much of the Body has not put these God-ordained mechanisms into practice. We've made excuses and explained away why healing isn't really for us and why the giftings of the Spirit are not for today. Or we've doctrinally acknowledged the giftings are for today but we don't put them all into practice in our gatherings. We've ignored or minimized teachings such as James 5 that tell us how to deal with the sick in our churches, and we've left out a key part of how we implement communion. What we've been left with is a Church body that is not operating in nearly the level of power that it is supposed to be operating in. We've gotten used to this low-power state where we just talk about God's sovereignty and "mystery" to explain why some people get sick and die. Brothers and sisters, this is not the way it is supposed to be.

Jesus told the religious leaders of His day that "for the sake of your tradition you have made void the word of God." (Matthew 15:6b ESV). Sadly, the same could still be said today. The church today can operate in the same type of power that the early church did, but if it wants to do so, it needs to start doing the types of things that they did! If we want Bible results, we need to do things the Bible way.

Chapter 12 – Baptism of the Holy Spirit

An important thing that is worthy to give consideration to for anyone really wanting to live the abundant life and flow in the power of God is the baptism of the Holy Spirit. The whole notion of a baptism of the Holy Spirit is foreign or unusual to some, while for others it primarily is thought about in terms of speaking in tongues. For those that are wary of (or downright scared of) speaking in tongues, this can be a particularly controversial subject.

I want to try to simplify and de-mystify things a bit here because honestly some of this can get a bit murky and there's lots of theological opinions out there. For myself, I tend to be a fairly simple guy. When I first started learning and hearing about this, I was initially a bit skeptical, but I made a decision. You know how on a multiple choice test, there's often an "E" response for "All of the above"? Well, I made a decision that whether I fully understood everything or not, I was going with "E" – I wanted everything that God had for me – I didn't want to live below what was available to me. I encourage you to adopt a similar attitude and just decide upfront that you want everything that God has to give you. I decided for myself that if I was going to "err" somewhere that is where I was going to do it. But I didn't "err" doing that and you won't either.

The idea of a baptism of the Holy Spirit came from Jesus. In John 20:22, after Jesus' resurrection when He appeared to His disciples, we read this:

> And when he had said this, he breathed on them and said to them, "Receive the Holy Spirit." (John 20:22 ESV).

Then at some point later, we read this:

> And while staying with them he ordered them not to depart from Jerusalem, but to wait for the promise of the Father, which, he said, "you heard from me; for John baptized with water, but you will be baptized with

the Holy Spirit not many days from now." (Acts 1:4–5 ESV)

"But you will receive power when the Holy Spirit has come upon you, and you will be my witnesses in Jerusalem and in all Judea and Samaria, and to the end of the earth." And when he had said these things, as they were looking on, he was lifted up, and a cloud took him out of their sight. (Acts 1:8–9 ESV)

This is the last thing Jesus told His followers right before He ascended to Heaven. Now here's a question: Why did Jesus breathe on some of His disciples and tell them to receive the Spirit (seemingly impart the Spirit to them), but then later told them to wait for another experience where the Spirit would come upon them and give them power? It seems here that there are two different experiences.

For those believers, the experience Jesus told them to wait for happened on the day of Pentecost:

When the day of Pentecost arrived, they were all together in one place. And suddenly there came from heaven a sound like a mighty rushing wind, and it filled the entire house where they were sitting. And divided tongues as of fire appeared to them and rested on each one of them. And they were all filled with the Holy Spirit and began to speak in other tongues as the Spirit gave them utterance. (Acts 2:1–4 ESV)

They were filled with the Holy Spirit and spoke in other tongues. The account goes on to show Peter preaching with power to Jews that had come to see what the commotion was. In part of that message, Peter says this:

This Jesus God raised up, and of that we all are witnesses. Being therefore exalted at the right hand of God, and having received from the Father the promise of the Holy Spirit, he has poured out this that you your-selves are seeing and hearing. (Acts 2:32–33 ESV)

Jesus sent the Holy Spirit, just as He had said He would do way back before He was crucified (John 16:7). The Holy Spirit came upon them and caused them to be filled with power and boldness, which affected their world around them.

Now, lest you think that this baptism of the Holy Spirit was only meant for them that day at Pentecost, the Bible shows something different. Sometimes people try to argue that the believers in Jesus prior to Pentecost weren't really "saved" until Pentecost when they were filled with the Spirit. Thus they say that the "born again" and "baptism of the Holy Spirit" experience always occur at the same time. Or they say that the Pentecost experience was a one-time thing, but that for us today, it's just that when we are "born again", we receive that powerful indwelling/filling of the Holy Spirit. An account later in the book of Acts sheds some light on all of this:

> 1 And it happened that while Apollos was at Corinth, Paul passed through the inland country and came to Ephesus. There he found some disciples. 2 And he said to them, "Did you receive the Holy Spirit when you be-lieved?" And they said, "No, we have not even heard that there is a Holy Spirit." 3 And he said, "Into what then were you baptized?" They said, "Into John's bap-tism." 4 And Paul said, "John baptized with the baptism of repentance, telling the people to believe in the one who was to come after him, that is, Jesus." 5 On hearing this, they were baptized in the name of the Lord Jesus. 6 And when Paul had laid his hands on them, the Holy Spirit came on them, and they began speaking in tongues and prophesying. (Acts 19:1–6 ESV)

Here, some time later, we have Paul running across believers in Ephesus. He asked them if they had received the Holy Spirit when they believed and they said they had not (they hadn't even heard of the Holy Spirit). Paul then went on to water baptize them in the name of Jesus (since they hadn't done that either), and then we are told in verse 6 that he laid his hands on them and the Holy Spirit came on them. Just like the believers at Pentecost, they spoke in other tongues and demonstrated God's power (i.e. began prophesying).

It is not fully clear from this account whether the disciples were already believers in Jesus or had basically only been following the message of John the Baptist (which was one of repentance), though it seems that they did know of and believe in Jesus but just were not aware of the Holy Spirit. Paul didn't just tell them that since they already believed in Jesus, they had the Holy Spirit too. No, he laid his hands on them and *then* the Holy Spirit came on them.

Now, the implication in Paul's question when he asked them in verse 2 whether they received the Spirit when they believed is that they were *supposed* to have received the Holy Spirit when they believed. But Paul must have known that that might not be the case sometimes or he would never have asked that question. And this is where the "catch" is I believe. I do believe that a person can believe in Jesus and receive the baptism of the Holy Spirit at the same time, and that this is actually the way it is *supposed* to be. The thing is though that just like Jesus won't force Himself on you, you have to want the Holy Spirit (be in receptive mode) in your life. Most evangelistic teaching out there talks about believing in and receiving Jesus, but doesn't at the same time talk about receiving the Holy Spirit and that the Spirit wants to empower their life. Thus people can make a decision to believe in Jesus and confess that decision with their mouth and become "born again", but not really receive the filling of the Spirit in their life at that time. It all goes back to "choice" and what people know or don't know. These Ephesian believers hadn't heard of the Spirit, so they couldn't really receive or want Him and His power. God worked with what they knew and He didn't baptize them in the Spirit when they didn't even know of the Spirit and weren't wanting Him.

Jesus and the Holy Spirit are two different and distinct parts of God with different roles. A person can receive Jesus and receive a new spirit that is born of the Holy Spirit, without actually having the filling / fullness of the Spirit operating in their life. If people aren't taught to want the Holy Spirit and His power, and are even taught explicitly against things that are evidences of that power (e.g. speaking in tongues, prophesying, etc.), then they are not in a position to really receive the baptism of the Holy Spirit. They may receive Jesus and become "born again", but they are going to be "born again" believers without much power. Which, coincidentally, describes a fair amount of the Church world today.

There are large parts of the Church that practically operate as if the Holy Spirit doesn't even exist. I know – I grew up in a part of the Body where very little mention of the Holy Spirit occurred except when we were reciting some doctrinal statement such as the Apostle's Creed. The Holy Spirit was talked about as being part of God, but I don't recall ever being clearly told that He was supposed to be playing an integral part in my life. All the emphasis was on God the Father and God the Son, but God the Holy Spirit was treated like the unpopular kid in school – you know he's there, but nobody pays him any mind.

For myself, I was a believer for about 10 years and constantly living defeated and feeling pretty powerless. I began craving *more*. I didn't understand much, but I read and heard testimonies from high-profile well-respected believers that mentioned having an experience subsequent to their initial salvation experience where they got an influx of power, and I wanted that too. That's where I made the decision I told you about earlier where I decided to mark box "E" – that I wanted ALL of God's power and everything He had for me. I wanted it all – Jesus, the Father, the Holy Spirit and everything entailed. I didn't understand about tongues and I had been taught to not really want it, but I decided I wanted everything God had for me.

I can't tell you the exact date of this as this was kind of an evolution over time for me, but I can tell you that there was a change in me. The Bible started becoming more alive to me in a way it hadn't previously. I started getting bolder. I started demonstrating more of God's power. And yes, eventually I even started speaking in tongues.

And, let's address address the speaking in tongues thing for a moment. Some parts of the Body teach that when you receive the baptism of the Holy Spirit that the evidence of that is speaking in tongues. They have good Biblical basis for that because that is what happened at Pentecost and also in the Acts 19 account above (as well as in Acts 10:44–46).

However, much like receiving the baptism of the Holy Spirit itself, if a person is dead-set against speaking in tongues, God isn't going to force them. God doesn't make people speak in tongues. They *get* to speak in tongues, but they don't have to. You can be baptized in the Holy Spirit and not immediately speak in tongues, however, speaking in tongues is I believe a primary evidence of being baptized in the Spirit and I believe that if a person is baptized in the Holy Spirit and is open to it, tongues will be a natural result. In my case, it was 2007 when I first did the tongues thing, and I really hadn't planned to do it. I was just lost in worship, singing to God and communing with Him, and then my singing switched from English to an unknown tongue for like 15 minutes. It seemed to well up from deep-within me (see John 7:38–39). I was very open to it at the time (it wasn't forced on me against my will) and I knew it was a beautiful thing, yet I also didn't really understand it and I was a bit ashamed of it in a sense because of wrong teaching I had previously received. Because of that teaching and misunderstandings regarding tongues, the experience was not repeated for a long time.

It took me about five more years before I really began speaking in tongues and that's only after I spent time studying it out and getting some understanding on some things. One of my earlier misunderstandings was I thought that God basically forced you to speak in tongues – that He came on you so strongly that you had to do so and that He opened your mouth and put the sounds in it. For years (we'll say since at least 2007), I would have stirrings in my spirit where internally I could feel my spirit praying. I now realize that as the same thing as speaking in tongues but without the vocalization. Once I began to realize that in order to speak in tongues, I myself needed to open my mouth and use my voice, and that the Holy Spirit would partner with me in that, things started falling into place. I also came to a place where I was willing to speak in tongues; I decided it wasn't something to be afraid of, but that it was a good thing. I reasoned that if the Apostle Paul thought it a good thing (1 Corinthians 14:18), then I probably should too. If it's from God, then it must be a good thing for me. So I asked the Lord for that and made myself open to it.

Some churches either actively or passively teach against speaking in tongues. They may acknowledge that it's a gift, but they don't make it seem as if it is something that believers should really want and they certainly don't make space for it in their gatherings. The Bible is clear when the Apostle Paul tells us: "So, my brothers, earnestly desire to prophesy, and do not forbid speaking in tongues." (1 Corinthians 14:39 ESV). There are a whole lot of churches around that do NOT desire to have anyone prophesy and also in essence have a de-facto (usually not official) ban on speaking in tongues, in direct opposition to this scripture. I don't know how else to say this but to just be blunt: this is wrong. Speaking in tongues is a good thing (as is prophecy by the way). In a church gathering, there needs to be order (that's much of what 1 Corinthians 14 is all about), but simply banning or ignoring tongues, prophecy, and other gifts (including the gift of healings) is not right. Without realizing it, what they basically have done is severely limit the Holy Spirit in their gatherings. The reason many churches today don't seem to have the same power and "oomph" that the early church had is because we've kicked out the Power source from our churches...Jesus Himself told us that power comes from the Spirit. And we've got churches that depend far more on their own wisdom and programs and systems and methodologies and traditions than they depend on the Spirit to lead and guide their services. That's just the truth.

There is a scriptural distinction between speaking in an unknown tongue to you for the benefit of others/giving a word of exhortation or similar in a tongue for the benefit of others versus praying in tongues for your own personal edification. In the first case is where it is a specific gift used for the Body to edify the Body and is where the gift of interpretation of tongues is utilized to understand the meaning. It also accounts for situations where you may speak a known language (unknown to you) for the benefit of someone else that does know that language (this happened at Pentecost). However, I want to focus on tongues as it relates to you personally.

Speaking/praying/singing in tongues is useful for you because it bypasses your brain. It allows you to have direct communication between your spirit and God without your brain getting in the way. "For one who speaks in a tongue speaks not to men but to God; for no one understands him, but he utters mysteries in the Spirit ... The one who speaks in a tongue builds up himself, but the one who prophesies builds up the church ... For if I pray in a tongue, my spirit prays but my mind is unfruitful." (1 Corinthians 14:2,4,14 ESV). Tongues help you to pray when you don't know what to pray (Romans 8:26) and it edifies you ("builds you up" as mentioned in the scripture above).

The other misnomer I had about speaking in tongues was that I assumed that some people got this gift and some people did not. It's actually a misunderstanding about the whole gifts thing in general, which I'm not going to get into too deep here, except to say that everything of the Spirit is available to you as a believer. You may have a specific overriding gift in a certain area, but it's not like you can't ever do anything else. It's not like the Spirit is saying: "Well, Joe, you get the gift of speaking in tongues. And Mary, you get the gift of prophecy. And that's all you can have." No, God might use you in a specific area more than others for the benefit of the Body (that's the whole purpose of the gifts), but all of the gifts are available to you as the Spirit works through you. You should make yourself open to all the gifts and to want everything God has for you. Further, when it comes to tongues, there's the gift of tongues for benefiting others, but then there's also you just praying/speaking in tongues for your own benefit as we've already discussed.

Now if unbelievers see you speaking in tongues, will they probably think you are completely loony? Yes. But they probably already think you are loony anyway. (That's a joke, friends.) Paul acknowledges in 1 Corinthians 14:23 that if unbelievers come into a church service and see everyone speaking in tongues, they will just think everyone is crazy. That's not necessarily a bad thing though – the Bible says that tongues are actually a "sign" for unbelievers (1 Cor. 14:22). In other words, it could maybe also spur thoughts among unbelievers like: "Woah – what are these people doing? What do they have or understand that I don't have that they would do something like this?" It's a power sign to them. Yet, given that it can also be perceived as lunacy, this is one reason why Paul pushed so hard that there needs to be order and said: "I thank God that I speak in tongues more than all of you. Nevertheless, in church I would rather speak five words with my mind in order to instruct others, than ten thousand words in a tongue." (1 Corinthians 14:18–19 ESV). So even the Apostle Paul who specifically said not to forbid tongues in church gatherings and talked about their benefits and how much he loved that he spoke in tongues, also saw limitations to that and conceded that when it came to actually teaching people, he would much rather be talking in understandable language. Tongues are useful and important and definitely have their place (both for corporate edification and also personal edification), but there also needs to be balance and order and wisdom used, particularly when you are in a corporate setting.

For the believer, the point in all this is that tongues isn't something weird or creepy. It's something for your benefit, and also potentially for the benefit of others, and is something you should want and desire! Don't let fear hold you back from something God has for you to be a blessing and help for you!

The baptism of the Holy Spirit is not just about tongues though. It's really about having the power to do all that God has for you to do. Many believers throughout church history bear witness with having a separate experience from their salvation experience where they received this power and they felt that this experience was crucial to their lives. Just a few that I know of because I've personally read their own words on the subject include D.L. Moody, Charles Finney, R.A. Torrey, and Charles Stanley.

In relation to healing or receiving something you need, the baptism of the Holy Spirit is important for several reasons. First, you will have the empowering to do things that you might not otherwise have. You will be in a position to receive giftings to help you. You will have the ability (if you are willing and want it) to pray in tongues which can help you in praying when you don't know what to do. For instance, you might find yourself praying in a tongue and then God reveal something to you as a word of wisdom that will help dictate your next course of action.

It's not just Jesus that we are to receive. We also are to receive the Holy Spirit. And how do we do that? We are told by Jesus that the heavenly Father will "give the Holy Spirit to them that ask him" (Luke 11:13b) and we are told in the same verse that the Holy Spirit is a "good gift."

Perhaps you have already done this. I recognize that sometimes this can get "muddled" with the initial salvation experience – that's one of the reasons why there is such confusion on this subject. But honestly, can I just say to you, that regardless of what you have done previously, if you haven't ever specifically just asked for the Holy Spirit and His filling in your life, might I suggest that now is a good time? Open your arms with your hands palm-up as a posture of receiving and ask for the Holy Spirit and His filling in your life. Ask for His power to live the life that God wants you to live and to do what He has for you to do. Be open to all He has for you. Decide that you want Option "E" – that you want ALL that God has to give you, including the ability to pray and speak in tongues. Say, "God, I want it ALL! Everything you have for me, I want, including tongues."

Then, whether you feel something or not, believe that you receive. Say, "God, I'm going to trust that as I open my mouth here and start using my voice to make noises other than my known language that you will meet me in that and empower that and that I will speak in a tongue." Then start doing so.

If you still have concerns or questions or don't feel like you understand this or you still are unsure about whether you are able to speak in tongues, I would suggest you seek out another believer or church that understands about the baptism of the Holy Spirit and ask them to help you to receive. Much like the Apostle Paul did with those believers in Ephesus in Acts 19, sometimes having someone else there that can help personally instruct you and lay hands on you can be a help.

The bottom-line on the baptism of the Holy Spirit as a whole is that this is an important part of really living the abundant life that we are meant to live. Living the abundant life means living in and living out of God's power through the Spirit. It is based in an understanding that we need His power and help to really accomplish all that He has for us.

Chapter 13 – Deeply Loved

We have spent a lot of time in this book so far stepping through key theological things that I believe are important underpinnings and key elements of being able to live the abundant life Jesus has for us. And that's all well and good, but Christianity and living the abundant life is more than just understanding theology. It's about experiencing the love of God, and I believe one of the major keys to really living the abundant life comes out of knowing how deeply loved we are and then letting that love transform us.

Most all believers know that God loves them on an intellectual basis. We all know that John 3:16 starts by saying: "For God so LOVED the world..." (emphasis mine). So I don't think there's any genuine believers out there that would argue with the statement that God loves people. We know this.

The problem is that while we do have an intellectual assent to this, really grasping God's love for us personally on a deep heart level can be another thing entirely. Most believers know God loves them. But there's knowing and then there's *KNOWING!*

The thing is that we all know ourselves pretty well. We know all the terrible things we've done. We know the terrible thoughts we've had; those thoughts that we wouldn't want anyone to ever know. We've all done and thought things that we are truly ashamed of. Because we know these things and all our shortcomings and ways we have failed through the years, it can be hard for us to truly on a deep level accept that we are deeply loved by God since we know that He knows us as we really are.

This can be even more likely if we have experienced significant rejection from other people in our life since we assume that God must really want to treat us the same way. Or if we had parents that were not the best at showing us affection, we might have subtly assumed that God is similar. It can be very hard for us to really truly believe and accept that God really does love us even while knowing all about us.

In addition, as we discussed way back in chapter two, many of us have been taught that God loves us while also being taught that He might be causing us sickness or causing loved ones to die. When that is one's view of God, one is only going to draw so close. Particularly if we have been through hard and painful situations, it is easy for our heart to (often subtly) question God's goodness and His love for us.

Sometimes what our head knows and what our heart knows are two very different things. Thus, when someone starts talking about God's love, it can be easy for us to think: "Oh, I know that. I know God loves me." And yet, there can be part of us on a core level that really *doesn't* know that. I truly believe that the degree to which we really grasp God's love for us in the pit of our being is a huge part in determining the degree to which we will walk in the abundant life that God has for us.

Our churches today may be known for lots of things, but love sadly often isn't at the top of the list. Jesus said, "A new commandment I give to you, that you love one another; as I have loved you, that you also love one another. By this all will know that you are My disciples, if you have love for one another." (John 13:34–35 NKJV). To God, love is to be the absolute central mark of a Christian.

Often times, reflecting our preferred view of God as harsh taskmaster rather than loving Father, we have tended to make ourselves more known in our culture for what we are against rather than what we are for. Our central trademark is to be love and is what we are supposed to be known by first-and-foremost, and yet we as a Church in general have far too often been more likely to come across as angry, arrogant, critical, and judgmental to our culture. I am definitely not saying that we as a Church should ignore or dismiss sin (that's a whole other prevalent problem), but I am saying that love always needs to rule and guide our actions and interactions, and far too often it has not. One key reason for that is simply that many of us have had trouble really receiving God's love for ourselves. If one hasn't really received and embraced God's love on a core level, it will be less likely they will be showing and sharing forth God's love with others in any significant way.

If the Apostle Paul were here praying for you personally today, perhaps one of his prayers for you would partially mirror what He prayed for some believers in his day: "that you, being rooted and grounded in love, may have strength to comprehend with all the saints what is the breadth and length and height and depth, and to know the love of Christ that surpasses knowledge, that you may be filled with all the fullness of God." (Ephesians 3:17b–19 ESV). We need to be really "rooted" and "grounded" in love. I join with the Apostle Paul in praying that prayer for you and me both. I pray that we would meditate on God's deep love for us and that we would experience this love flooding every nook and cranny of our being.

Many believers approach Christianity on a transactional basis. We hear that we have a sin problem that God did something about through Jesus and we accept God's gift to us in Jesus. Transaction complete. Yet, Christianity isn't supposed to just be a transaction, but a two-way relationship with the God that made us. And at the core of that relationship is love.

Did you know that God the Father loves *you* as much as He loves Jesus the Son? Sound blasphemous? Well it might sound that way, but it's what the Bible actually says. God the Father loves you with the same love with which He loves Jesus the Son. In other words, the same love between God Himself as the Trinity is the same love He has for you! I know you probably don't believe that, but Jesus Himself actually said it. He did so in John 17 in His prayer to God the Father for His disciples and those that would believe in Him (i.e. you and me). Here's a portion of that prayer with a few parts that I've bolded to stand out:

> 20 "I do not ask for these only, but also for those who will believe in me through their word, 21 that they may all be one, just as you, Father, are in me, and I in you, that they also may be in us, so that the world may believe that you have sent me. 22 The glory that you have given me I have given to them, that they may be one even as we are one, 23 I in them and you in me, that they may become perfectly one, **so that the world may know that you sent me and loved them even as you loved me.** 24 Father, I desire that they also, whom you have given me, may be with me where I am, to see my glory that you have given me **because you loved me**

before the foundation of the world. 25 O righteous Father, even though the world does not know you, I know you, and these know that you have sent me. 26 I made known to them your name, and I will continue to make it known, **that the love with which you have loved me may be in them, and I in them.**" (John 17:20–26 ESV, emphasis mine).

Note in verse 23 that Jesus prays that we would KNOW that we are loved even as Jesus is loved. We don't need to earn the love – it's already an established fact – but a key issue is whether we KNOW it or not. Then we are told in verse 24 that Jesus was loved before the foundation of the world. Finally Jesus prays in verse 26 that the same love with which Jesus has been loved would be in us!

In other words, the same love that loved Jesus before the foundation of the world is the same love that God has for you! That's some mind-blowing, serious love!

If we're honest with ourselves, if we boil everything down, don't we all just really want to be loved? So much of what we do and say is geared towards trying to get acceptance from others. In fact, lots of the trouble that people get themselves into is because they are trying to meet this love need on their own and end up getting hurt by others or hurting themselves in the process. We all want to know that we are loved. Deeply. Unconditionally. We want love.

God, being the source of true love and it actually being His very nature, is the one in whom we are meant to first and foremost have our love-needs met. People can and will let us down; they are flawed just like you and I are. No person is capable of 100% meeting our needs. But God IS capable and is always there for us and always loves us. You, right now, are deeply, deeply loved. This God that loves you has called you into a close relationship with Himself – as close of relationship as exists between God the Father and Jesus the Son! Did you notice from the same John 17 passage above that Jesus not only talked about us being loved with the same love, but He also said that He would be IN US (vs. 26). That's a pretty close relationship... You don't get closer than that.

Friend, God – being God – already knew before the foundations of the world who you would be. He knew all of your mistakes and failures before you made a one of them. And yet, He loved you then and He loves you now. His very nature is love. God is love (1 John 4:16). He has always been love. He always will be love. There's no need to fear. "There is no fear in love, but perfect love casts out fear. For fear has to do with punishment, and whoever fears has not been perfected in love." (1 John 4:18 ESV). God is not out to get you and He's not out to punish you. He already laid all your punishment on Jesus. Jesus took your punishment. He knows what you've done and what you've thought and Jesus paid for all of that on the cross. What God has for you is not wrath, but love, and He calls you to bask in His love.

You may remember that earlier in this book we looked at Isaiah chapter 53, which is an Old Testament portion of Scripture that talks about Jesus the Messiah. That chapter ends talking about Jesus bearing our sins and then immediately in the next chapter (remember, chapter divisions did not exist in the original manuscripts), it starts talking about some of the results of this and how we should be rejoicing. It is told from God's perspective to us and He says this:

> "This is like the days of Noah to me:
> as I swore that the waters of Noah
> should no more go over the earth,
> so I have sworn that I will not be angry with you,
> and will not rebuke you.
> For the mountains may depart
> and the hills be removed,
> but my steadfast love shall not depart from you,
> and my covenant of peace shall not be removed,"
> says the LORD, who has compassion on you. (Isaiah 54:9–10 ESV)

God made an unconditional covenant back after He sent the flood in the time of Noah that He would never again send a flood to cover the earth (Genesis 9:11). Just as He made that unconditional covenant, God also just as strongly is saying that He has made another covenant, a "covenant of peace", in which He has sworn that He will not be angry with us, will not rebuke us, and that His steadfast love (or kindness) will not depart from us. This "covenant of peace" will not be removed and it was given by our God who "has compassion" on us.

Religion, even in the name of Christianity, has told all of us that God really is angry and in a bad mood a lot of the time – that when we mess up (even as believers), that God is waiting to whack us over the head. That's not the case, friends! It's just not true! That doesn't mean God likes us sinning – sin very much hurts us. God will work with us if we are in sin and I will tell you right now that He will not tolerate it in your life precisely because He loves you and wants what is best for you. There is a disciplining of the Lord and He will definitely work with us and work on us, but it's not anger. This picture of a God up there waiting to strike you because of something you've done has got to go.

God is not mad at you! You don't need to fear Him or His wrath any more. God's wrath has *already* been poured out! Jesus took the wrath that you deserved. Your sins have already been dealt with. The war is over! Jesus was the proof and fulfillment of the "covenant of peace" between God and man. You have been brought to the banqueting table to feast and God has put a banner over you of love (see Song of Solomon 2:4). "In this the love of God was made manifest among us, that God sent his only Son into the world, so that we might live through him." (1 John 4:9 ESV). Jesus is proof of God's love for us and we are meant to live life through Jesus. We are told by Jesus, "As the Father loved Me, I also have loved you; abide in My love." (John 15:9 NKJV). We are to live in, to abide in love. As we abide in Jesus' love, we live our lives through Him and we truly experience the fullness of life as we are meant to experience it – full, abundant life.

God isn't interested in you having a "transactional relationship" with Him where you just get things from Him because you pulled the right levers (be it faith or otherwise). He's interested in you having a deep relationship with Him. He wants you to crawl up on His lap. He wants to hold you. He wants to look in your eyes and tell you that you are incredibly precious to Him. That you are cherished.

You are loved. All that your heart has ever really wanted is met in Him. He wants your life and His life to be intertwined – your heart to beat with His heart. He wants you with Him, forever. You are His. He made you and He knows you – far better than any person ever could. He knows the good, the bad, the ugly – and He still wants you. He's calling to you to let go, to fall into His arms and trust that they will hold you and never let you go. He will never run from you, but He wants you to not run from Him. He calls you to dwell in Him – to dwell in love – to dwell in Life. Abundant, full Life.

This is what our life here on this earth is all about. Knowing our God and being restored to Life the way it was always meant to be – the way it was before the Fall of mankind in the Garden. It's about being restored to relationship with our loving Creator that made us and made this entire world. It is all about relationship before it is about anything else.

Many Christians approach their Christian walk like one would approach a Rubik's cube. They are looking for the right formula to "make it work." All they want is someone to tell them what to do so they can get what they're after. They basically want a magic formula. Thus we're drawn to books and videos with titles such as: "5 Ways to Have a Great Marriage" or "10 Ways to Overcome Fear" or "7 Steps to Experience Peace" or "10 Keys to Walk in Divine Health", etc. We just want someone to tell us what to do.

This can even happen with stuff that I've addressed in this book. Some people learn about about faith and "speaking to their mountain" and having a good confession – speaking positively – and they integrate that into their lives as a formula. So for instance, they develop a set of rules to see their healing come to pass such as praying X amount, speaking 10 confessions a day, reading healing scriptures every day, never saying anything negative, and so on. I'm not saying some of those things aren't good, but healing specifically, and Christianity in general, is not about a formula.

Many people get so caught up chasing what they're after that they miss the relationship. They get so caught up chasing their healing that they miss the Healer. They get so caught up chasing provision that they miss the Provider. They get so caught up chasing freedom that they miss the One that has set them free!

What God most wants from you is for you to be in close relationship with Him. He wants you. And He wants you to want Him. Not His stuff, but Him. His stuff is yours – that's a perk of being in relationship with Him. You are an heir and you get the stuff too. It's a natural byproduct of the relationship and it is all available for you. But many times Christians really are chasing after all the stuff (be it forgiveness, healing, peace, financial blessings, whatever) instead of chasing after the Giver of the stuff. This is where some of the "faith movement" in the Body of Christ has errored in times past and given themselves a "bad reputation" with much of the rest of the Body in the process. They've often put the emphasis on the stuff at the expense of the relationship with the Giver of the stuff. If you chase after the stuff instead of the Giver, you will eventually end up finding yourself frustrated, guaranteed.

God wants you. He loves you. It wasn't Adam that cried out to God in the Garden after he sinned, but it was God that went looking for Adam and basically asked, "Where are you?" (see Genesis 3:9). I don't believe He was asking that angrily. I believe He was a loving Father seeking His child. God hasn't changed. He's interested in you and me and where we are at and what's going on in our lives. He created us for fellowship with Him and deep, intimate relationship with Him. Through Jesus, God has restored us to this place of fellowship and relationship with Himself. But, still, far too often, much like Adam & Eve did after their sin, we try to run and hide and do things our way. Adam & Eve tried to depend on themselves to cover their nakedness instead of looking to their Daddy and trusting in His provision for them. We still pull the same nonsense today even as believers in Jesus. We're always trying to depend on ourselves and our efforts instead of resting in the provision that God has provided for us in Jesus. When we rest in Jesus, what we are really doing is resting in God and His love for us.

Genuine Bible faith is about resting in Jesus and His sacrifice for you. People that aren't in faith are in their flesh, trying to do things themselves to get what they are after. That goes for people that haven't ever trusted in Jesus and aren't "born again", and it also goes for some Christians that are looking for some blessing. Often times believers that get a hold of a truth such as that God wants them well and start learning some of the things like I've shared in this book then get into a snare in trying to MAKE something come about (such as their healing) through all the things that they DO. Now don't get me wrong, there are some things you should do to put your faith into action. We've already talked about some of that and will be talking about that even more in a later chapter. But you need to be careful that you don't start depending on what you are doing. If you aren't careful, the object of your faith can subtly shift from Jesus and His sacrifice for you and what you have through Him, to you and what you are doing. At the end of the day, your faith needs to stay rooted and grounded in Jesus Christ and what is available to you because of His sacrifice for you. That is where you plant your flag and make your stand. That is where you rest.

I encourage you to believe God's Word to you for whatever your need is and confess it. I encourage you to stand in faith and trust God for what you need. I encourage you to take hold of all that Jesus died to give you. Just don't lose sight of the big picture. What God most wants from you is you. He wants your heart, your trust, your love as you rest in, abide in, dwell in, bask in, dance up and down in, His Love for you! He wants you! Don't just settle for His stuff. Go after *Him*. And you'll find the stuff is there for you too.

There's no magic formula to get what you're after. There are principles that can help or hinder things in your life, and faith (or lack thereof) is a big one of those principles. But it's not about coming up with just the right combination of things that you do to get God to move in your life. It's about looking to your Daddy in trust and assurance, resting in what He's provided for you in Jesus. In your quest to walk in the blessings of God (whatever your needs may be), don't lose sight of this big picture.

The real Good News of Jesus is truly incredible. When you really stop and think about the fact that our God loves us so much that He "freely gives us all things" (Romans 8:32), it can be quite overwhelming. We know all the wrong things that we have done and thus it can be easy to feel unworthy to receive all that God has for us, which can sometimes hinder us receiving those things. That can be the case when it comes to receiving Christ's sacrifice on your behalf for forgiveness of sins, and it can also be the case when it comes to receiving Christ's sacrifice on your behalf for health and wholeness or other needs.

The reality is that none of us in ourselves are worthy. But the great news is that it's not based on our worthiness. We are made righteous through Jesus and it is because of this righteousness that gets conferred upon us that we are able to be fully blessed by God. We don't deserve these blessings in ourselves, but we aren't in ourselves anymore but are rather "in Christ", and God delights in giving them to us. Jesus made the way for us to truly live the abundant life!

This abundant life is to be a lifestyle though. It comes as we live in all that God has provided for us. God isn't interested in His children overcoming a temptation one time or seeing a healing one time, and then going on their merry way. He wants you to live in Him and walk in victory and health the rest of your days. God's desire isn't that you run from crisis to crisis having to beg Him for help, but that you receive and live in the blessings He has provided for you.

What happens sometimes is Christians will have some problem (perhaps they are sick or have a financial problem) and cry out to God and maybe even believe God for their answer, and then when they receive it and the "crisis" has passed, they set God over on the shelf and only come visit Him periodically. God wants a close relationship with you where you are walking with Him daily, dwelling in and experiencing all the blessings He has for you. He is not interested in being your Part-time God.

We are to live our lives in and through Christ, with full dependence on, and faith in, Him because of His sacrifice for us. God wants you to draw near to Himself through Jesus. He wants you to know how loved you are and for you to live your life in response to that. He wants you.

> So we have come to know and to believe the love that
> God has for us. God is love, and whoever abides in

love abides in God, and God abides in him. (1 John
4:16 ESV).

This, as we have already discussed, tells us that God Himself IS
love. When one is truly abiding in love, they are actually abiding in
God, because all genuine love actually springs from Him. He is the
source of true, genuine, unfiltered, untainted love. It is who He is.
God IS love, and if you remember from your mathematics teaching,
"is" equates to "equals." Thus the mathematical equation is God =
Love.

1 Corinthians 13 is an oft-quoted chapter of the Bible; it is frequently shared at weddings or other events where the context is
human love. Here is one of the most commonly shared passages
from that chapter:

> Love is patient and kind; love does not envy or boast; it
> is not arrogant or rude. It does not insist on its own
> way; it is not irritable or resentful; it does not rejoice at
> wrongdoing, but rejoices with the truth. Love bears all
> things, believes all things, hopes all things, endures all
> things. Love never ends. (1 Corinthians 13:4–8a ESV)

Since we have already established that God IS love, meaning
that God = Love, everywhere you see the word "Love" in the above
passage, you could substitute the word "God". God is patient and
kind with you. He doesn't envy or boast. He isn't arrogant or rude.
He won't force you by insisting on His own way in some selfish
manner. He isn't irritable with you or resentful. He does not rejoice
when you do wrong, but rejoices with the truth. God bears all
things, believes all things, hopes all things, and endures all things.
God never ends. God never fails. Love never ends. Love never fails.

You are deeply loved and cherished by God Almighty. The old is
gone – the shame, the guilt, the feelings of unworthiness – that is all
the past. Let it go. You are a new creation in Christ, and that new
creation is entitled to ALL the benefits of the Kingdom, including
health and wholeness. All is yours and you can make a choice to

receive what God has freely provided for you out of His love. Receive His love and His blessings for you today!

I would like to share a poem/song I wrote titled "This Is What I've Been Looking For" that I would encourage you to read as your own:

> This is what I've been looking for,
> This is what I have sought,
> to know deep down and really grasp,
> that I am loved by God;
>
> By my Creator that made me,
> And cherishes who He made.
> Oh my heart, rejoice in love,
> no longer be afraid.
>
> I am a child of God;
> I'm an heir with Jesus Christ.
> I receive my inheritance purchased for me
> by my Savior's sacrifice.
>
> I have been set free;
> I am no longer bound.
> All blessings are mine in Christ,
> I receive my royal crown.
>
> For I am royalty by my new birth,
> born into a royal family.
> I receive all the promises that are mine,
> By the position bestowed to me.
>
> And I know all things are possible,
> Yes I can do anything.
> There are no limitations,
> for children of the King.
>
> And I rejoice and lift my hands,

and I bow in humility,
with gratefulness to this One
who has so loved me.

This is what I've been looking for,
Yes this is what I have sought,
to know deep down and really grasp,
Oh I am loved by God.

May you be rooted and grounded in God's tremendous love for
you, and as you receive all of His love and blessings He has for you,
may you shine forth as a bright witness to all you come in contact
with.

You are loved.

Chapter 14 – A Balanced View

In talking about living the abundant life, one of the subjects that we have spent quite some time on is that of faith, and specifically faith as it relates to health and wholeness. In the last chapter, we also spent some time emphasizing the importance of understanding God's love for us. The trick when talking about all of this stuff (faith in particular) is to maintain proper balance and that is what this chapter aims to help accomplish. Those that are in the "faith camps" of the Body (those that emphasize using faith for healing or other needs) probably really loved what I had to say when I have talked about using our faith. This chapter, however, provides balance that you don't often see in teaching along these lines and thus I'll just prepare those that are in that boat up front by saying that what I'm about to say could potentially ruffle a few feathers.

Sometimes it can be easy for people that are real gung-ho on having and exercising faith to lose sight of some things. In other words, some people see the trees, but miss the forest. In doing so, they can make some rather significant errors. I have met people that are so pro-faith, that that's all they talk about. And honestly, they sometimes downright appear "out to lunch" or very uncaring. Some of the most "disconnected", "cold-feeling", "fake-appearing", judgmental, arrogant Christians I have ever met are some I've come across in the "faith camps" of the Body. There is a balance with things and we want to make sure we stay in the proper balance.

Having faith is a good thing and exercising that faith through action is a good thing. Speaking positively (and not negatively) is a good thing. But some people just plain go to extremes, whereby they are constantly analyzing everyone's speech or can't even be honest when people ask them a simple question like "How are you doing?" They might have had the worst morning ever, have a major migraine going on at the moment you ask them, and they'll still respond with something super-spiritual-sounding like "I'm blessed – God is good" because they are afraid to say something negative that might "counteract" their faith. You know what? I'm not saying that we should be negative, but I do think that God is a God of truth and thus we want to live in a place of truth. We need to drop some of the nonsense. If you've got a migraine and someone asks how you are doing, it is perfectly okay to be honest and say: "I've got a migraine right now." Now you can also say something like, "But I believe I'm healed in Jesus and that the pain must leave in Jesus' name – would you agree with me?" But honestly, if I hear one more "faith person" tell me: "I'm blessed", every single time I ask them how they are, I think I'm going to scream! Yes, we are blessed in Jesus. But I didn't ask you that. When I ask you how you are doing, I am asking "What's going on in your world right now?" "How is life going?" Whether things appear to be going good or bad, we are still blessed and God is good and we don't want to lose sight of that and start speaking negatively about things, but we can also be honest and upfront with people about what's going on in our lives. That's not a negative confession. That's called being honest. Which is something God really likes... It is possible to be real with people without talking bad about ourselves or others. We need to drop the super-spiritual-Christian-face and related lingo and just be real.

This does require wisdom because it can definitely be easy to start talking negatively or in a way where we really are just looking for sympathy from others and depart from a place of standing in faith. Some people are also ones that it isn't necessarily wise to fully explain or say much to because they wouldn't understand or might say things that would make it harder on you to stay in faith. So I'm not saying we shouldn't use wisdom. I DO get that sometimes just saying something simple like "I'm blessed" is the better route to go, particularly if you have been prone to having a real problem speaking negatively or if those around you tend to be negative. I just also know that it has frustrated me to no end when I ask somebody how they are doing and every single time I ask that question, I never get any more information beyond just that they are "blessed." It's a conversation stopper. My goal was to find out what was going on in their world, and yet some people seem to think being in faith means you just put on your super-Christian-smile face and talk about how you are blessed and say "Praise the Lord!" every three minutes. That's not what faith is about. I'm not saying we shouldn't be positive (we should), but faith needs to operate in an environment of truth.

God does want us operating in faith and trusting Him, and as I have already shown, our faith can enter into the equation in the degree to which we walk in and experience the blessings of God. Specifically, it is our faith in Jesus and resting in His sacrifice for us and all that's available to us through that. So faith is definitely really important.

But while God likes faith, we have also talked about how our God is also a God with deep love for us. Out of His love, He is merciful and compassionate towards us and sometimes He intervenes in our lives largely because of this. For instance, while there are many Bible accounts where Jesus healed where faith was obviously in operation on the part of the one receiving healing, there are others where that is not clearly showcased.

In Matthew 14:14 we are told, "And when Jesus went out He saw a great multitude; and He was moved with compassion for them, and healed their sick." (NKJV). Jesus loved people and cared about them and He healed out of His compassion. That doesn't mean there wasn't at least a smidgen of faith in operation on the part of the people – after all, even coming to Jesus for healing showcases some level of faith – but the emphasis here is on Jesus' compassion for the people. We serve a merciful God – it is part of His character.

This is something that some "faith people" seem to have a harder time grasping. While I do believe that God wants us believing the truths that I've spelled out in this book and using our faith and God-given authority, do you know what else faith can look like? It can look like trusting that God is a good and merciful God and appealing to Him on the basis of His mercy and compassion.

In the early 1980's, my mother was very sick and in the hospital and didn't know much of what I've shared in this book. I was only a young child at the time. The devil was working overtime to try to take her out and was afflicting both her body and her mind. She was depressed and having suicidal type thoughts and her body was having major problems. She told me how a turning point for her was when she just cried out to God and made a decision that she wanted to live because she wanted to be here for her children (including me) and asked for God's mercy on that basis. She knew that He wanted her to be a mother for the kids that He had given her and that's where she appealed to Him for healing. She told me that she absolutely believed God honored that "mother's prayer." That actually happened two other times in my mother's life and I have heard similar stories from others. Believing that God is a good God who cares about you and your family and appealing to Him on that basis is an act of faith. Crying out to God on the basis of His mercy can be a faith act.

However, it also can be an ignorant faith act. If you don't know the truths as spelled out in this book that it's God's will to heal you and for you to walk in health and that He's already provided healing for you through Jesus, and you just cry out to God begging Him to heal you and have mercy on you, He might do that even though you aren't sure that He will or wants to heal you. That's still exercising an amount of faith in accordance with what you know (since even calling out to God does require some faith), but since you are not appealing to Him based on what's yours and what He's declared is true in His Word but instead on His intervening separately from what He's already provided, it does become more of a "God prerogative" whether He sovereignly intervenes or not and makes a "special case" for you. In other words, you are not coming to Him based on what He's already done for you in Jesus; instead you are coming in ignorance and basically asking Him for a separate special miracle for you. He can and does do that sometimes. But sometimes He does not. Why He does or doesn't in these situations can indeed be a bit of a mystery. And if He doesn't, it doesn't mean He's not good or doesn't care about your pain.

In John 11:5, we are told that Jesus loved Lazarus and Mary and Martha. When Lazarus died, even though Jesus knew He was going to raise him from the dead, it still hurt Jesus to see Mary and those with her weeping over him. He was "troubled" (vs. 33) and we are told in the shortest verse in the Bible that "Jesus wept." (John 11:35). Again, even though Jesus knew Lazarus was going to be raised shortly, He still wept and was troubled inside when He saw the pain of those affected. Never doubt that Jesus cares about your hurt and pain. But sometimes He doesn't intervene on His own and I don't know that anyone can fully understand that except to put it in the context of the larger understanding about hurt and pain that was explained back in chapter two.

For me, I just know that the best place for me to stand is in faith based on what His Word tells me is mine. As we grow in knowledge and learn, we should be putting our faith into practice based on His Word. We need to move beyond just begging God for things and instead stand based on the truth of the Word. You can't go wrong banking on the truth of the Word. At the same time, never forget that your God also actually cares about you and loves you and is merciful. It's just who He is.

It is out of His care and concern for you that brings me to another point that often times isn't really considered. We've talked before about how we as human beings are tri-part beings: we are a spirit, we have a soul, and we live in a body. God cares about us in our totality and is looking at the big picture. As humans, however, when we look at ourselves or other people, we tend to see ourselves and them very narrowly. This particularly happens when dealing with physical infirmities, where we only tend to really consider the physical issue at hand.

God isn't nearly as concerned about your physical healing as He is about you. All of you. When He looks at you, He doesn't just see a physical problem that needs to be fixed, He sees you. He knows you. Every part of you. And while God is for us being physically well, He really is for us being well period – in every respect of our being, not just regarding whatever our physical need is. God wants us healthy and whole in every respect. And as I've already shown, the same promises and scriptures that deal with physical health and healing also deal with health and wholeness across-the-board.

So let's just get real practical here for a moment. I'm going to use a fictitious situation here to make a point. Let's say there's a Christian man who is having a problem with a joint in his elbow hurting and causing severe pain. He believes that Jesus paid for that hurt and carried it away with His work on the cross and that he doesn't need to carry it too. He's declaring the Word and believing God for his elbow to no longer be hurting. He even goes to a healing meeting and healing ministers pray over his elbow, but yet there still is a problem. It still keeps hurting. The pain from his elbow is causing

Him to really draw close to God and seek God because he doesn't know what else to do.

Now, let's introduce another fact. Suppose this guy also has a real problem with lust and pornography. In other words, he's got an ongoing sin issue that's a stronghold in his life. I'm choosing this particular issue for my example because recent studies have shown that the vast majority of men, including Christian men, have this problem (it's also an increasingly significant issue for women). It's just a rampant one that's out there so it's easy to pick on, but you could substitute all manner of other things of an "ongoing nature" such as gluttony (another big one). The guy is just in a regular habit of disobeying God's Word when it comes to the subject of lust, and because of his sin, he also regularly deals with guilt and shame and feelings of discouragement and hopelessness, leading to depression.

Now, let's add a third fact. Let's say this guy also was really hurt by someone in his past that he hasn't quite been able to let go of. He still holds a real grudge against that person and harbors anger and bitterness and unforgiveness towards them.

When God looks at this guy, what does He see? Does He just see a guy that has a hurt elbow? No, He sees the entire picture. He sees all of the areas in the man's life where he needs healing and wholeness, even if the man himself doesn't realize he needs healing in those other areas. For instance, the man might not even really see it as a problem that he is still harboring anger and unforgiveness towards someone. But God does. He sees all the hurt and pain caused from all that is not right in this man's life and how those things are keeping him from really being all that God intends for him to be. He sees and cares about the hurt elbow, but He also sees and cares about all the rest too.

As humans, we don't see all that stuff when we look at others. We don't usually even know about it. But the reason I'm using this example is because it's a lot closer to reality for most people than someone just having only a physical problem. Many people that are looking for physical healing also have areas where they need emotional healing and/or to walk in freedom in regards to sin-related issues. God knows all of this and He cares about it all.

God also knows that all of our symptoms (be they physical, emotional, or sin-related) often ultimately spring from the same root problem. We are inter-related beings and our emotional state can affect our physical state (and vice versa). If a person is harboring bitterness, that can manifest in various ways physically in the body. Likewise, for a person who is basically a "slave to sin" in a specific area and is not walking in the victory Jesus purchased for them over sin, that can also affect their emotions (e.g. causing them to get depressed, feel hopeless) and their body (any number of physical maladies). In fact, the sin can lead to emotional hurt which can then lead to physical hurt. A person that is depressed all the time, for instance, is in a ripe position for physical issues to manifest. We are inter-related and God sees all of that and how each part of us affects the rest of us.

Because God is looking at us in our totality, I believe He works with us where we are at. God is not only interested in just healing a hurt elbow if the root issue isn't dealt with. Don't misunderstand me. I'm not saying He wouldn't heal the elbow. He does heal things independent of other things and health can manifest in such an area simply by exercising faith in accordance with His Word, but at the end of the day God is wanting you well across-the-board. Thus, since God is looking at the big-picture view of us, I do believe He does work with us in things such as in our sicknesses to help bring healing in other areas of our lives as well.

You might recall that similar to my fictitious example above, I also shared back in chapter two a little bit from my own story along these lines. As a Christian, I had struggled for years with addiction and had a lot of emotional hurts and pain where I was very sick in my soul – stemming from things in my childhood such as a lot of rejection. I also had serious struggles with physical sickness. Often I had intense battles in all three of these areas raging at the same time or in the same timeframe. It is my personal testimony that God, while not causing my emotional hurts, addictions, or physical sickness, has at different times used one of those things to bring about a greater good in another. For instance, when I was really sick physically, that brought out a whole lot of fear and anxiety in me that I realized was also a problem and thus I was able to work on letting go of the fear to Jesus. I also found that physical sickness helped illuminate some things and bring healing to me as far as longstanding addictions.

I of course am not saying that God caused my sicknesses or addictions or fear. I'm not saying that God causes us to be sick to teach us things. But I have found that God will work with us where we are at because His goal is health across-the-board. God can use sickness in a person's life to help bring about a greater good. God does not want you physically sick, He doesn't want you emotionally sick, and He doesn't want you beholden to addictions or sin of any kind. Understanding this big-picture view is important and is something that I think many just don't give consideration to. God is looking at all of you and wanting all of you well and whole and walking in victory.

Regardless of where you are at and what you have been dealing with in your life, I encourage you to just keep pressing forward with Jesus, looking to Him in faith and standing on the Word of God. If you have a physical need, stand on the Word for your physical healing. If you have an emotional need, stand on the Word for your emotional healing. If you have a need to experience greater freedom over sin, stand on the Word for that. In Jesus, you are free, you are healed emotionally, and you are healed physically. It's all found in Him and what He's provided for you.

One reason I am talking about the love of God, the mercy of God, and the fact that God is looking at people in their totality, is because some well-intentioned Christians that believe as I do that faith is important, have ended up coming across as unfeeling and judgmental when dealing with sick people and simply treating their problems as a "faith transaction", rather than truly showing the love of Jesus and compassion of Jesus to them. Faith is important, but so is love. And in fact, faith works through (or by) love (Galatians 5:6). We need to be loving towards people, not criticizing them or telling them the reason they are still sick is because they don't have enough faith. Even if there could be some truth that a faith-related issue is why they aren't seeing the result they're after, we can help stir up people without accusing them or just making them feel like they aren't "good enough." I'm not saying some blunt talk might not be in order sometimes, but love should rule the day in all of our interactions and we want to consider both ourselves and others in the light of God's big-picture view. God is gracious and merciful and loving and patient, and we want to be showing forth the same.

In considering a balanced view on things, given that a lot of this book has talked about healing, there's something else that I have to mention that isn't usually discussed in books like this. And that is the fact that while I do believe that God wants us well while we are here, there is a time for each of us where we will "die." I put "die" in quotes because if you remember from an earlier chapter, as believers we don't actually die. But there will be a time when your purposes on this planet will be no more and it will be time for you to go Home. Again, I do believe that God wants us well while we are here. However, the natural aging processes in our bodies are still at work. I do believe that faith can change that to a degree, but eventually if you live long enough, you will reach a point where it will be time to go and trade this mortal body for your immortal body.

Now, I don't believe that a person necessarily needs to die sick. We know that the actions of others, such as through persecution or just bad choices, could also affect us and end our life here. But, ideally, you will walk in health and just decide in submission to the Lord to go home when the time is right and He calls you, and basically give up your life here (which could appear as a sudden heart-attack or similar in the natural). I don't think it needs to be some debilitating life disease that takes you out. God wants you well and you can experience and walk in victory in health here. However, I also don't know anyone that has managed to do this perfectly. In any event, there will be a point at which your time is up and on that Day you will experience God's ultimate healing in the fullest sense.

I mentioned my mother a bit back. She had several illnesses where the devil tried to take her out over the years, including several bouts with cancer. In the fall of 2008, she was not visibly sick, but I started sensing in my spirit that something was wrong and heard "Get her affairs in order." God really started working with me on being willing to let my mother go, which started bringing up all sorts of pain and fear and emotion in me because my mother and I

were very close. I tried to encourage her to see a doctor but she did-
n't want to (out of fear). Long story short, after a number of months,
it became clear that she was getting very sick and she went to a doctor and had tests done. She had very serious endometrial cancer.
After consulting with one of the top doctors (at a top hospital), we
were told that there wasn't much they could do, that chemo wouldn't
likely work, that surgery wasn't safe, and that she could literally die
any day (the doctor wouldn't even get our hopes up by saying she
had weeks or months). This was a very scary time for both of us and
I can't tell you the level of fear I had – it was off the charts. And I
also should mention that I was very sick at this time as well and this
added stress certainly didn't help me either.

But my mother made a decision to believe God. Neither of us
had really been taught about healing, but we started learning a little
bit. We had people pray over her in faith. She saw my pain and fear,
and as my mother, she prayed a "mother's prayer" much as she had
done when I was a little boy and she was in the hospital. She chose
to fight in faith and adopted the attitude that "It's not over until God
says it's over" irrespective of what some doctor says. She really
prayed and believed God for Him to heal her. I was full of a lot of
doubt and unbelief because of my fear, but she believed God. She
chose to do chemotherapy and believe God for Him to work
through it even though the doctors had given little hope with that.
That was where she put her faith. And you know what? He did. She
had a tremendous response. She ended up living almost three more
years when the doctors weren't even willing to give her three days.
She eventually went home to Jesus after a recurrence of the cancer.
It was during this recurrence in 2011 that we really started learning
much more about healing: attended healing services where they
were teaching about healing, read books on the subject, listened to
healing scriptures, and so forth.

There was something really strange though. In early 2010, right
after she had experienced the miraculous result and we were believing she was completely well, God continued to intensely work with
me to be willing to let my mom go just as He had while she was
sick. It didn't let up even though she was visibly much better. It was
definitely God and He had my number. He literally had me walk

through a very hard "Gethsemane" experience where I was willing to let go and surrender my mom to Him. In other words, there was a clear knowing in my spirit that her time was at hand. If some "faith person" wants to argue with me about that, they can, but I know what I know. As incredible as it may sound, God actually had me walk through a lot of the grief process long before she actually went to Jesus. God worked with me to be willing to let her go in my heart, which after much wrestling I did in April of 2010 and she lived over two years after that.

Now, by the time she passed, we had been studying healing significantly for over a year. I had started making tremendous progress in my own health as I started grasping things and exercising my faith, however she was not. She was having a harder time "getting" the healing truths that we were learning about. We were praying for her healing and even though God had worked with me earlier to be willing to let her go, I was still believing God for her healing here. To this day, I don't know or fully understand all the variables, but I do know a few things.

About a week before she passed, before we actually knew how bad of a state she was in (she actually went rapidly downhill in the span of 1 day), I was talking with her because she was really struggling with finding purpose for her life. She was feeling like maybe her purpose had been completed. I tried to encourage her with some things but I honestly told her that this time around, unlike in 2009, she couldn't use me as her reason to stay here because I wasn't in that place anymore. I told her that God had worked with me to be willing in my heart to let her go in such a way that I wasn't clinging to her and I had done that so that that was no longer a block in my life. I told her I was still wanting and believing for her to be here, but that she needed to talk with God and have Him give her vision for her future – that only God and her could do that.

A few days later, she mentioned to me that she had talked with God and heard from Him and she seemed to have a peace about it, but she didn't tell me what He had said. To this day, I don't really know. I do know one thing she had done in the days and weeks before she passed is latched on to the verse Psalm 90:10 that basically says that a person's years are 70 (or if you've got strength, 80) and she had just turned 70, so she latched onto that as meaning that her time was up. That's a misapplication of Scripture because that was part of a lament of Moses in regards to the children of Israel that had disobeyed God and were wandering in the desert. He was describing what he saw with them, not what should be. According to Deuteronomy 34:7, "Moses *was* one hundred and twenty years old when he died. His eyes were not dim nor his natural vigor diminished." (NKJV). So Moses himself broke what he said by 40 or 50 years, living to 120 years old in great health. So my mom latching on to that Psalm 90:10 verse to think that we are only supposed to live to 70 or 80 wasn't valid.

But the reason I bring all this up, is there was a sense with my mother that her time was up – that she had fulfilled her purposes. And honestly, I was sensing the same thing (though not vocalizing it and doing my best to believe despite that gnawing sense). There was a clear sense that her calling was done – that God had called her to be a wife and mother and raise up her children and her calling was done. She sensed it. I sensed it. And no matter how much we were still trying to do our part to believe for healing (the day she went Home, she wrote out some healing scriptures and faith declarations!), she went into the arms of Jesus. While she was fading in the hospital, I prayed one of the most sincere and hardest prayers I've ever prayed. I told Jesus that He knew I had already let go of my mom to Him in my heart prior, but that I still really wanted her here. But I told Him that if the purposes that He had for her here were done, then I was willing to let her go into His presence. But that if those purposes were not done, to bring her healing and health and that I was really trusting Him for that in that case. Basically, I fully gave it to Jesus because He was the only One that really fully knew what the deal was. It was raw and it was honest and He knew my heart. And Jesus led my precious mother out of this world and into His arms.

Again, "faith people" can (and some probably will) nitpick this all day long. "Well, you just weren't really believing in faith for her healing here." Maybe. Maybe we didn't do everything right. As I said, even with the variables I know, there was definitely some doubt and unbelief going on. But I also know that what my mom and I both sensed was that her time was at hand. You know, whether a person is sick or not, their time can be at hand. I don't believe that just because Moses lived to 120 years-old that that means that is a formula for everybody – that everyone is supposed to live to 120. Now don't get me wrong – I think that's a good one to plan for! But I believe that we all have a calling and purposes and God works with us as we are and also with our desires, and one person's purposes could be completed at 70 years old and one at 120 years old. When your purposes here are fulfilled, I don't care if you've got physical sickness or disease going on in your body or not, your time can be at hand for you to go Home.

With that said, I have to give a strong and serious caution here, because the devil can whisper to you that your purposes are done and your time is at hand. I think everyone should plan to live to be at least 120 and believe God for full health all the rest of their days. In Psalm 91, which shows us a picture of God's blessings as we dwell in and abide in Him, God talks of giving us "long life" to satisfy us. Most of us desire a long and fruitful life here, and I believe that is available in Jesus. All I'm saying is that there will come a time at some point where God will call you out of this earthly home as it currently is and into your true Home – your dwelling with Him forever.

We are all here to fulfill God's call on our life. But there will come a time when our time is over here. The trick is not to let the devil take us out before our time. He will try, I assure you. He's whispered his lies to me several times over the years. We need to be very careful here. If you are sick, and especially if you are older and sick, don't let the devil whisper to you that your time is over. I think our default position as believers should ALWAYS be to believe God for life and health here. If you are sick, believe God for your healing. That is a safe position. Because just to make the point here, even if you were to end up dying, at least you will have gone out trying to be in a posture of faith, rather than one of defeat or submitting to sickness. Fight the good fight of faith. Make that your "go-to position." The worst that happens is you go see Jesus. So just don't worry about it and choose to always adopt a position that "It's not over until God says it's over" and "I'm going to believe for health no matter what." Your position should be one of trusting in God for health in your body.

We do need to be led by the peace of the Lord and I believe God will speak to us as we seek Him and listen to Him, but our strong default position is always to go for life and health here. The devil would love nothing more than to take us out and keep us from doing all God has for us to do, so we need to have a high awareness of, and vigilance against, his schemes.

Chapter 15 – Overcoming Objections

Throughout this book, we've touched on various theological issues of significance where the view I've presented differs somewhat from some common views out there in the Body of Christ. This is no more true than with the related issues of God's sovereignty, whether He afflicts believers with sickness, and whether healing is in the atonement.

As we have discussed before, it is common in some Christian circles to talk about God in terms of Him orchestrating every detail of our lives and our world. Basically that God is controlling everything and causing everything to happen that He wants to happen in order to fulfill His will. Again, people often adopt this worldview because they think it is comforting to put everything on God (it's also rather convenient, I might add...) But doing so largely, or even completely, negates our freewill choice because at the end of the day, it doesn't really matter what you do because God has His will and He will have His way with everyone.

What I just described is a worldview that permeates a whole lot of Christianity to one degree or another. And when one has that worldview, it affects how they view God and how they see and live their Christian life. If everything is all just up to God, then that means all the bad we see in our world is His fault too and thus that God doesn't always want us well. When one believes that, even if they think it's comforting to believe God just must know what He is doing, there will be core doubt and distrust of God (whether they realize it or not) that will keep them from drawing in too close because one never knows what kind of mood God might be in. It renders people passive and sitting ducks to just accept everything the devil throws their way (all the while thinking it's from God), and it leads to people living weak, powerless, ineffective lives. In my opinion, this worldview is one of the absolute most damaging things EVER in the entirety of Christianity. And it's rampant – it's literally everywhere.

This theological perspective comes out of a complete misunderstanding of Scripture. It relies on staring intently at certain "tree" verses of the Bible while missing the "forest" of the entirety of the

Word of God. It also completely misses the point of what really happened at the cross.

We have already discussed that God is indeed sovereign in the sense of being the Creator of whom there is no equal and that He has all power. You can find plenty of scriptures that talk of God's power. And you can find plenty of scriptures that talk of God intervening in the affairs of our world in various ways. I do not deny this. But all throughout the Bible, over and over again you find God constantly working with and responding to the choices of people. And the foremost choice that we are called to make, that the whole Bible points to, is a choice to put our faith in Christ.

When believers in Jesus read the Bible, it needs to be read through the filter of you being "in Christ" and with the perspective of the whole Biblical narrative. If you don't do this, you're going to find it easy to get mistaken doctrine because God and mankind related to each other differently at different times. If you go trying for instance to take verses in the Old Testament that reflect how mankind related to God under the Old Covenant with the law and hold them in high esteem as to how we should relate to God now, you are likely going to find yourself in error because we as believers in Jesus Christ are not to relate to God in those same ways. We are under a completely different covenant with Jesus at the center. And in this New Covenant exists abundant life with blessings galore. It is where Jesus in the ultimate gift of love took our punishment on the cross as the wrath of God was poured out, and we, through our faith, receive that gift of grace. God's justice has been satisfied and what remains is His love and blessings for us. We become new creations, and when God looks at us, He sees us in Jesus.

Not everything you read in the Bible is appropriate theology for believers under this New Covenant. Any number of verses could be brought up by someone to object to the case I've made in this book, but those verses need to be examined in light of this "big picture" view of the entire Biblical narrative as a whole and need to be filtered through the lens of the cross.

With that general statement said, there are some specific scriptural instances that people often bring up to counter things I have presented in this book. I have tried to already address some of them as I have gone along. For instance, way back in chapter two, we already talked about Paul's "thorn in the flesh" and the book of Job. However, there are other common scriptures that people tend to throw out there and so I want to address those. Even if you already have fully bought everything as I've presented it, I think it important to look at these because they are things that might be brought up by well-meaning pastors or teachers. This may not be the most "exciting" chapter, but it is an important one.

Unlike some that tend to avoid arguments that people put forth or just dismiss them outright because they differ from their view, that's not where I'm coming from. I am not interested in believing a lie any more than you are. My goal is to know the truth and plant myself there. If I'm wrong on something, I want to be proven wrong. I don't want to blindly hold on to some view if it can't stand up to scrutiny.

The fact of the matter is that I have considered the main scriptures that people use to put forth a contrary view to what this book presents. I had to consider those scriptures long before writing this book in order to even reach the position that I have come to because I USED to be on the other side. I grew up being taught the other view! As God began showing me things and working on me, in order to make a switch in my position, I had to thoroughly satisfy for myself that such a switch was scripturally valid and justified. What I found was that while there are some scriptures that can come across a certain way (especially when viewed through a "filter" of being predisposed to believing that God controls every event in our lives or that healing isn't God's will for everyone), after studying them all out and balancing them with the rest of the Word, I satisfied myself that the position as spelled out in this book is the one that has the strongest scriptural support behind it by far. I encourage you to study these "seemingly-contrary" scriptures as well, balance them with other scriptures in the Bible, and come to your own conclusions with the Lord.

God talking to Moses in Exodus 4:11

When God talks with Moses from the burning bush and calls Moses to lead His people, one of Moses' concerns is that he doesn't speak well.

> 10 But Moses said to the LORD, "Oh, my Lord, I am not eloquent, either in the past or since you have spoken to your servant, but I am slow of speech and of tongue." 11 Then the LORD said to him, "Who has made man's mouth? Who makes him mute, or deaf, or seeing, or blind? Is it not I, the LORD? 12 Now therefore go, and I will be with your mouth and teach you what you shall speak. (Exodus 4:10–12 ESV)

This seems to show in verse 11 that God is saying that He makes people mute, deaf, and blind, doesn't it?

Many translations are worded similarly. However, there are also a number, including the KJV and NKJV, that make a rather significant word change. See if you can spot it – here's verse 11 in the King James: "And the LORD said unto him, Who hath made man's mouth? or who maketh the dumb, or deaf, or the seeing, or the blind? have not I the LORD?" (Exodus 4:11 KJV). Did you notice anything different? In place of the word "him", we have the word, "the." Rather than it saying that God makes *him* mute or deaf and so forth, we are told that God makes *the* mute ("dumb" in KJV English) or deaf and so forth.

Here's the deal: In the original Hebrew, neither "him" or "the" are there. It literally more or less reads "Who makes mute, deaf, seeing, blind..." Some translators decided to put "him" there because they assumed that's what God meant. And some put "the" there.

You might wonder why it matters? Well, if it says "him", that personalizes it and makes it seem to say that God causes people to be mute or deaf, etc. Thus that seems to imply that God actively chooses for some people to be born with an infirmity, which then means that God obviously doesn't want all people to be well.

But with a "the" rendering, then it can be taken to be saying that God makes all people including those that are mute and deaf and blind. It can become a general statement that God is the creator of all – that He has created even people that are mute and deaf and blind, without actually implying that God himself caused them to be mute and deaf and blind.

Consider the passage above from this perspective: Moses was complaining about his speech. God wants Moses to realize that God is BIGGER than that problem by saying that the One who MADE his mouth and indeed all people whether they have impediments or not (notice vs 11 references both "seeing" and "blind" people), is with Him and will help him (vs 12). That perspective fits very nicely with the context. And in this case, it doesn't mean God is saying that He actually specifically made people to be blind, mute, etc.

The reality is that there are deaf and blind and mute people, and God still ultimately is their creator, but you have to remember that God works through the biological processes of humanity. He set in motion the way that human beings are created back when He created men and women in the book of Genesis, so in a sense He is the creator of every human being, but He does that through the natural human processes that He set up. Those processes, however, have been tainted by sin. Some people are born blind or mute due to this, but that does not mean that God chose person A to be blind or person B to see, etc.

Blind Man in John 9

After just considering Exodus 4:11, it seems appropriate to go to the account of the man born blind in John chapter 9 as it deals with the same issue (with a twist). I love this story; it takes up the whole chapter and is unique to the Gospel of John. There's lots of great stuff in it, but we'll focus on the first few verses as that's where the controversial part is:

> 1 Now as *Jesus* passed by, He saw a man who was blind from birth. 2 And His disciples asked Him, saying, "Rabbi, who sinned, this man or his parents, that he was born blind?"

3 Jesus answered, "Neither this man nor his parents sinned, but that the works of God should be revealed in him. 4 I must work the works of Him who sent Me while it is day; *the* night is coming when no one can work. 5 As long as I am in the world, I am the light of the world."

6 When He had said these things, He spat on the ground and made clay with the saliva; and He anointed the eyes of the blind man with the clay. 7 And He said to him, "Go, wash in the pool of Siloam" (which is translated, Sent). So he went and washed, and came back seeing. (John 9:1–7 NKJV)

Alright, so here we have a guy that was born blind. His disciples, obviously reflecting a common opinion of the day, assumed that for him to have been born blind, someone must have done something wrong and God must have been punishing the guy, so they ask Jesus who's sin caused his blindness (vs. 2). I find that fascinating, especially since the guy was BORN blind – how could it have been *his* sin? Maybe I'm missing something, but as far as I can see, if sin was the issue, it would have had to have been his parent's sin, since he was born blind and didn't have an opportunity for his own personal sin to enter the equation. So I find it interesting that (1) they assume it was sin, and (2) they aren't sure whether it was his own sin or his parents' sin. If I was Jesus, I might have responded, "Oh, you silly little men, how could it have been his sin?" But Jesus just rolls with it.

Jesus answers their question point-blank in verse 3 by telling them that someone's specific sin wasn't the issue. And here's where the controversy starts. The way the text appears, it seems like Jesus is saying that the reason the man was born blind was basically for the Glory of God – so that the "works of God should be revealed in him." (vs 3 NKJV). In other words, it seems that God chose to make this man be born blind so that God would get glory later on. Now, before we even get into talking about this, doesn't something about that just strike you wrong? If it doesn't, it probably should! I don't know about you, but a God that would purposely afflict a person that hadn't done anything wrong with a debilitating condition for years solely so He would get glory, doesn't sound like someone with very good character – it sure doesn't sound like a God I'd want to follow. Yeah, I know all the lingo: "well, He's God and we just have to trust Him and His sovereignty that He is doing what's best." Maybe you feel different than me, but I think most people if we're honest, would have to admit that God doing something like this just strikes us as really "unfair" and I think we would have good reason in feeling that way. It *would* be an unfair and unjust God that inflicts sickness on babies just so that He could get glory years later.

Guess what? Whether you agree with my thinking that such a thing would be "unfair", the good news is that there is actually a very logical and rational case for why what it seems like this text is saying isn't exactly the case.

First let me state that though I have used the NKJV to showcase this portion of Scripture, most English translations are similar, so I don't want it to appear that I'm picking on the NKJV – this is a broader translation issue.

Remember that in the original Greek text, there is no punctuation and no verse divisions. Punctuation and verse divisions were added by the translators where they felt it was appropriate to do so for the English. Such things can be affected by their own biases and views of God. They might have assumed that what Jesus was saying was that the reason for the man's sickness was to bring God glory and thus that influenced how they punctuated and set up the verse divisions. Go re-read verses 3–5 again as shown previously. Now consider the same exact text of Jesus punctuated differently: "Neither this man nor his parents sinned. But that the works of God should be revealed in him, I must work the works of Him who sent Me while it is day; the night is coming when no one can work. As long as I am in the world, I am the light of the world." There are two changes here: (1) ending the first sentence after "sinned", and (2) changing the period after "him" to a comma. Even only making this second alteration changes the entire implied meaning! If you read it this way, what it says is that Jesus answered the disciples' question regarding whether it was the man's or parent's sin by telling them it was not. He answered their question. Then He goes on to tell them that since He was sent to the world to do works at that time, that He should heal the man so that the works of God will be evident. In other words, reading it this way does not suggest that God purposely caused the man to be born blind. Just the change of one period (which does not exist in the original text) to a comma affects that!

Even setting aside the theological implications of God causing a man to be born blind simply so He can heal him later, just on a language basis – looking at the words themselves – it makes much more logical sense for it to be punctuated this second way. In the first way, the "works of God" part is attached to the "sin answer" Jesus gave and then the rest of what Jesus says regarding His working is another thought separated from what He said about the "works of God." In the second revised way, Jesus answers the disciples' question and then starts His next thought talking about the "works of God" and His purpose in working as one related thought. It's a much more "clean cut" way of dealing with the text. Also, just a sidenote, but the Greek word used for "but" after the word "sinned" could also be translated "Nevertheless", which if the translators had gone with punctuation like the second way showcases, it is conceivable that they might have decided that that would be a better fit to start off Jesus' next statement regarding His works.

Although what I've put forth regarding the punctuation is a perfectly valid way of looking at this and explaining a differing view of that seemingly difficult verse, if you don't like it, there's actually another issue that also sheds light here that doesn't even require changing the punctuation that most English translations use. This one's a tad complicated, but it also gets into a translation decision. Let's go back to Jesus' words in verse 3 as translated: "Neither this man nor his parents sinned, but that the works of God should be revealed in him." (Jn 9:3b NKJV). The word "that" is the Greek word "hina" (transliterated). Greek scholars will tell you that when "hina" is used with a subjunctive verb, it can be used to express either purpose or command – to express why something happened or to express an order or command for something to happen. It is up to translators to look at the surrounding text to determine whether it should express purpose (known as a "purpose clause") or a command (known as a "command clause"), and sometimes translations differ.

For instance, in Mark 5:12 where the demons plead with Jesus to enter the pigs, this exact same "hina" issue comes up. In some translations (such as the KJV and NASB) it was translated as expressing purpose as in "Send us into the swine, that we may enter into them." In other translations (such as the ESV) it was translated as expressing a command as in "Send us to the pigs; let us enter them." (Mk 5:12b ESV). Do you see the difference? It's the exact same Greek "hina", but when translated, one expresses purpose ("that we may enter") and one is of a command-type form (just "let us enter").

The same "hina" situation ("hina"+subjunctive verb) occurs in John 9:3. Most translations render it as a "purpose clause." Thus you see the word "that" which seems to suggest that Jesus is saying that while the man and his parents didn't sin to cause his problem, the reason *that* he was born blind was so *that* the works of God would be revealed. However, as mentioned, rendering it as a "purpose clause" in that way produces some theological concerns in the light of other scriptures. For instance, the Bible's summary of Jesus' work in Acts 10:38 tells us that Jesus "went about doing good, and healing all that were oppressed of the devil". (KJV). It doesn't say that Jesus healed those oppressed by God or even the devil *and* God – it only mentions the devil! Nowhere in the healings recorded in the gospels do we find anyone clearly called out to have been afflicted by God, but we find several where the devil/demons are clearly identified as being involved in the sickness/disease. Afflicting a person solely to gain glory sounds a whole lot more like a work of the devil than it does of God, yet by rendering the "hina" part of John 9:3 as a "purpose clause", it makes it appear that it's God's fault. Instead of rendering it as a "purpose clause", if it was instead rendered as a "command clause" (same exact Greek text), it would appear something like this: "Neither this man nor his parents sinned, but let the works of God be revealed in him." That's a noticeable difference! It changes it from Jesus ascribing the man's blindness to God to instead simply saying that the works of God should be revealed in him. This makes much more sense given that in the following verses Jesus goes on to make the case for why that should be so.

You might wonder why the translators didn't translate it as a "command clause." The obvious guess is that they assumed that Jesus in His answer was actually telling the disciples why the man was blind. And that isn't necessarily true. The disciples basically asked whether the man's sin or his parent's sin was the cause and Jesus answered that question. The translators then likely assumed that Jesus went beyond that to explain what WAS the cause, but that would have been an assumption on the translators' part. If they assumed that's what Jesus was doing, then they would have translated it, as they did, as a "purpose clause." But if Jesus never intended to say any more about the cause but rather to just go into what He was going to do about it, then it should have been rendered as a "command clause." Since the "purpose clause" way conflicts with other scriptures and the "command clause" way does not, I believe it should have been rendered in the latter form.

So there you have it: I've given two different and entirely rational and valid reasons to explain why a differing view of John 9:3 than what it appears on the surface is in order. Generally speaking, I am always a bit wary whenever someone tries to tell me that what a verse plainly says isn't what it is really saying. It actually tends to be one of my pet peeves because often what the person is saying it is *really* saying doesn't have much solid to back it up but rather relies on flimsy (and often circular) evidence. In this case though, there is a reasonably solid case to be made as I've showcased above. Even if you aren't fully convinced by my explanations, at the very least it should be enough to give you pause to realize that this isn't the "slam dunk", "God made this man blind" verse that it can appear.

Lazarus in John 11

The story of Lazarus and his resurrection by Jesus from the dead as related in John 11 is fascinating. Like the story of the blind man in John 9, we'll just look at the first part of it, but the whole chapter is definitely worth a read!

> 1 Now a certain man was ill, Lazarus of Bethany, the village of Mary and her sister Martha. 2 It was Mary who anointed the Lord with ointment and wiped his feet with her hair, whose brother Lazarus was ill. 3 So the sisters sent to him, saying, "Lord, he whom you love is ill." 4 But when Jesus heard it he said, "This illness does not lead to death. It is for the glory of God, so that the Son of God may be glorified through it." (John 11:1–4 ESV).

After saying this, Jesus interestingly waits two days before starting out to Lazarus, and before He gets there, Lazarus dies. Jesus knew that this was going to happen (vs 15) and is the one to break the news to His disciples that Lazarus had died ("fallen asleep"). Long story short, He tells His disciples and Martha and Mary that this will all be for the glory of God. He gets Martha exercising her faith (vs. 21–27) and then He specifically tells Martha that her belief enters into the equation of Lazarus being raised from the dead in verse 40 where He says, "Did I not tell you that if you believed you would see the glory of God?" (John 11:40b ESV). In other words, like we've talked about previously in regards to many healings, Jesus made clear that her faith played a role in this miracle coming to pass. Jesus' implication was seemingly that if she didn't believe, her brother would not be raised. But she did. He then of course raises Lazarus from the dead.

There's all sorts of good stuff in there that could preach multiple sermons, but I want to go back to the beginning in verse 4 as this is the verse in question that naysayers sometimes bring up. Like the John 9:3 passage relating to the man born blind that we've already discussed, this is another verse that people use to try to say that God in His sovereignty causes sickness so that He can be glorified.

I'm just going to point out something. Nowhere in this account does Jesus ever say that God caused the sickness. He does say in verse 4 that it won't end in death and that it would bring glory to God and specifically to Jesus. And that is exactly what happened. John 12:10–11 shows us that many Jews came to believe in Jesus because of the raising of Lazarus. The fact that Jesus knew that Lazarus was going to be raised from the dead and that through that, Jesus would be glorified, does not in any way insinuate that God caused Lazarus to be sick so that Jesus would be glorified. That's a leap that you can't make from the text. Lazarus was sick, yes. And yes, Jesus could have healed him. But He waited two days and then went to him, knowing that by the time He got there Lazarus would be dead ("asleep") because He knew God wanted to use this to glorify Himself. The fact that God *used* Lazarus' sickness does NOT mean that God *caused* Lazarus' sickness. That's the faulty logic people have. They assume that just because God used the situation with Lazarus, well that must mean that God intended it all along by causing Lazarus to get sick in the first place just so He could glorify Jesus. There's nothing in the text that says anything of the sort. The only way people see this story that way is if they are reading their Bible through a "sovereignty filter" where they are looking for passages to bolster a view that they already have.

And what view is that? It's the ever-pervasive view that people have that God is just the puppet-master up there and we're just the puppet on the string doing whatever He wants to do. It's this extreme view of the sovereignty of God where we have little say in our own lives but everything that happens to us in our life is because God wanted it to happen. As we've talked about before, that is a comforting view for people because it eliminates any personal responsibility.

And that's really why people use stories like this one of Lazarus to try to bolster that view, so that if they or a friend or family member get sick, well maybe it's just because God wants to glorify Himself through that person. If a person embraces that, of course what happens is they become passive and basically "submit to the sickness" because they think they are "submitting to God." It's actually incredibly sneaky of the devil to get people to embrace sickness as a blessing from God. Sickness is not now, and never has been, a blessing from God. Sickness is a curse brought about because of sin back in the Garden of Eden! God doesn't cause people to be sick so He can bless them! But He most definitely can use sickness for His glory, just as He did with Lazarus.

God working with people where they are at and using sickness to bring about good does *not* mean that He wanted them sick in the first place or caused them to get sick. God can use a sickness for His glory. And you know how He can most use a sickness for His glory? By bringing you healing as you exercise your faith and trust in Him! You can be healed and God can get glory. But don't ever assume that God made you sick just so He can get glory. That is wrong, wrong, wrong. You walking in health and wholeness and testifying of God's divine health and life that He died to provide for you – that is how God would like to get glory from your life – by you being a showcase to the world of what walking in victory in this life through Jesus is all about. That is how God would ideally like to get glory from your life. He's not interested in causing you to get sick and then healing you to get glory. But if you do happen to be sick, as you look to Him, God can work with you where you're at and heal you and He can certainly use that for His glory.

One of the few times we have record of Jesus crying is in this segment of Scripture. The shortest verse in the Bible is John 11:35 where we are simply told that "Jesus wept." Jesus wept after He witnessed Mary and all those with her weeping, and He was "troubled" (vs. 33). It really hurt Jesus to see others hurting, even though He knew what was going to happen. Do you think God caused Lazarus to get sick even though He knew it was going to inflict pain on many, just so He could get some glory from his rising? How callous do we think God is!? The answer of course, is that many people do think He's really callous. That He didn't care about hurting people as long as more might believe in Jesus. But Jesus demonstrated God's heart here. Jesus loved Lazarus and He loved Mary and Martha (John 11:5) and He wept when He saw the pain of those that knew Lazarus, even though He knew what was going to happen. Friends, God loves you and He doesn't want you sick, but rather well. He's not inflicting you with sickness to bring Himself glory and we need to let that incredibly dangerous view go.

Trophimus & Epaphroditus

There are two people that Paul mentions in his writings that people sometimes try to bring up when it comes to the subject of whether God always wants people well or not. The first is Trophimus and the second is Epaphroditus.

Let's start with Trophimus. The verse in question is this one where Paul says, "Erastus stayed in Corinth, but Trophimus I have left in Miletus sick." (2 Timothy 4:20 NKJV). That literally is all it says there regarding Trophimus but people try to draw out some doctrine because Trophimus was sick and Paul said that he left him there sick. The implication that some make is that since Trophimus was still sick when Paul left, that means that healing must not have been God's will for Trophimus since even the "GREAT PAUL" couldn't get the man healed.

All I can say is trying to draw any kind of doctrine out of that one line summary statement without any of the details isn't even remotely fair or valid. We don't know anything about Trophimus' sickness, what Paul may or may not have done, and anything about Trophimus' condition other than that he was "sick." Perhaps Paul prayed for him and he was starting the road to recovery when Paul left but was still sick. Who knows? We don't know anything about this. Further, even if Paul prayed for Trophimus and he was still sick, that doesn't mean anything when it comes to the truth of the Word regarding healing. Even people that are praying in faith for their healing still might deal with sickness for any number of reasons. The fact that Trophimus was sick does NOT prove that God didn't want him well. That's an incredible leap to claim that just because a man is sick that that means that God wants him sick. That's like saying that a man that is depressed is so because God wants them depressed. Or that a man that is in adultery does that because God wants them to. It's ridiculous logic and springs out of the extreme sovereignty of God view we've already talked about. God could want him well and he still be dealing with sickness for various reasons. But again, we've got virtually nothing to go on with this account relating to Trophimus.

With Epaphroditus, we've got a tiny bit more to go on, but it really is only a tiny bit more. We're told about him in Philippians 2:25–30 and the two key verses are 27 and 30 where Paul says: "Indeed he was ill, near to death. But God had mercy on him, and not only on him but on me also, lest I should have sorrow upon sorrow. … for he nearly died for the work of Christ, risking his life to complete what was lacking in your service to me." (Philippians 2:27,30 ESV).

So here we have it: This guy Epaphroditus apparently was working himself really hard for the work of Christ (seemingly not taking care of himself while pushing himself too hard) and he got sick and almost died. Paul says that he was spared by God out of God's mercy not only for his own sake, but also for Paul's sake because Paul loved and was ministered to by him.

You know what? I don't care how super-spiritual you are, if you push yourself hard enough and don't take care of this temple (your body) God has given you, you are opening yourself up to get sick. It doesn't actually say that's what happened in this man's case, but it is implied when it tells us that he almost died and risked his life to do Christ's work where there was a void of service. It makes it sound like he felt he needed to do a whole lot for Jesus and pushed himself so hard that he almost died. That may or may not be the case, but that's the implication.

Some people try to say that because it just mentions God's mercy and doesn't say anything about faith that that proves that healing is just all up to God, whether He wants you to be well or not. You know, I suppose if there weren't countless other passages in the Bible showing that faith can be an important factor for healing and showcasing God's will for healing, such a view could at least be halfway excused. But that's not the case. There's a whole lot, as several other chapters in this book have proven.

We don't know anything about what this guy was believing for – where his faith was at for healing – nor that of Paul, since the text does not tell us. The fact that it doesn't tell us doesn't mean it wasn't a factor, however. In fact, when Paul mentions God's mercy sparing him, how do we know that Epaphroditus and/or Paul weren't believing God for his healing at the same time? We don't. Maybe they weren't and God just did sovereignly on His own intervene to bring healing. But we don't know that either. We pretty much know nothing about this and thus using this account to try to bolster some position that God might want a person sick and that faith isn't a concern is a rather large chasm to cross given the lack of details. At the end of the day, mostly what this story does is just tell us that this guy Epaphroditus got sick and almost died, but that he didn't die. Great! Praise God!

Timothy's Stomach Ailment

In a similar way that Paul mentions a one-liner about Trophimus being sick, he gives a one-liner piece of advice to Timothy on the topic of sickness: "No longer drink only water, but use a little wine for your stomach's sake and your frequent infirmities." (1 Timothy 5:23 NKJV). The fact that Paul references using wine but doesn't say anything about praying for or believing God for healing is something that some people use to try to make a case for why God doesn't want to heal some people.

As with Trophimus, we have very little to go on here. We can see from the verse that Timothy was having frequent ailments, apparently stomach-related. And we can see that Paul suggested he use a little wine to help. And that's pretty much all we can see.

Considering that there are other occasions recorded in the Bible where Paul prayed healing prayers and/or mentions faith in that context (e.g. Acts 14:9, Acts 28:8–9), we have to keep that in mind when reading a one-liner like this that doesn't mention those things. Simply because Paul didn't mention them to Timothy in regards to his ailments doesn't mean Paul and/or Timothy weren't praying to God or believing God. It's just a one-liner practical piece of advice. In those days, it was commonly believed that a little wine could help with certain conditions. It would be like if I knew that a person had some issues with acid-reflux and I told them, "Hey, maybe don't drink as much soda or coffee but instead drink more water." It's the same type of practical advice-giving. There's nothing wrong with this! Even if a person is fully trusting God for health in their body, we still are called to take care of this temple and if we've had problems in a certain area, perhaps wisdom dictates that we do some practical things to help ourselves out to help avoid those problems.

There's nothing wrong with this and it doesn't necessarily indicate a lack of faith.

Trying to draw any conclusions about whether God wants people (or even just Timothy) well from this one passing reference to some stomach problems that Timothy was having isn't really valid. People use this verse to say that God must not have wanted Timothy well or else he wouldn't have had these problems, but that's an assumption – it's not something told to us by the text. Again, people that say these kinds of things are people that hold the extreme sovereignty view where God is just completely controlling our lives, so that if we are sick, then it must be because God wants us sick. That's an opinion that some people have and then when they get to verses like this, they just assume that the verse is backing up their view, rather than just letting the text speak for itself. In other words, they read into the text something that isn't there. The text doesn't tell us that God didn't want Timothy well. The text doesn't tell us that Paul and Timothy prayed for healing and God turned them down. All the text shows is that Timothy was having some stomach issues and Paul suggested a practical help in using a little wine. That's it.

Teaching of the Sparrows

In Matthew chapter 10, Jesus shares some teaching that I believe is often misunderstood on two different fronts.

> 28 And do not fear those who kill the body but cannot kill the soul. Rather fear him who can destroy both soul and body in hell. 29 Are not two sparrows sold for a penny? And not one of them will fall to the ground apart from your Father. 30 But even the hairs of your head are all numbered. 31 Fear not, therefore; you are of more value than many sparrows. 32 So everyone who acknowledges me before men, I also will acknowledge before my Father who is in heaven, 33 but whoever denies me before men, I also will deny be-

fore my Father who is in heaven. (Matthew 10:28–33
ESV)

The first misunderstanding I believe relates to what Jesus said
about fearing God. Jesus has been telling His disciples that they
will experience persecution from other people, but then He tells
them not to fear those people because they really don't have any
lasting power – that they might be able to kill your body (your
shell) here in time but they can't destroy your soul eternally. He says
in verse 28 that if you are going to fear somebody, it shouldn't be
people who don't have that eternal power, but rather should be God
who does have that power. People sometimes take this to mean that
we should be cowering in fear of God because God might send us
to hell. However, this interpretation I believe misses the entire point
of what Jesus is getting at. It is focusing on one verse while missing
the overarching point.

Notice that right after Jesus makes that statement about fearing
God, He then goes into talking about sparrows and how if God
places great value on sparrows, how much more value He places on
you and me – that He cares so much about you that He even has
numbered every hair on your head. In verse 31, He tells us to "Fear
not." But wait! I thought we were supposed to fear just a minute
ago? Jesus goes on to explain why we as believers in Him don't
need to fear in verse 32 where He tells us that those that
acknowledge Him before men, Jesus will also acknowledge before
the Father. This gets back to the whole "In Christ" thing we talked
about before. Those that believe in Jesus and confess Him as Lord
are in Jesus and have Jesus as their defense. The whole point of
what Jesus is saying it seems to me is something like this (this
would be my paraphrase): "Listen, if you're gonna fear somebody, it
shouldn't be people, but rather the God that has power to destroy
eternally, but if you believe in Me and acknowledge Me before others, you don't need to fear because I've got your back. God loves
you more than even the sparrows and He knows all about you and is
concerned for you. Because of that, you don't need to be afraid of
God – the Father loves you and cares for you and in Me you are secure." That's how I see this portion of Scripture, but religion has

poisoned a lot of us (myself included for many years) to just hone in on this part about fearing God because we think He might just decide to throw us in hell out of His sovereign will. Doing that I believe really misses what Jesus is trying to convey about the heart of the Father and the value of relationship with Jesus.

The other misunderstanding that comes out of this portion of Scripture is found in verse 29 where it says that not a single sparrow falls to the ground apart from God the Father. People take that to mean that God in His sovereignty causes sparrows to die and thus God in His sovereignty might not want you and me well and might want to kill us too. Like the fear issue discussed above, I would start answering this by again saying that even putting the emphasis there is missing the whole point of what Jesus is saying. But setting that aside, it also doesn't actually say what some are assuming, or at the very least is kind of ambiguous as far as I can see.

This same basic story is also given in Luke 12. In the Luke account, in place of the sentence where it talks about a sparrow not falling apart from God, it says "And not one of them is forgotten before God." (Luke 12:6b ESV). So in the Luke account it just summarizes by saying that God knows all the sparrows and doesn't forget them.

In the Matthew account it does say that a sparrow doesn't fall apart from the Father, but I believe putting that together with the Luke account and also the rest of what Jesus says, that it doesn't seem that Jesus is trying to make some point about God killing sparrows but rather that God knows the sparrows individually and that even WHEN one falls to the ground, He knows it and sees it and cares and He is with them.

I quoted the ESV version of the Matthew passage for clarity purposes, but in the King James (KJV) it doesn't even use the word "apart" but rather the word "without" – that a sparrow doesn't fall *without* the Father – which is more in line with what I just said. Some translations add the word "will" to the end of the sentence as in meaning that they don't fall apart from the Father's will. But the word "will" appears to me to be a translator addition because that apparently was what those translators assumed was being conveyed or intended, but as far as I know, literally the text just ends with

"Father." It really on face value isn't making any statement as far as I can see about God possibly wanting or causing sparrows to die, and it's unfortunate to me that some translations kind of make it seem that way by adding the word "will" there. Again, neither the KJV or the ESV do that.

Regardless, the point Jesus is making isn't that God might want sparrows to die, but that God cares about the sparrows and that if He cares about them, how much more He cares for you and me! God loves you and is for you. Using this passage to try to bolster a claim that God in His sovereignty might act to make a person sick or kill them is not fair or in-line with what Jesus was talking about.

Paul's Teaching on Submitting to Authorities

When dealing with the subject of God's sovereignty, a portion of Scripture that sometimes gets brought up is Paul's teaching on submitting to authorities as given in Romans 13. We'll just look at the first few verses for time's sake.

> 1 Let every person be subject to the governing authorities. For there is no authority except from God, and those that exist have been instituted by God. 2 Therefore whoever resists the authorities resists what God has appointed, and those who resist will incur judgment. 3 For rulers are not a terror to good conduct, but to bad. (Romans 13:1–3a ESV)

This particularly tends to be quoted in pulpits around election times to tell us that regardless of the outcome of an election, God is the one that establishes who He wants so that whoever wins it is because God wanted them to win and we need to just trust Him. This type of thinking I believe to be flawed for several reasons. It first of all assumes that what Paul is talking about is that God sets up specific people to be the ones in authority. I don't deny that it could be read that way, but doing so creates other issues which I will get to in a moment. I rather see it as Paul talking about authority as a structure. When he says in verse 2 that all authority comes from God, I don't take that to mean that every person in authority is in authority because God willed it, but that God has established and appointed all authority as in that God intends structures (and people as a part of those structures) here that govern us in our earthly kingdom. When it talks about God appointing authorities and that those that resist what God's appointed will face judgment, I don't think that is referring to specific individuals, but the general concept of the authority – we are supposed to have a healthy respect for authorities over us.

With that said, verse 3 is key because it mentions that a reason why we are supposed to submit to the authorities is because rulers are basically looking out for our good and only are a "terror" to those that are bad, not to those that are doing good. And that right there is what shoots down the notion of reading Romans 13 to try to say that regardless of who a leader is and what they do that God wills them there. Because you and I both know that throughout history (and even currently) there have been and are plenty of leaders that have acted contrary to that. The obvious example of course is Hitler. He may have had authority and even had a majority support of the German people who at the time wanted him over them, but he most certainly WAS a "terror" to those with "good conduct" – which runs counter to what verse 3 says. I didn't quote verse 4, but it goes on to say that those in authority are God's servants that are here for our good. Is there anyone who would like to stand up and say that Hitler was God's servant who was here for our good and was only a terror to evil people and not good ones? I didn't think so... Actually, the really sad thing is that there ARE people who would say that – who take their sovereignty view so seriously that even Hitler must have been established by God and used by God in killing millions of people for some greater purpose in the big picture (i.e. the re-establishment of the state of Israel in 1948). Again, people confuse God's foreknowledge of things (such as prophecies in the Bible regarding the nation of Israel) and even God working with situations as they are, with God actively choosing or wanting to kill millions of people (many of them His own Jewish people mind you) to accomplish something He wants.

Back to Romans 13 though, the truth is that what is discussed in it is clearly also assuming that the rulers are actually righteous. There's plenty of passages in the Bible that show that lots of people in authority were set up when they weren't God's choice or clearly acted in ways contrary to what God wanted. One can find loads of examples with the kings in the Old Testament for instance – where we then find that they committed terrible acts. So trying to use this to say that God just sovereignly puts whoever He wants in authority over us and that no matter what, we just need to submit to whatever they say and do is going too far.

The reason this matters is because people read passages like this and they don't balance it with the rest of the Word and then they build doctrines that extend beyond even just God's sovereignty with earthly governing authorities, but also into God's sovereignty in general. People use passages like this to paint a picture of God as one that is basically just doing whatever He sovereignly wants in regards to people. Which again just serves to make everything all about God and His will, and completely serves to diminish the role of our human choice.

As we have discussed before, God allowing something in concert with our free will and God wanting something are not the same thing. This is an error that many Christians make – they assume that if God allows it then He must want it. But that's faulty logic. All through the Bible you find God interacting with people on the basis of their choices and this hasn't changed – God still works with us in our choices.

Life of Joseph

In the story of Joseph in Genesis 37–50, there are a bunch of statements made relating to the sovereignty of God that people sometimes use to bolster a view counter to what I've presented. I know you probably know the story, but let's do a brief overview of it anyway.

Joseph's father loved Joseph more than all of his brothers and his brothers hated him for that. Joseph had some dreams about his brothers and parents bowing down to him and he tells those dreams to his brothers. He told them the first dream and they hated him more for the insinuation that he would rule over them (Gen. 37:8) and then after he has a second dream, he goes right ahead and shares it with them. His brothers were so angry with him that they were going to kill him, but at the last minute they ended up deciding to sell him as a slave to some traders who then took him to Egypt and sold him to Potiphar, a high-ranking official of the Pharaoh. Potiphar's wife tries to have sex with Joseph, but Joseph refuses, and in retribution, she lies and says that he tried to rape her. So Joseph is thrown in prison where he stays a very long time. At one point he helps a fellow inmate, the chief cupbearer, by interpreting his dream about how he would be restored to his position and asks him to talk to Pharaoh on his behalf when that happens. However, the cupbearer forgot Joseph and doesn't mention him to Pharaoh for two years after Pharoah has some dreams that need interpreting. Joseph is summoned and interprets the dreams as meaning that in the land there will be seven good years followed by seven years of famine. He suggests Pharaoh appoint someone to oversee gathering food during the good years so that there will be ample supply in the lean years. Pharaoh appoints Joseph to that position and indeed makes him the second most powerful person in all of Egypt.

During the years of famine, his brothers end up coming down to Egypt and bowing before him in order to get grain and after a lengthy period and different visits, he eventually reveals himself to his brothers. He basically tells them not to worry or be upset and says that God was the one that sent him to Egypt and not them. He tells them: "And God sent me before you to preserve for you a remnant on earth, and to keep alive for you many survivors. So it was not you who sent me here, but God. He has made me a father to Pharaoh, and lord of all his house and ruler over all the land of Egypt." (Genesis 45:7–8 ESV) He later tells them, "As for you, you meant evil against me, but God meant it for good, to bring it about that many people should be kept alive, as they are today." (Genesis 50:20 ESV).

I don't deny that Joseph said these things or that the whole story of Joseph can easily be taken to mean that God just arranged the whole thing, including Joseph's long imprisonment, regardless of the behavior of individual people, because God wanted to use Joseph to save people. I both understand how Joseph could have come to the conclusion he did as well as how people reading the story could come to a certain conclusion.

However, let's get practical here. Yes, Joseph had some dreams from God. God knew what was going to happen. But Joseph was the one that decided to flaunt those dreams to his brothers (even after he saw how angry they were after he shared the first one). Did God make Joseph tell his brothers these dreams rather than keep them to himself? His brothers were the ones that were so angry that they took him off to kill him. Did God make his brothers angry and want to murder their brother? When they decided to sell him for monetary gain, did God make them want to sell their brother to be a slave? Did God make Potiphar's wife try to come on to him and get him to sleep with her? When he didn't and Potiphar's wife lied and accused him of rape, did God make her do that? When Potiphar was enraged and unjustly threw Joseph in prison, was it God that caused him to do that? When Joseph was in prison and told the cupbearer's dream and yet the cupbearer didn't do as Joseph asked for two years, was it God that caused the cupbearer to ignore Joseph and leave him in jail another two years?

Do you see the problem here? Yes, God knew what was going to happen ahead of time. Yes, God did use Joseph to save the lives of many, including his family. Yes, God was with Joseph the whole way and gave Joseph favor (even in hard situations). But seriously, if one is going to argue that God caused all those people to act in certain ways (even ways that were explicitly sin and counter to how God tells us He wants people to act) so that He could have Joseph spend many years in prison and then have him later be a key figure in saving people's lives, that's where I think one needs to do a double-check.

I don't deny that there is a bit of mystery with some of this stuff. The line between God's sovereignty and man's freewill choice has been debated for centuries. But when one starts adopting a position where all of the actions of people are completely negated by God who is just manipulating everyone as a puppet-master, that's where one is getting into an extreme view that I don't believe is remotely supported by the whole of Scripture.

While it's fairly clear from the story as related that Joseph seemingly attributes all that happened to God, what's not clear is that that necessarily means that he was right on that. For instance, in Genesis 42:25, we are told that Joseph gave orders to replace the money and put provisions in his brother's sacks before they left Egypt, but later when they return to Egypt he tells them that it was God who put the money in their sacks (Gen. 43:23). So Joseph has this thing of broadly attributing to God. Thus I think we probably need to take a little pause before extrapolating too much from some of his statements.

By the way, while mentioning Joseph, one thing that is clear is that God was not only with Joseph, but He helped Joseph prosper and succeed wherever he was. God was wanting things to go well for Joseph (see Genesis 39:2–5 and Genesis 39:23).

Life of Jesus and Paul

Finally, the last thing I want to look at isn't so much a specific segment of Scripture, but a general argument that gets used. It's one I have personally heard many times. When one starts talking about the blessings that are available to us in Jesus, someone will make statements like: "Paul suffered greatly in incredible ways", "Paul was physically infirmed", "Paul was poor", "Jesus was poor", "Jesus suffered and so will you" and so forth. The reasoning is that if the life of Paul or Jesus contradicts, then those blessings people talk about of health or prosperity or whatever must not be for us.

We've already talked a little bit about the suffering thing several chapters back, but it IS true that Jesus and Paul both suffered. It is also true that you and I, if we're doing this Christianity thing right, will experience some form of suffering for our faith too (it might not be on that level but still...) That's actually a promise in the Bible. And that's not because God wants it for us because He's trying to punish us – it's just the way it is. If you stand up for Jesus, you are going to get persecuted by rebellious unbelievers – that's just part of the territory. But you know what? It's one thing to say and acknowledge that, and it's another to extrapolate that we are just meant to be sick and poor and that God doesn't want us well and prospering.

On the physical health front, we really don't know Paul's situation there. We do know that he did experience physical issues as a result of persecution, but we don't really know much beyond that. I already addressed the whole "thorn in the flesh" thing back in chapter two, so I won't reiterate that except to remind you that the Bible doesn't say Paul's thorn was a sickness. With emotional health, we do know that Paul talked about experiencing discouragement and despair and so forth, but when you read his writings, you see a picture of a guy that didn't camp there but knew how to rejoice in Jesus.

Paul experienced some very hard situations as a result of persecution by fellow humans that exercised their freewill choice to persecute him, but that has zero bearing on whether God wanted Paul well and living in joy and peace and prospering in His life, or whether such things were available to Paul because Jesus purchased them for him. You just can't make that leap and yet that's what people do.

On the financial front, let me just be blunt and say that we don't really know the full financial state of either Paul or Jesus. It is true that Paul lived a life of giving and not hoarding money as that is fairly evident from his writings, but that doesn't mean that he didn't have funds to work with. It would appear from various scriptures that Paul was not really ultra-wealthy, but he must have had some funds to work with to accomplish what he did. As for Jesus, people say that because He walked around and didn't have a regular "place to lay His head" that He must have been poor. Look, I haven't seen Jesus' personal financial statements, but I do know that He and His disciples had a treasury with a treasurer to manage it (the infamous Judas Iscariot). People that are poor usually don't need a treasurer. And Judas was even able to steal from the treasury which is something you wouldn't think he would do unless he felt he could get away with it because there was so much there. Jesus also interacted with a bunch of important people and had lots of followers, so a claim that Jesus was financially poor just strikes me as not being very likely.

But the thing is, none of these arguments really matter anyway. They are just a smokescreen so people can defend living a miserable life and put all responsibility over on God by saying that whether we are well or sick or prospering or full of lack is all just up to God based on whatever He wills for you at any given time. After all, if everything is just solely up to God and God doesn't definitely desire us to be well and healthy and walking in freedom and prospering in all areas of our lives, then it lets us off the hook. People will fight to the death to defend their view that life is just supposed to be full of misery. It's actually comforting to them in a strange way.

Here's the reality: There is trouble in this world. There is persecution. Hard times or circumstances may affect you. And none of that has any bearing on what is available to you in Jesus. In Jesus, you have everything you can ever need, and that includes health and wholeness and freedom and joy and love and peace and prosperity and victory.

The Choice

You have to make a choice: Either God is a puppet-master making everything happen in your life (both good and bad) and that He could want bad for you, OR God is for you and has provided blessings for you in Jesus that you can apprehend and walk in and that He does not ever desire you to be sick and broke and depressed and beaten down by sin. Really, it's that simple. A lot of the church world has tended to at least somewhat go with option one. This book is all about proving option two and it's the view that I believe the whole of Scripture backs up.

You might notice that in all these discussions of sovereignty and freewill, I have avoided using some common theological terms that people banter around. That's on purpose, because my experience is some people love to get sidetracked in a deep theological thicket of weeds. When you get down to it, there's really just the two pretty simple choices that I outlined. As I said at the beginning of this chapter, I encourage you to weigh all these things yourself and come to your own conclusions with the Lord. For me, I've considered both sides and I've made my choice. Settling this issue is a key thing because it will drastically affect how you approach living your Christian life. You are not likely to fully live an abundant life here if you don't truly believe on a core level that God really WANTS you to live an abundant life here.

Chapter 16 – The Heart of the Money Matter

Note: If you skipped ahead to check out this chapter because you saw the word "money" in the title, you need to give yourself 10 lashes and go stand in the corner. Well, okay, you can spare yourself the physical punishment, but seriously if that's you, you do need to go back and read all the preceding chapters before jumping into this one as they all set the necessary background for this chapter.

In discussing living the abundant life, we have talked a fair degree about health, but I purposely have avoided saying much about finances thus far. The primary reason for that is simply that making the case that God wants us healthy is an easier and more direct case to make than that God wants people prospering financially. In addition, just on a personal note from my own life, for me as one that was coming from a place of skepticism, it was easier to accept the healing truths than to accept the prospering ones.

Talking about finances is a tricky proposition because it tends to be quite the touchy subject with people in multiple ways. One of these is that many people are very skeptical of "prosperity teaching" and this partly is because there HAS been some out-of-balance teaching put forth in this area that I would say is sketchy at best. There are times where I myself have found myself frustrated at the way the subject of finances has been handled by various teachers, even teachers that I very much respect or have agreed with otherwise. So if this subject is one that tends to make you wary, let me just say upfront that I totally understand!

I also should probably just be forthright in saying that this chapter, even more than those before it, is probably going to be the hardest for me to avoid hitting people's nerves on because people tend to be fairly polarized on this subject and the view that I believe best squares with Scripture as a whole doesn't really fit neatly into either of the predominant polarizing views out there. Like many things people tend to get worked up over, I believe there's a balance to be struck. So I'm going to ask you for some extra grace and that you please not tune me out right away if I hit a nerve, as you will likely find I will pour a lot of salve on that nerve later if you keep reading! :)

Whenever the subject of the believer's relationship to wealth is brought up, it tends to be portrayed in one of two ways by pastors and teachers. The first (and I dare say the most popular) is that God could want to give you wealth or He could not, but it's just a matter of what He chooses for you based on what He feels is best for you. This springs from the same sovereignty worldview we've already talked about that says that God could want you healthy or not want you healthy based on how He's feeling or deciding for you on a given day – that it's all just up to His sovereignty.

With this view, it is often also assumed that you really shouldn't WANT to want to have a lot of wealth – there is an emphasis given on the dangers of having a lot of money. If God does choose to bless you financially, then it's usually then seen as your job to give at least a majority of it away. In many circles, you're somewhat made to feel "guilty" if you have an abundance of wealth and live in a nice home or drive a nice car, etc. And this is doubly-true of pastors and those in ministry – if a pastor is observed driving a fancy car, or heaven forbid, they own a private jet, there are some people that will angrily come out with their fingers-a-waggin' talking about how that pastor should be ashamed and is a "wolf in sheep's clothing" that is just out to "fleece the flock." [I'm probably striking some nerves – please don't tune me out yet!]

This way of viewing wealth is usually put forth by very well-meaning people that believe in keeping an eye on the dangers of having a lot of wealth (because, they point out, the Bible talks a lot about the dangers of great wealth). Some even take their concern of having great finances so seriously that they go a step further and choose to make a "vow of poverty", where they believe God wants them to live poor and to just give everything they have away. Whether someone goes to that extreme or not, this whole overarching view of the way believers should relate to finances lends towards people not really expecting to prosper and instead emphasizes how we should just be content with how things are. So, for instance, if you are poor, you should be content in being poor.

The other common view (though less so) that is out there is that God wants all believers to financially prosper and have great wealth. Those that that hold to this view obviously emphasize how God wants people to prosper and, given this focus, often this has come across either blatantly or sometimes just subtly as a focus on money for personal material gain (i.e. to have a bigger house and expensive car, etc.) There are teachers that promote this view who talk about how if you desire a bigger house, you should confess that with your mouth and believe for it, etc.

It is also very common for those that hold to this view to talk of giving money away in order to receive much more blessing from the Lord. For instance, if one goes to a church with a pastor that believes this view, it is quite possible they will be hearing a fair bit about how "we cannot out-give God" and that as we give (and usually the context is giving to the church/ministry that the speaker is representing), God will bless us much more beyond what we could give.

It is understandable then that to some believers that hear this view, it can definitely seem that the focus is put on "me and what I can get" – that it is a message that appeals to our fleshly greed. And it can also sometimes appear that pastors/teachers who are promoting this view can be trying to manipulate believers for the sake of getting more finances for their church or ministry, or even themselves. Thus there has been a pretty notable backlash in Christendom pushing back against this view, which is sometimes dubbed the "prosperity gospel" by those that reject it.

So there you have it – that's an incredibly simplified, ultra-basic overview of the 2 main views. As you were reading my descriptions above, chances are you already have identified that you find yourself more in one camp than the other. However, like many things that us church folk love to squabble about, there are legit points to be made on both sides, but it requires a willingness to move beyond our feelings and look at the other side without just instantly dismissing them.

We have already talked a lot about the sovereignty issue and how God is a good God who wants us well in all respects. I just don't see how that doesn't apply to our financial situation as well. Why would God want a bunch of broke followers, where all the wealth is controlled by the unrighteous heathen? Why would God want His people to be poor beggars?

I believe God is not only totally fine with, but desirous of, His people to be financially prosperous. In the Bible, there were several wealthy individuals where it's not even hinted that it was a problem for them being wealthy. For instance, Abraham (the father of our faith), David, Solomon, and Job were all very wealthy. Speaking of Job (who you might recall we talked about way back in chapter two), we are even specifically told at the end of the book how God gave Job twice the wealth that he had had (see Job 42:10). The devil had wanted to hurt Job, but God wanted to bless him.

When the children of Israel conquered the ungodly in the land of Canaan that God had given them, Joshua told some of them: "Return with much riches unto your tents, and with very much cattle, with silver, and with gold, and with brass..." (from Joshua 22:8b KJV). God was not opposed to His children having wealth. Indeed, God had earlier pronounced they would be wealthy if they obeyed Him in the blessings He declared for them under the Old Covenant.

> And the LORD will grant you plenty of goods, in the fruit of your body, in the increase of your livestock, and in the produce of your ground, in the land of which the LORD swore to your fathers to give you. The LORD will open to you His good treasure, the heavens, to give the rain to your land in its season, and to bless all the work of your hand. You shall lend to many nations, but you shall not borrow. And the LORD will make you the head and not the tail; you shall be above only, and not be beneath, if you heed the commandments of the LORD your God, which I command you today, and are careful to observe *them.* (Deuteronomy 28:11–13 NKJV)

This sounds to me like God wanted His kids to prosper! By contrast, the curses God pronounced in the same chapter if they didn't follow Him talked (among other things) of how they would be negatively impacted financially and would not prosper. But that certainly wasn't what God wanted. His desire was clearly for them to be blessed in all areas, including financially. Being poor has never been one of God's blessings.

Now this was under the Old Covenant which as we have already previously talked about was a performance-based covenant with God. You might also recall how we discussed that in the book of Hebrews, the New Covenant that we have through Jesus that is based on faith in Him rather than our perfect performance, is declared to be a better covenant. If the new is better, I would expect it to at least offer as many benefits as the old, wouldn't you? Was God wanting to bless the children of Israel financially, but not wanting to bless His children today? I don't think so...

When Jesus began His earthly ministry and went to His hometown of Nazareth, this is what He read about Himself:

> "The Spirit of the Lord is upon me,
> because he has anointed me
> to proclaim good news to the poor.
> He has sent me to proclaim liberty to the captives
> and recovering of sight to the blind,
> to set at liberty those who are oppressed,
> to proclaim the year of the Lord's favor." (Luke 4:18–19 ESV)

Jesus starts right off the bat in describing His earthly ministry by reading from Isaiah 61 and the first part of that ministry description declared that He was anointed to proclaim good news to the poor. Now I know that many when they read that think "poor in spirit" and I concede that perhaps could be one way of looking at it (the Hebrew in Isaiah 61 could also mean "humble" or "meek"). But in its Greek form as related in Luke, the word seems to pretty much mean poor in a financial sense and that is almost always how the same Greek word for "poor" is used in the rest of the New Testament. Also, in the rest of this passage, it then goes on to talk about freedom for those bound and also physical health (recovering of sight to those blind). Again, I understand this whole thing could just be "spiritualized" to say that Jesus isn't really talking about people that are financially poor or physically blind. But if you just take it at face value, it seems that Jesus is making a quite encompassing statement – saying that He has come to affect us across-the-board and that He is proclaiming God's favor on humanity!

I'm not remotely claiming that I think this means Jesus is saying the Good News that He came to bring is that you can have 20 million dollars. What I am saying, as we've talked about in previous chapters, is that being in relationship with God through Jesus isn't meant to just only be about getting to go to Heaven when you die, but that there's much more encompassing benefits available here and forever. That God wants us to prosper across-the-board in all respects and that we have that available to us through Jesus.

You may remember the verse that I shared many chapters ago where the Apostle John declared His heart: "Beloved, I wish above all things that thou mayest prosper and be in health, even as thy soul prospereth." (3 John 2 KJV). That was John speaking, but why do we think God's desires for us would be anything less? In this verse, besides mentioning being in health, it mentions a desire for prosperity (and the implication, at least partially, is financially).

Proverbs 10:15 says, "The rich man's wealth is his strong city: the destruction of the poor is their poverty." (KJV). Speaking of the righteous man, Psalm 112:3 says, "Wealth and riches shall be in his house: and his righteousness endureth for ever." (KJV).

In 2 Corinthians 8:9 it says, "For you know the grace of our Lord Jesus Christ, that though He was rich, yet for your sakes He became poor, that you through His poverty might become rich." (NKJV). People that are against the whole prosperity message tend to point out that this verse is misapplied by those that support that message – that it's clearly talking about poor and rich in spiritual terms – that Jesus was "rich" in heaven and then came to earth as a baby and had to grow here and so compared to how it was for Him in heaven He was poor, but that by His coming and dying for us we have become "rich" through Him in that we now have eternal life. Honestly, I am pre-disposed to somewhat agree with that assessment. Except there's one thing I have a problem getting around. This verse is a quote from the Apostle Paul to the Corinthian church where he was specifically talking to them about financial giving and was trying to spur them on to give. So the clear immediate context is actual finances, not some spiritualized concept. Now if what we've already talked about in this book is true, that in and through Jesus all we need is available to us and we are joint-heirs with Christ, then this verse could probably be taken in multiple ways. But the context does very much suggest it's at least partially about finances.

In any event, I think it's quite clear that God is not opposed to wealth in-and-of-itself and that being poor has never been a blessing from God. On the subject of giving, there are numerous scriptures that talk about giving that support the notion that when we give that we can be financially blessed in return (e.g. 2 Cor. 9:6–11, Luke 6:38, Proverbs 3:9–10, Proverbs 11:25).

Taking all of this together, on a macro-level, I do believe that God desires His children to prosper in all areas of our lives, including financially, and I do believe that all things are possible and available to us through our relationship with Jesus. I also believe that the same principle of faith that works in other areas can work in the financial area as well, including when we give.

So far, all the prosperity "faith" people are cheering me on: "WOOHOO!! Preach it brother!" Well, I hate to pour cold water while we're all jumping up and down, but there's more to the story. Those that point out that there are warnings in Scripture relating to having a lot of money are not wrong...

> "How hardly shall they that have riches enter into the kingdom of God! For it is easier for a camel to go through a needle's eye, than for a rich man to enter into the kingdom of God." (Luke 18:24b–25 KJV)

Jesus said this in response to a rich young ruler who had asked Him what he needed to do to inherit eternal life. You can read the whole story in Luke 18:18–29, but basically the ruler had told Jesus that he kept all the commandments from his youth, but Jesus then zeroed in on and exposed the ruler's heart when He told him to give away all that he had to the poor and to come follow Him (Jesus). Instead of responding favorably, the man grew very sorrowful and that is when Jesus said what He said above about how hard it is for a rich man to enter the kingdom of God. After Jesus said this, the people around Him asked Jesus, "Who then can be saved?" (vs 26), and Jesus responds by saying that "The things which are impossible with men are possible with God." (vs 27).

This portion of Scripture gives rise to several questions such as: (1) "Does Jesus want all rich people to give away everything to the poor?", (2) "Is giving away everything really the means to inherit eternal life?", and (3) "Why is it so hard for rich people to enter the kingdom of God?"

The ruler seemingly had come to Jesus full of pride: pride in his adherence to the commandments as well as pride in his wealth. He had the gall to say he had kept all the commandments since his youth! That would be quite something if true, but it wasn't and Jesus knew it. Not only had he probably broken many or all of the others at some point in his life, but at the very least he broke the first one, which is where God says to put no other gods above Himself. Upon seeing the man's prideful response, Jesus doesn't argue with him by telling him that he's not correct in regards to keeping all the commandments. Instead, He plays along but just goes straight to highlighting the issue that shows that the man's got a problem even with the first commandment – that his wealth had become a stumbling block for him.

So to answer the questions posed above, no, we can't extrapolate from this interaction with this one man that Jesus wants all rich people to give away all of their wealth. And no, doing so isn't really the means to gaining eternal life. After Jesus told the ruler to give away his wealth, He also told him to come follow Him (Jesus). Had the man gotten his heart right and chosen Jesus over his wealth and placed his faith and trust in Jesus rather than his wealth, he absolutely would have inherited eternal life. That was the issue. And that leads us to the answer for the third question of why it is so hard for those with great wealth to be saved. Not only here, but in plenty of other places in Scripture, it is made clear that being wealthy can be a real trap because there is a real temptation to trust in your wealth instead of in God.

In one of Jesus's parables, He told a story of such a man that fell into that trap. Picking up with the man speaking to himself:

> And I will say to my soul, "Soul, you have ample goods laid up for many years; relax, eat, drink, be merry.'" But God said to him, 'Fool! This night your soul is required of you, and the things you have prepared, whose will they be?' So is the one who lays up treasure for himself and is not rich toward God." (Luke 12:19–21 ESV)

In our culture today, one of the chief goals of many is to "be successful" by having a lot of money so you can "live it up" and have no worries. Here, Jesus is going straight to the heart of the flaw in that mindset – that trusting in riches can only get you so far and won't help you one iota on the day you have to stand before God. It can literally be your downfall.

> But those who desire to be rich fall into temptation, into a snare, into many senseless and harmful desires that plunge people into ruin and destruction. For the love of money is a root of all kinds of evils. It is through this craving that some have wandered away from the faith and pierced themselves with many pangs. (1 Timothy 6:9–10 ESV)

The problem isn't being rich in and of itself; it's that those that are so focused on just wanting to be rich and are coveting and craving money for themselves easily cross a line where they are looking to money to be their answer instead of God. It does not say that money itself is a root of (various) evil, but that the love of money is. When it comes to money, there is a very real and very strong temptation to place its importance in one's heart over God, and when this happens, the pursuit of wealth becomes all about fulfilling one's fleshly desires and this leads to all sorts of troubles.

> As for the rich in this present age, charge them not to
> be haughty, nor to set their hopes on the uncertainty of
> riches, but on God, who richly provides us with every-
> thing to enjoy. (1 Timothy 6:17 ESV)

There is absolutely nothing wrong with being wealthy, but it is important that those that are wealthy have the proper perspective. Here we are told that those that are rich are not to be haughty or put their hope in their riches (which are uncertain), but instead on God (who is certain) and who is the One who Himself richly provides us with everything. God is a good giving God. He is a provider and He provides for our enjoyment! I've already stated that I believe He wants His people to prosper in all areas, including financially. But what He doesn't want is people looking to riches instead of Him. God cares about the heart. He cares about motivations.

In 2 Chronicles 1, God told Solomon that he could ask Him for anything, and Solomon told God he would like wisdom and knowledge so he could better govern the people. God's response was, "Because this was in your heart, and you have not asked riches or wealth or honor or the life of your enemies, nor have you asked long life—but have asked wisdom and knowledge for yourself, that you may judge My people over whom I have made you king— wisdom and knowledge *are* granted to you; and I will give you riches and wealth and honor, such as none of the kings have had who *were* before you, nor shall any after you have the like." (2 Chronicles 1:11b–12 NKJV).

Again, God loves to bless. He is totally cool with you being wealthy! But He cares about your heart and your motivations a whole lot. Psalm 49:5–6 talks of the iniquity of those "that trust in their wealth, and boast themselves in the multitude of their riches" (Psalm 49:6b KJV).

We have talked a bit about faith in this book and I've already stated that I believe faith can be exercised for finances the same as for other things. And all the prosperity faith people said "Amen!" But in the famous "faith chapter" of Hebrews 11, one of those called out for his faith was Moses, and part of why he was acknowledged was because he "considered the reproach of Christ greater wealth than the treasures of Egypt, for he was looking to the reward." (Hebrews 11:26b ESV). Moses knew that more important than being physically wealthy was being wealthy in terms of His relationship with God. He knew where his priorities needed to be and he was willing to give up his temporal riches provided for him in Egypt to follow God.

It's about the heart. While I do absolutely agree that God is a good God who loves to give and wants people to prosper financially, I also acknowledge that there is a very real danger in having a lot of wealth because, quite bluntly, it is very easy for the heart to even be subtly deceived on these things.

When I see people that are all just focused on having money to get things for themselves, where money is a chief goal for them, I just think that's a tricky place to be. This is where I have tended to get frustrated with some faith teachers that teach prosperity. While I often agree with much of the underlying theology, what happens is that the strong emphasis is usually placed on what a person can get, and how they can be blessed so much and get so much back from God if they just believe, and how as they give, God will return back to them many times over, and things like that. I'm not saying there's not a Scriptural basis for those things. What I am saying is that it tends to be pretty one-sided and come across as a very "me-centered" theology that appeals to our fleshly desires. It's VERY clear from Scripture that we need to be very careful of our heart as it relates to money! Money can be a wonderful tool or a terrible curse in our lives, depending on how we approach it.

On the other side, there are those that have a "poverty mentality" where they don't know how to (or even have the want to) exercise their faith for finances and don't believe God wants them to prosper. That is not the case – God wants His people to prosper financially and He is perfectly happy for you to have wealth. But He wants your heart in the right place too and He knows the danger that having a lot of money can pose. Regardless of our current experiential state in any area of life, we are called to be content and to be in peace. But that doesn't mean that we can't have a desire for something different. The issue is whether it's a pure Godly desire or selfish fleshly greed. The issue is of the heart.

It is NOT a bad thing in-and-of-itself to desire to be prosperous financially! You just need to check your motivations for that – to continually check your heart! Is your reason for wanting wealth so that you can have big giant houses, a maid, expensive sports cars, etc? I mean, is that your goal? Or how about this one: is it so you can know that your future is financially secure and you won't ever have any worries? Or maybe it's so you can prove to yourself and to the world that you "made it" – that you are a "big success"? There can be a real fine line with some of this and we can very easily deceive ourselves to think our motives our pure when they are not. God is happy for you to have finances, but He also doesn't want you trusting in your riches or using your riches to find your identity. Nor does He want you using your riches to prop yourself up and look down on others while you play with all your toys!

But you know what? If your genuine desire is to have wealth so that you can be an example of the goodness of God and can significantly bless others in Jesus' name, that can be a solid thing! God isn't opposed to you having nice things, but He does want your heart right.

> Honor the LORD with your wealth
>   and with the firstfruits of all your produce;
> then your barns will be filled with plenty,
>   and your vats will be bursting with wine. (Proverbs 3:9–10 ESV)

I am convinced that one of the chief reasons why God instituted tithing and the concept of firstfruits (giving out of the first of the results of your labor) among the nation of Israel was precisely because He wanted His people to keep their hearts in the right place where He would be first. Regardless of whether we as Christians are bound to keep the tithe or not, we are still called to be givers (and cheerful ones at that – see 2 Cor. 9:7) and the principle of honoring the Lord first still stands. Whether you currently have a lot of wealth or a little does not matter as far as this goes – the principle is the same no matter where you are on the spectrum. God is a giver, and we're called to be givers too.

Earlier it was mentioned that some people get tripped up on the apparent financial excesses showcased by some pastors and Christian leaders. For instance, sometimes pastors or other Christian leaders get in the headlines for things like having private jets and so forth. Again, I do believe that the model in the Bible, particularly in the New Testament, is one of abundant giving (as opposed to hoarding), and I do believe that money is an area that can (and does) easily trip up leaders. I personally would also urge that leaders use wisdom as to how things can appear. But you know what? Some pastors and teachers are so prominent and have so many varied speaking engagements around the country or world that a private jet might just make good ministry sense. Even if it doesn't, unless I have some direct responsibility regarding them, before I go pointing at them, I probably should examine my own heart. If someone is taking advantage of God's people, believe me, they'll give an account for that one day... But I'd suggest that rather than pointing fingers, a better plan is to check our own hearts, and then start believing God for increase in our own lives! Don't let the apparent (or actual) misdeeds of others allow you to use that as an excuse to keep you in a place of less than God might have for YOU!

You don't have to live poor and broke, barely making ends meet. If you keep your heart fixed on the Lord and keep Him number one, there is no reason why you cannot have wealth and use it in a way that is very God-honoring. You can believe God for finances to meet all of your needs and to also allow you to be a greater blessing to others. As a child of God, you are a co-heir with Jesus Christ, and you have all resources at your disposal. You can use your faith to believe God for your needs as well as over-and-above your needs. Like health which we've talked about previously, it's not really that you are believing to "get something" as it is to lay hold of that which is already yours because of the position you have thanks to your Savior! As you believe and then speak and act in line with what you believe and what God shows you to do, you can see definite changes in your financial position. Just remember to never forget Who is your source and to always be mindful of how you are viewing money and to keep it from occupying a place in your heart that it is not meant to occupy.

The heart of the money matter is indeed the heart.

Chapter 17 – Our Treasure

In this book, I have been trying to make the case to you from the Word that God not only CAN heal you or set you free, but that He WANTS to and actually has ALREADY provided health and freedom and provision and indeed everything you could need in this life through the atonement paid for by Jesus, and that we can receive what we need and walk in the abundant life through faith.

Regardless of your need, step one in really seeing it come to pass is that you need to be convinced that God loves you, that He wants you well and whole, and that He has already provided the payment for your full health and wholeness and prosperous blessed living through Jesus' sacrifice. This is where the biggest battle occurs. You have to believe that God wants you well and living the full life He has for you even more than you do; that He is on your side and not trying to oppose you. The reality is that many people struggle with really believing these things. People speak and act out of what they truly believe. Step one is to get these truths rooted in you – deep in your being.

Knowing information in your head on an intellectual level is one thing. Knowing it in the pit of your being is another. It needs to become revelation knowledge in your heart, where you believe it to such a degree that you just "know that you know" that it is true and will then act on it in faith. If you aren't to that place, don't despair. Just keep pressing forward to study and grow and marinate yourself in the Word as it relates to these things. After finishing this book, you might want to go back and re-read it and also spend time considering God's love for you.

Specifically in the context of physical/emotional healing, you can check out some of the Resources in Appendix D, go through and read all the examples of healing in the New Testament, and basically do everything you can to marinate in these truths. You need to be absolutely 100% convinced that health and wholeness are yours, that it is your right as a child of God, and that God wants you well in every respect of your life.

In 2011, I was really sick but had started learning a whole lot about healing and I listened to dozens and dozens of healing messages where I was taught different facets regarding what the Word says about healing. Although I "believed" it in my head, I still remember the day I crossed a "threshold" of sorts. I was sitting in a local park reading a small book with some healing scriptures in it and as I was going through them, faith just welled up in me, and I realized: "Yes, this really is true, and I can bank my life on this!" Once I really settled that in my heart is when things began to change.

A related issue here is that many people have some doubts about the Bible as a whole. You need to be completely convinced that the Bible is God's Word and can be trusted. You're going to have trouble really believing what the Bible says regarding healing or whatever need you have if you aren't even sure you can trust the Bible.

Lots of people like to play fast-and-loose with the Bible, taking the parts they like and discarding or dismissing the parts they don't. They'll explain why what God clearly says in the Word isn't really what He meant to say. Now one definitely does need to consider passages in the Bible in the light of both the immediate context as well as the entire Biblical narrative and that can affect how one interprets or should apply passages. But the bottom-line is that you need to be in a place where you just make a decision that you are going to trust the Bible as the standard for your life. If, for instance, there's an opinion you have that contradicts what God has said about that subject in His Word, you have to come to a place of admitting that it's not the Bible that's wrong and you need to adjust yourself to its teachings, and not try to conform it to your thinking. If you haven't ever done so, you should perhaps study regarding the reliability of the Bible in order to satisfy yourself. When you do, you'll find there is plenty of evidence to support it – far more than any other book.

The Bible can be trusted. Yes, God really did make this world. Yes, He really did create the first humans. Yes, those humans really did rebel and bring sin and death into this world. Yes, Jonah really did get swallowed by a great fish (and Jesus Himself referenced it later!). Yes, Jesus really was conceived by the Holy Spirit and born of the Virgin Mary. Yes, Jesus really did rise from the dead. Yes, we really are saved by grace through faith in Jesus. Yes, health and wholeness really is ours through Jesus. Yes, Jesus really will come back one day. You have to settle in your heart that what the Bible says is indeed true and you are going to put all your chips on it and choose to live your life based on it, whether that's "culturally popular" or not (and it's definitely not right now).

You also are going to have to reconcile your experiences with what you are learning from the Word of God. For instance, if you have had family members or friends that have died that you prayed for, especially if they were Christians that seemed to be believing God for healing, you are going to have to reconcile that. I discussed my mother previously. When she went home to Jesus, while there was part of us both that I think in a sense "knew" she was going as I've already mentioned, we were still believing for her healing here. The day she passed, she had written out a bunch of faith declarations about her being well! Believe you me, I had to reconcile that all with God. I couldn't believe God for my own health and I certainly couldn't be writing this book to you if I hadn't.

I literally sat down several months after my mom passed, and with all of my emotions swirling around, just started working through my thoughts by writing them down. I wrote down the variables that I knew, and the things that I didn't know. God brought some things to my remembrance and I realized that while she was believing for healing, there was also part of her that really wanted to go Home and that she was conflicted on a deep level. I also realized that there were a bunch of things that I just plain didn't have data for – that there were variables in the mix that I didn't have any way to measure or evaluate. The bottom-line is I realized that I could not base my theology on healing based on my mom's experience, or anybody else's experience for that matter. I had to solely base my theology on healing on the Word of God and what it tells me. You will have to come to the same place, where what you saw happen or didn't see happen with someone else isn't your marker stick to determine whether God's Word is true. You have to make a decision that God's Word is true regardless of whether anybody else's experiences or even your own experiences, seem to bear it out. Our experiences are not the standard for whether what the Bible says about healing or anything else is true or not. It is true simply because it is God's Word, and God doesn't lie. That doesn't mean there aren't people out there that haven't proved out what the Bible says, because there are. There are plenty of testimonies out there that bear out what the Word says.

We've talked a fair bit about faith in this book, but not a whole lot about unbelief. Unbelief and doubt are the antithesis of faith. The fact is that many of us have been conditioned to doubt God's Word when it comes to really living the abundant life here and now. We've been taught that God doesn't necessarily always want us well and whole and that health isn't definitely ours in Jesus. We've been taught that even for believers in Jesus, God picks and chooses who He wants to bless and that it's all just up to His sovereign will. We might somewhat believe the truth, but getting fully sold-out to it can take awhile for some of us because we've heard so much contrary teaching, which has caused us to not really expect much. We've been infused with doubt and unbelief regarding what the Word says is ours. Our culture is constantly bombarding us with messages that fuel doubt and unbelief towards God, and sadly a fair part of the church does the same (under a "religious cloak").

Unbelief can hinder you experiencing all that God has for you. There's a fascinating bit of Scripture in Mark 6. Referring to Jesus in His hometown of Nazareth, we are told, "And he could do no mighty work there, except that he laid his hands on a few sick people and healed them. And he marveled because of their unbelief." (Mark 6:5–6a ESV).

In His own hometown, Jesus basically was only able to heal a few sick people (and the implication is people with minor ailments). Nothing like many of the other towns where we see multitudes healed. It doesn't say that Jesus *would not* do mighty works; notice that we are told that He *could not* do mighty works, and the reason we are given is because they had a lot of unbelief. "But I thought Jesus was all-powerful and could do whatever He wanted because He was God?" Yes, He was God, but He interacted with people's faith and what they wanted. People in His hometown did not believe in Him and even took offense at Him (Mark 6:3). Their unbelief limited what Jesus was able to do for them.

There's another fascinating story in Mark 8 of a blind guy Jesus ran across in Bethsaida.

> 22 And they came to Bethsaida. And some people brought to him a blind man and begged him to touch him. 23 And he took the blind man by the hand and led him out of the village, and when he had spit on his eyes and laid his hands on him, he asked him, "Do you see anything?" 24 And he looked up and said, "I see people, but they look like trees, walking." 25 Then Jesus laid his hands on his eyes again; and he opened his eyes, his sight was restored, and he saw everything clearly. 26 And he sent him to his home, saying, "Do not even enter the village." (Mark 8:22–26 ESV)

Now, Bethsaida was a city full of unbelief. We know this because Jesus says this about it in the Gospel of Luke: "Woe to you, Bethsaida! For if the mighty works which were done in you had been done in Tyre and Sidon, they would have repented long ago, sitting in sackcloth and ashes." (Luke 10:13b NKJV). Jesus actually issued them a "Woe!" – that's serious. They were full of unbelief, and that unbelief hindered Jesus.

Back to the account of the blind guy. Notice in verse 23 that Jesus took the hand of the blind man and led him out of Bethsaida before healing him. And in verse 26, He then tells the guy to not go back to Bethsaida. It appears that Jesus couldn't heal the man in Bethsaida due to the unbelief factor in the city. In addition to our own unbelief, this shows us that the unbelief of those around us can affect us also; there can be an "atmosphere of unbelief" that can hinder us. It also is interesting that even when Jesus laid His hands on the man, the first time he received only a partial healing. It took a second time of Jesus laying His hands on him for his sight to be restored. This is the only account I am aware of in the Bible that we have record of Jesus not instantly being able to heal someone completely. Was the problem with Jesus here? Did Jesus just not have it all together that day? I don't think so. I think that even this man had been influenced some by Bethsaida such that there was some unbelief that was hindering him fully receiving from Jesus, and it took him receiving a partial healing for the faith to well up in Him to knock out the unbelief so that he could fully receive. This is an assumption – the text doesn't actually tell us this – but I think it's a logical one.

In James 1, in regards to asking for wisdom and receiving that wisdom from God, James tacks on this important piece of information: "But let him ask in faith, with no doubting, for the one who doubts is like a wave of the sea that is driven and tossed by the wind. For that person must not suppose that he will receive anything from the Lord; he is a double-minded man, unstable in all his ways." (James 1:6–8 ESV). The context was asking for wisdom, but there's a principle here that can apply to lots of things. Doubt and Unbelief can keep you from seeing your answer. The phrase "unstable in all his ways" used to always bother me a bit because it seems rather harsh. But the truth is that if a person is kind of believing but also doubting, they are going to go back and forth and be all over the place which makes them not in a stable, sure position.

It is perfectly possible to both believe and have unbelief at the same time. Remember the father of the epileptic boy? When Jesus told him that all things were possible to those that believe, the man responded, "Lord, I believe; help my unbelief!" (Mark 9:24b NKJV). This was not an ideal position for him to be in. Now, Jesus worked with him where he was at, but you get the clear impression when you read the story that he just barely "skated by." The less unbelief you have, the better position you are going to be in.

So, you may be wondering exactly how to get rid of unbelief? There's only one real way that I know and that is to spend time meditating on the Word and building yourself up in the truths of the Word. Our world is constantly throwing doubt and unbelief our way. The less time you're listening to the world, and the more time you're listening to the Word, the less doubt and unbelief you'll have and the more faith you will have. To use a specific example, if your need is healing, the more teachings you can listen to and receive regarding healing and the more you study this subject, the less unbelief you will have when it comes to healing.

This is the whole concept of "fasting" – it's you setting aside some natural stuff for a bit (e.g. eating and/or perhaps certain things such as a media fast) to really extra focus on God and the truth of the Word without fleshly distractions. If you're sick, a no-food fast may or may not be a wise thing, but you can definitely do a "media fast" which in our culture is a huge deal. You want to just spend a lot less time listening to the world and a lot more time listening to what God says. And don't be afraid to cry out to Jesus just like the father of the epileptic boy did asking for His help.

Fast or not though, we need to always guard ourselves in regards to what we allow ourselves to take in and meditate on precisely because in the faith vs. unbelief equation, we want the faith side to be the stronger of the two. This is where I'm really about to go to meddling, so brace yourself!

In our society today, we are bombarded with media. Between television, movies, music, and the Internet, and our zillions of devices to consume that media on, we are continually surrounded with media options. Most people consume a lot of media – whether that's television shows, videos on the web, news stories on the web, or what have you.

You need to realize that the media you consume can affect you. The Bible tells us: "Be not deceived: evil communications corrupt good manners." (1 Corinthians 15:33 KJV). If you are constantly watching and reading the news for instance, you are likely going to have a negative and cynical outlook, because the news just by definition of it reporting news in this sinful world, is going to be predominantly negative. For instance, if you watch a news story or read a social media post about a shark attack occurring, that could cause fear to rise in you to not let you or your kids go to the ocean for fear of similar happening to you. Or if you constantly are watching news opinion shows where there's intense talk and rhetoric, you might find yourself more apt to be frustrated or agitated. These things can affect us because words (and I would say images also) have power.

Likewise, if you are in the habit of watching television shows or movies that are focused on murder and death (e.g. solving crimes or medical dramas), and yet you are very sick in your body and wanting to be well, can I just as nicely as I can, tell you that that is not smart? If you are sick in your body and wanting to be well, but the media that you consume is focused on death and murder, that's just not a very wise plan. Or if you've had a lot of issues with anxiety and feel "stressed" a lot, but yet you like to watch the latest scary movies, what you are doing is basically feeding and magnifying those issues in your life. You are consuming content that is not helpful to you. Those kinds of things can introduce (perhaps even subtly) doubt and unbelief and fear into your heart.

I used to like a show from the 1980's and 1990's called "Murder, She Wrote." Although it had a reputation of being a show for older women because the star was an older woman, I found it an entertaining show and it was popular enough that it ran for 12 seasons. As far as "murder/crime/mystery" shows go, this one was ridiculously tame compared to today's standards. I owned a number of seasons of this show on DVD. When I was really sick though, I realized that it just wasn't helpful to me with the major life-and-death battle I was in, to be continually watching shows where the focus was on solving a murder and where you see all the drama of people and why they commit murder. Eventually, even after I had started feeling some better, I realized that they probably weren't *ever* likely going to be helpful for me, so I literally threw out those DVD's in the trash.

I still enjoy that show in my flesh and I've seen a few episodes subsequently on television, and I don't consider it the end of the world that I did so. I'm not trying to be ultra-legalistic or dogmatic here on this point. But all media can either help you or harm you (it's either life or death to you), and the plain truth is most of it will harm you. For me personally, I couldn't see a scenario where watching that show would ever actually bring life and health to me, so especially given the seriousness of the health issues I had been facing, I made a decision to pretty much cut it from my life. I'm definitely not saying you need to do the same, but it is worthwhile to consider your media intake with the Lord because you might need to adjust some things for your specific situation. You might need to cut some stuff out, even if your flesh really likes it, simply because it's just not going to be a help for you.

As a Christian, you just plain need to be very selective in this department. You need to watch what you watch. You need to guard your eyes and ears from things that might stir up stuff like doubt, fear, unbelief, hopelessness, discouragement, and so forth (not to mention all the other junk that can get stirred up by most of our modern media – things like lust, greed, anger, envy, pride, etc.).

We are told in Philippians 4:8, "Finally, brothers, whatever is true, whatever is honorable, whatever is just, whatever is pure, whatever is lovely, whatever is commendable, if there is any excellence, if there is anything worthy of praise, think about these things." (ESV).

These are the kinds of things we are told to put into our minds and think on. If a believer spends their days and nights listening to worldly music, watching worldly TV shows and movies, engaging in worldly entertainment, focusing on the world's gadgets and gizmos, etc. then it probably shouldn't come as a big surprise why they are not living the victorious, abundant life God wants them to live. I mean, if a movie has inappropriate language and/or sexual situations (stirs up lust) and/or messages and themes contrary to Scripture (e.g. "revenge", "living in fear", "having sex before marriage is ok", etc.) then we really need to ask ourselves what part of that is true, honorable, just, pure, lovely, commendable, excellent, and praiseworthy. Right?

What goes in, will come out. You cannot consume content on a regular basis with vulgar language and contrary stuff and not have it affect you. I know people fool themselves into thinking they can. They are wrong, plain and simple. What you put in, will affect you, and will come back out one way or another.

Jesus said "For where your treasure is, there your heart will be also." (Matthew 6:21 ESV). I have found this verse applies to a lot more than just money.

Jesus also said "For out of the abundance of the heart the mouth speaks." (Matthew 12:34b NKJV). What is in your heart WILL come out of your mouth.

When it comes to media, while you want to spend the bulk of your time watching/listening to stuff that's going to specifically build yourself up in the things of God, that doesn't mean you can't take in any other media also. It does mean though that you need to be careful and selective. For instance, I love to watch some good, clean, classic TV shows that will cause me to laugh and feel positive. I also love watching some good, clean comedians. Not only is there nothing wrong with that, it can potentially be good. But it does mean choosing shows and content that are going to be helpful for you or at the very least not harmful to your faith.

A word of caution: Don't assume that just because something has a "Christian" label that it's automatically "ok." Even some supposedly "Christian movies" or "Christian music" can be sending harmful messages (you might recall that I opened Chapter 2 discussing such a Christian film). There are certain Christian songs that when they come on the radio, I change the station, simply because they promote a view of God that runs counter to what God has shown me and could potentially cause doubt or unbelief to rise in me. You want to try to keep out as much negative or faith-countering stuff as possible because you don't want that stuff in your heart.

This concept also doesn't just apply to media, but to church and Christian teachings. You need to watch the teachings you are allowing yourself to take in and meditate on. If you have specific areas of your life where you are not living the abundant life, you want to be listening to teaching that is going to helpful for you and not counter your faith.

In early 2011, with sickness being a major issue for myself and my mother, we made a switch in the church we attended. We had been attending a church that while had some good general teaching, didn't believe or emphasize some of the key truths in this book and occasionally the pastor would even preach concepts outright counter to them. As God started using other pastors and teachers to show us some things, we started attending a church that did a "healing school" service every Sunday night, where essentially they would teach a passage every week highlighting something about healing. Week after week, God was speaking to us and we were growing in our knowledge and building our faith in this area (an area we had long neglected). We realized that given the seriousness of our medical issues, we really needed to focus on these things because that was what we needed.

Our other church we had been attending was I believe teaching on end-times-related stuff on Sundays and the book of Jeremiah during the week. While that teaching might be nice and definitely has its place, that wasn't what we needed at that moment. Particularly when dealing with major circumstances, you want to be in an environment that's meeting you where you are at. If you are physically ill or fighting major battles with depression or whatever, it might not be best for you to be doing a study on the book of Revelation, but rather instead to take that time and energy and put it towards studying the subject of healing or the joy of the Lord or faith or whatever relates to your situation, and building your faith up to receive what you need. It's not that the other is wrong, but sometimes you just need to focus on certain things and not other things depending on where you are at. And actually, just a side-note, but given the prevalence of sickness and disease in our world and the fact that it is a major area where we can be attacked, it's really best to study and receive teaching on that subject regularly even if you aren't currently sick so that you will maintain a faith posture in that area. Prevention is really a much better plan than trying to deal with things and build yourself up in faith once you are sick.

What we meditate on and let in our lives can powerfully affect us. And even things that are good things are not always the most helpful for us to be focusing on in a given situation. You know, if I've got a major disease in my body that's trying to kill me, perhaps it's not the best time for me to be singing or listening to songs about going to Heaven and how wonderful Heaven will be. Those might be great songs and there absolutely might be a place for them, but if I'm really sick and the devil's trying to take me out, perhaps it's not the wisest thing for me to be focusing on. Of course, being with Jesus for all eternity IS our hope and it will be awesome and I do think there is a degree to which that always needs to be in our mind. But if I'm really sick and that's what I really start meditating on as opposed to really believing God for health in my body here and now, I'm putting myself in a place where I'm in essence allowing and even embracing the sickness in a sense.

There's a time and place for things and maybe that's not the time where I need to be singing songs about how wonderful it will be to go to Heaven and listening to teaching about the awesomeness of Heaven. Maybe that's a time where I need to be singing songs about God's power and about how I am well in Him and listening to teachings on all I have in Jesus and building up my faith and so forth. I'm not saying there's always a "one-size-fits-all" thing here, but these are worthwhile considerations. What we allow ourselves to dwell on and meditate on affects us, often far more powerfully than we realize.

It all comes down to where we are going to put our focus. If we want to truly live the abundant life, part of that involves making a decision to avoid continually allowing stuff in our lives that is going to stir up unbelief and counter our faith. Perhaps watching some of those documentaries on television on those learning/science/history channels that often seem to exist solely to try to poke holes in the Bible or the existence of God or the goodness of God is something that needs to be cut out. I'm not saying we shouldn't study things and know what we believe and why, but once you reach the point where you do know the truth, it might be time to stop letting in the falsehoods put out by people that are full of unbelief, because it might potentially cause unbelief to rise in you.

We need to be proactive with this stuff. The reason this is all important is because unbelief once it gets lodged in our heart becomes a part of our core belief system. And then out of that, our mouth will speak. Which means that we will be speaking forth doubt and unbelief. Which given the power of our words and the authority we have, is a very unwise thing to do. We want to be speaking forth words of life, not death. We want to be speaking forth words of faith, not unbelief or doubt.

It comes down to what we truly are going to value. In our fast-paced culture, many believers just live on a diet of all sorts of media that isn't helpful for them and maybe only give God a few hours a week of their time (if that). That just plain isn't a recipe for success in living the abundant life. We need to be spending regular time talking with Jesus and meditating on the Word, and at the same time, minimizing media and content that will not be helpful for us.

We've talked a fair bit in this book on some specific big items related to living an abundant life, such as physical/emotional health, finances, having the power of the Spirit, knowing God's love, and so forth. But living an abundant life encompasses so many varied facets. It's a person that is able to remain at peace when storms are raging all around. It's a person that is known for being generous and freely giving of themselves. It's a person that is able to rejoice with those that rejoice and weep with those who weep and that truly cares about others. It's a person that is full of hope when others are full of despair. It's a person that is able to be a peace-maker while all the world around is throwing mud at one another and promoting division. It's a person that is known for being a blessing wherever they go. And on and on.

Living the abundant life that Jesus has for us pretty much requires that we spend time with Him and His Word and renew our minds to all that is ours in Him. It's a process and it requires continual active participation on our part. The fact that you are reading this book says that you desire to live the life Jesus has for you. But it's about more than just reading a book. It's about a lifestyle.

Living the abundant life is going to require commitment and effort on your part. You will be swimming upstream against a culture that is trying to tear you down and "keep you in your place" at every turn. You know the saying "misery loves company?" Don't expect an unbelieving culture to applaud you or make it easy for you to live abundantly. And although it's been implied throughout this book, I guess I should just go ahead and fully state this outright: You cannot expect to really live the abundant life if you aren't willing to fully follow Jesus and live as He wants you to live in all areas of your life.

Again, I share the wise words of Jesus: "For where your treasure is, there will your heart be also." (Matthew 6:21 KJV).

May we guard our heart from unbelief and doubt.

May we stir ourselves up in faith.

May Jesus be our treasure.

Chapter 18 – Practically Living the Abundant Life

The title of this book asks the question, "Where's the Abundant Life?" The answer is that it is found in Jesus and what He has provided for us, but we get to choose the degree to which we walk in it. Jesus' whole purpose in coming to this earth and dying for us and rising again was to provide us abundant life. While all genuine believers in Jesus will one day experience this life in all its true fullness on the day we depart to be with the Lord, it's not meant to just begin on the day we go Home. Christ's abundant life is available in the here-and-now, but we have a part to play in the degree of abundance that we practically will experience here. It does not just completely come to pass because God wills it for us, but it requires our active participation. Just as coming to Jesus in the first place requires active participation on our part, so does walking out really living the life God has for us here.

In the last chapter we talked about the importance of meditating in the Word and spending time building our faith up as opposed to giving our attention to things that might fuel unbelief. Knowing the truth on a core-level is the first step to practically living the abundant life. Indeed, the main purpose that I believe God really has for this book is to aid people in this process as this is where there has been too much of a void in the Body of Christ.

With our heart established in the truth, it is time to then act on that truth. We have talked previously that faith is not just a noun, but also a verb. Faith speaks. Faith acts.

Your prayers should be prayers of faith, reflecting that you believe that God has already provided your answers for you. Take the authority that you have in Jesus and speak to your body, speak to your emotions, speak to your situation! Because you are in the kingdom of God and a child of God, an heir with Jesus Christ meant to reign in life, you have the authority of the kingdom backing you up. Jesus gave us authority. He also told us we would do the things that He did, and more. Jesus lives inside of you through the Spirit. He is in you and you are in Him. You have His authority. It's like having the signet ring of the king. Just like in an earthly kingdom, a son of the king has authority over things and people under them, so you in the kingdom of God as a son/daughter of the King have authority. When it comes to your body and life, that is a stewardship from God for you, and your body is the temple of the Holy Spirit. Your body and soul (including emotions) are subject to your authority as a child of God. Thus you can speak to your body and emotions, and they must obey. This is the attitude you must take.

When it comes to your body, declare your body well and command it to line up with the Word that says that you are already healed because Jesus carried your sicknesses and diseases away. He carried them so you don't have to. Curse any sickness or disease in your body and bind it up and cast it out in Jesus' name. Command any evil / demonic spirits such as spirits of infirmities and diseases to leave you and be-gone in the name of Jesus. Declare yourself well and whole and see yourself that way. Speak and pray healing scriptures over your body and life. In Appendix B, you will find a sample prayer that you can use as a guideline, and in Appendix C, you will find several healing scriptures.

If you've been struggling with feeling depressed or discouraged or hopeless, speak to those emotions and command them to leave and be replaced by the peace and love and joy of Jesus Christ. Declare that you will not allow yourself to be depressed, but will find your joy in the Lord.

One might say, "Well, it's not that simple." You know what? As long as you have that attitude, it certainly won't be. You have to get to a place where you are sick and tired of being sick and tired – where you are sick of living below the life that Jesus purchased for you to live. You have to get intense about this stuff!

As long as you can tolerate sickness or depression or anxiety or sin or poverty or lack in your life, you WILL! You have to come to a place where you just plain won't tolerate it any more. You must make a clear decision that you will not allow the devil to steal and rob from you any longer and that you WILL experience all that Jesus paid the price for you to have! You must get absolutely serious about this. What you can tolerate, you will experience. It's amazing the things we have just learned to "put up with." If you can live with a rash, you will. If you can live with having acid-reflux, you will. If you can live with being anxious or fearful, you will. If you can live with overeating or being an addict, you will. And on and on this goes. You have authority over your life and what you permit or allow, you will experience.

There's a story in John chapter 5 of a guy that was an invalid who had been at the Pool of Bethesda for 38 years.

> 5 Now a certain man was there who had an infirmity thirty-eight years. 6 When Jesus saw him lying there, and knew that he already had been *in that condition* a long time, He said to him, "Do you want to be made well?" (John 5:5–6 NKJV)

Jesus saw the guy lying there and knew he had been there a long time with his infirmity and he asked him a very pointed question: "Do you want to be made well?" (John 5:6b NKJV). Jesus might ask you and me the same question. We really need to be honest with ourselves and examine ourselves deep-down. Do you really want to be well?

Sometimes people say they want to be well, but there is a part of them on a core level that is deeply afraid of actually being made well. Especially in the case of a person that has had a long-term condition, living without that condition can actually seem scary because it means that everything will change. Strange as it may sound, sometimes people actually become attached to their disease or condition and have made it such a part of their identity that the thought of living without it scares them because it means things will change. Us human beings tend to become comfortable with what we know and the thought of change can terrify us. Perhaps it's the realization that if you're made well, disability payments from the government might stop, or perhaps it's just the general uncertainty of what the future holds / how you will function. Some people also have identified with their condition so much that part of them has actually relished getting sympathy and affection from others because of their condition, and the thought of losing that scares them on a deep-down level.

Fear is powerful and can really hinder people from living the abundant life they were created to live. This is one of those things that we might be deceiving ourselves on – we might be subconsciously in fear and not really realize it. Thus I encourage you to ask God to show you if you have any fear about being made well or living in all that He has for you. If you sense that there's some fear there, I encourage you to really bring that before the Lord and ask Him to help you with that. You're going to have to make a choice to either give in to the fear and stay stuck or let go of the fear and trust that your God will take care of you and help you.

You need to settle in your heart that you are done living below what God has for you. You need to decide that you are willing to do all you need to do to see what Jesus purchased for you become a practical reality in your life.

A big part of living the abundant life is taking your authority and not allowing the devil to put things on you. You do have authority over your life. As a believer in Jesus Christ, the devil only has the authority over you that you give him. And sadly most believers just passively let the devil walk all over them. You have to decide that you are not going to allow that any longer but are instead going to resist him.

When a headache first starts, THAT is the time to say, "NO!! I will not allow this in Jesus' name – headache and pain be gone and any demonic spirits get away now in the mighty name of Jesus Christ!" Fight that battle then! If you don't and permit that headache or just tolerate it, then don't be surprised if it gets worse or you end up with migraines or whatever. I will just tell you that it is MUCH easier to stand in faith at the outset than once you've allowed those things and they've been able to take root in your life. If you are finding yourself starting to think anxious or fearful thoughts, make a choice to resist those thoughts. Open your mouth and in faith say something like: "I refuse you fear and any spirits behind fear and I command you to leave my life now in Jesus' name."

Look, I'm not trying to oversimplify things, but really this is a core issue. This is why the Bible tells us to take all thoughts captive to the obedience of Christ:

"For though we walk in the flesh, we do not war after the flesh: (For the weapons of our warfare are not carnal, but mighty through God to the pulling down of strong holds;) Casting down imaginations, and every high thing that exalteth itself against the knowledge of God, and bringing into captivity every thought to the obedience of Christ;" (2 Corinthians 3–5 KJV).

It doesn't matter what the thing trying to come against you is – if it is contrary to what Jesus has for you, then you need to say "NO! I will not have this in my life!" You need to not allow the devil to give you imaginations or arguments or in any way set up strongholds in your life in ANY area. Not just in the area of sin and temptation, but any area. You know what? Something as "simple" as a headache is contrary to the knowledge of God that God has provided health for you in Jesus. It's something trying to exalt itself in your life and you need to say: "NO! I will not allow this because I am healthy in Jesus because of what He has provided for me and a headache has no place in me, so be gone now!" And when I say you need to say it, I mean you need to say it. Speak it out (obviously where practical – otherwise under your breath or whatever). Your words are powerful and are an establishing force where you are declaring what you believe. It is putting your faith in action for you and God and all the angels and demons to see.

As human beings, we are dramatically affected by words. Words have inherent power within them. You know as well as I do that this is true. If a parent says: "You're stupid and you'll never amount to anything" to a child, you know as well as I do that will negatively affect that child. But if a parent says: "You're really smart and I know you're gonna do great things" that can affect the child positively. Or that if someone says something kind to you that can easily help make your day, but if they say something hurtful, it can potentially ruin your day (not that you have to let it do so because you shouldn't, but you get the point).

Words have power and they are either bringing life or they are bringing death. According to Proverbs, "Death and life are in the power of the tongue: and they that love it shall eat the fruit thereof."

(Proverbs 18:21 KJV). The tongue can be used to bring the fruit of death or the fruit of life. What you speak will be the fruit that you yourself eat.

You need to speak positively and use your words to speak faith based on the promises of God. And ideally, as mentioned, you really want to do this at the outset when the devil first tries to put something on you. If you start sensing cold-like symptoms in your body and you start going around telling people "I think I'm coming down with a cold", don't be surprised when you end up in a full-blown sickness because by saying things like that, it basically gave your approval and consent. A much better way to use your words in a situation like that would be something like: "I am healthy in Jesus and I refuse to have a cold! Sickness leave me now in the mighty name of Jesus!" I have personally experienced several times where by taking the latter approach instead of the former, symptoms that in previous years would have become a full-blown sickness event for me either immediately left or were on a much milder scale.

Currently as I am writing this, the world is in chaos because of COVID-19, a new flu bug and people have been in a lot of fear and anxiety regarding it. Every so often these major things come up, but even outside of that, there's always sickness and disease going around and what we might call the the "regular" flu alone kills many people worldwide every year. As a believer in Jesus, with His provision and His promises, fear has NO place in our life. We are not supposed to cower in fear because of some bug, no matter how terrifying the world and the news wants to tell us it is. Rather we take our authority and declare that bug cannot have any place in our life and we absolutely refuse its presence. We declare that we are healthy in Jesus and we don't allow ourselves to expect to get sick. I'm not saying we shouldn't do practical things too (e.g. washing our hands) and use our God-given wisdom, but we aren't to live in a state of fear, but rather faith in Jesus and what is ours in Him. We use the choice God has given us to choose to align ourselves in faith with His truth, instead of embracing sickness (even subtly) through fear and unbelief.

While it is ideal to deal with things ahead of time or when they first start creeping up, even if it's something you've already been dealing with in your life for a long time, the principle still stands. If you say things like: "I don't think I'll ever be healed" or you go around telling everyone how sick you are and recounting your list of symptoms to people, you are speaking fruit that you are going to eat, and that fruit's not going to help you. If you've been having a problem with your eyes for the last 10 years, don't keep telling people about your terrible eye problem. Remember, faith sees the answer as already done even while you may not actually be seeing it yet. So if someone asks you how your eyes are doing, don't just say: "Terrible! I don't think they'll ever get better." Instead, you can say, "Well, I've been still having some problems, but praise God, I believe they are healed and God's working that out!" See the difference? You aren't denying the problem symptom, but you are declaring the greater truth that you are healed.

You have authority over your life. What you allow will be allowed. If you speak negatively over yourself regarding sickness and disease, that can affect you and either open the door for more sickness or keep you from seeing your healing, even if part of you is trying to believe God for healing. Instead, you should speak words that are positive and helpful. Speak the healing scriptures. Declare yourself well in Jesus' name.

If you've had a problem with drinking alcohol excessively, for goodness sakes stop identifying yourself as an alcoholic and telling people that you are an alcoholic! (despite what some "12 Steps" program might say...) You are NOT an alcoholic in Jesus; speak forth your true identity in Jesus and see yourself living free of abusing alcohol in Jesus because of the freedom over it that He won for you! If you keep telling people that you are an alcoholic, don't be surprised if that continues to be a major problem or battle in your life. Rather, use your words to declare your freedom in Jesus and how no alcohol or anything else has any power over you because Jesus has made the way for you to live a life of self-control.

You have to see yourself well and living the life God has for you and speak in accordance with that. If you continually say that you are sick or an over-eater or a smoker or a sex addict or full of lack and that's what you speak because that is how you see yourself, you in essence are continually cursing yourself because you are not seeing yourself as God sees you but rather are affirming those things in your life. You are not speaking through the lens of faith in accordance with what the Word says is yours, but instead are merely focusing on fleshly symptoms. You need to look past those things and declare the greater reality of what is ALREADY yours, whether you have really been experiencing what you are wanting or not. You need to get your eyes off the symptoms and on the truth.

Do you see yourself as sick trying to get well, or do you see yourself as already well resisting sickness? Do you see yourself as a rotten sinner trying to get free, or do you see yourself as already free in Jesus resisting temptation? How you see yourself matters a lot. You might recall that we talked before that this is a key principle of faith. You must see yourself in line with what the Word of God says is yours, whether you actually are seeing it yet in your body or life or not. You have to exalt the Word of God OVER your fleshly experiences. It's a greater reality. As you do that and continually speak in line with what the Word says is yours and use your words to speak faith (and not doubt), you will be in a place where your fleshly circumstances must submit to the truth of who you are and what is yours already because of Jesus.

These aren't just psychological mind games you are playing either. When you line your thinking up and speak in accordance with the Word in faith, you are actually putting yourself in sync with the true reality of who you really are in Jesus. In that place, every part of your being must line up to this reality.

As mentioned earlier, when you have thoughts that are contrary to Jesus' best for you, you need to take those captive and not allow them to take root in your life. However, it's not enough for us to just resist those things by resisting the devil; we also need to embrace the truth and look to God. We are told, "Submit yourselves therefore to God. Resist the devil, and he will flee from you. Draw nigh to God, and he will draw nigh to you." (James 4:7–8a KJV). This principle applies to any struggle we may have. If you've had an issue with anxiety and a fearful thought comes, it's not enough to just tell the fearful thought to go, but at the same time you need to submit yourself to God and draw near (nigh) to Him. You need to actively embrace the truth of who you are in Him – that He is your

Daddy and loves you and you can trust Him and have no need to be afraid. Use your mouth to speak positive, faith-filled words (and perhaps some Bible verses you've memorized on the subject) instead of speaking forth fear-laced words that will cause you to spiral down the anxiety hole.

In addition to your own words, you also need to watch words that are spoken over you. For instance, many times when someone is sick tells someone else that they are sick, those well-meaning people will say things that are not helpful because they are used to speaking and thinking negatively.

As a part of health issues I was having, I experienced significant unexplained weight-loss. I eventually reached a place where I was really believing God and standing in faith that the weight loss would stop. Then I got a phone call from a friend and they asked me if I had continued losing weight. I answered honestly and said, "yes." This person then immediately said to me, "Pretty soon you'll just be a skeleton and we won't be able to find you." Now the person cared about me and meant well, but that was a terrible thing to say. Had I let those words into my heart, they could have really affected me and brought me down (spiritually, emotionally, and physically). If I had latched onto that and expected to become a skeleton, rather than expecting the weight loss to stop in the name of Jesus, I might not be here today.

I immediately told that person (in a friendly tone) that I was believing God was working and that I would be fine. As soon as I got off the phone, I specifically and vocally rejected those words spoken over me and made sure that I was not letting any part of those words take root in me. You may have to do similar. Guard your heart from negative words spoken to you and over you by others. People mean well and don't realize what they are doing, but words can hurt you if you are not careful.

In contrast, however, something that can be very helpful is having brothers or sisters that will stand with you in faith and will speak blessings (and not curses) over you. If you are unwell in any area of your life, something very practical that you can do is to go to other brothers and sisters that will stand with you in faith to pray for you and with you. If desired, you can go to your church elders (or whatever leaders/pastors you can find that will pray in faith) and ask them to anoint you with oil and pray the prayer of faith over you per James 5. Then believe that what it says is true that you will be well. You could go to a person that has the gift of healing and ask them to pray for you. When you are prayed for in faith, exercise your faith together with them and declare that you are well – that it is done – and don't change your confession!

When you partake of the Lord's Supper, believe that Christ's body which was broken for you, was broken for you to be well and whole and that Jesus paid the price for sickness and disease in His body so you don't have to. Believe that as you eat the bread and drink the cup that the bread and wine, as being/representing the body and blood of Jesus, are literally bringing health and life to your body and soul and meeting your specific needs and declare that in faith.

We have talked a lot specifically about health in this book, but there is an element that we haven't really touched on yet that we need to: that of doctors and medicine. I have not really mentioned them thus far because they have no bearing whatsoever on the truths of God's Word and that is where I wanted to put the focus. However, this is obviously a subject worth discussing in figuring out how to practically live the abundant life.

God does NOT need doctors or medicine to enforce healing in your body. Doctors and medicine, however, can be used by God. Doctors and medicine are "natural means", but God has gifted some people in those areas and a lot of medicine is at least somewhat based on substances and sources that God has created on this planet. God can take the "natural means" and make them "supernatural" for you. I want to say very clearly that I am not opposed to doctors or medicine! However, there can be a terrible trap here.

Most of us have been conditioned to just trust doctors and their medicine and look to them to "heal us." A pill is not your healing agent. God is your healing agent. A doctor is not your healer. God is your Healer. Do not put your faith in any doctor or pill. Doctors are not God – they are fallen, fallible human beings just like you and me and they make mistakes all the time. There's a reason why it's said that they "practice medicine." They're just "practicing" – they do the best they know to do, but there's a whole lot medically that doctors understand little to nothing about and for many conditions can't offer much hope beyond just trying to treat some symptoms. Don't put your faith in doctors for your healing. Put your faith in God. The Bible says, "It is better to trust in the LORD than to put confidence in man." (Psalm 118:8 KJV). It also says "that your faith should not be in the wisdom of men but in the power of God." (1 Corinthians 2:5 NKJV).

Doctors love to prescribe drugs. And if you have a side-effect, they'll likely prescribe another drug to combat that side-effect. Then when that drug produces a side-effect, they give you another one, or keep switching them up, or whatever. It can truly be a vicious cycle. I am reminded of the woman with the issue of blood in Mark 5 where it says of her in vs 25–26: "And there was a woman who had had a discharge of blood for twelve years, and who had suffered much under many physicians, and had spent all that she had, and was no better but rather grew worse." (Mk 5:25–26 ESV). Notice she suffered much under doctors and spent all her money on them trying to get well, but just got worse and worse. Sounds like she was in a downward spiral to me. But what did she do? She apparently came to her senses and she stopped putting her faith in all these doctors and their "cures", and instead put her faith in the only One who really could make her well. She became determined in her faith, she spoke in accordance with her faith, took action in accordance with her faith, and Jesus stated that it was her faith that made her whole.

So often we run to the doctors and their supposed "wisdom" without exercising faith in the healing that is available to us as a child of God. I'm not saying this to condemn – I've done the same thing. Nor am I saying that doctors don't have their place. I absolutely believe God can work through doctors. But I also believe that the devil can too. The overarching question is one of where we're going to put our faith.

Doctors can possibly be a help to you even if you aren't trusting God because they do have some understanding on certain things and a medicine can help simply because it makes changes in your body that help you. As mentioned, they can also possibly be a harm to you or deal with some symptom issues without solving the root problem. But if you do go the doctor/medication route, as a Christian, how much more effective things can be when you get your faith in the mix and believe God to work through them! God is ultimately where you need to see your help as coming from, not doctors or medicine.

Whether you should go to a doctor or take a medicine I think is a personal decision between you and God and not one that anybody should condemn. One consideration in deciding what to do can include your level of faith. In other words, you need to be realistic about where you are at. Particularly if you aren't fully sure you can stand on the Word alone or you feel doubts or unbelief in you that is hindering your faith, then that might be something to consider in deciding to see a doctor. You should still go to the doctor in faith though. In this case, you believe that God will use the doctor to help you and then trust that as you see the doctor and take any medicine that God is using that for you.

You need to be honest with yourself about where you are at. It can be harder to stand in a situation when the symptoms are blaring you in the face. I saw an incredible, well-documented testimony of this guy that had a tumor growing on the outside of his chest and it got so large he literally had to use a bra to hold it. It was a nasty affair and they showed numerous pictures of it. But the guy had been in a church that taught on faith and that believed in healing, and against the advice of the doctors, he chose to not have surgery to remove the tumor. He instead decided to trust that God would take care of it. This whole thing went on for several years. Not months. Years. That's years where he woke up every morning staring at this giant, nasty mass on his chest.

Eventually he got a much clearer revelation on how he was already healed in Jesus and he stood in faith on that fact. And you know what? The tumor did eventually die and get smaller and smaller until it was gone.

As I was watching the testimony several years back, I had a few thoughts and one of them is that I knew that for where I was at that I wouldn't have been able to stand in faith like that; I probably would have been in a lot of fear and wavering all over the place.

The other thought I had is that maybe the guy should have trusted God in removing the tumor through the doctor. He might have been able to shave off some time. On the other hand, maybe this guy was truly following the leading/peace of the Lord and doing exactly what he sensed God had for him to do and that if he had done it another way, the result might not have been the same. I don't know. And that's my point. We need to be honest with ourselves about where we are at and recognize that God knows where we are at too. Ultimately we need to be seeking and listening to God for ourselves and doing what we feel He would have us do. If you sense you should go to a doctor or pop a pill, do it in faith and trust God with it. If you sense you should not take a medicine or go to a doctor, do it in faith and trust God with it.

Specifically in regards to medicine, I encourage you to be very prayerful before just stopping a medicine. I am not encouraging anyone to just stop their medication. I also am not saying you shouldn't. I'm saying you should seek God. On a practical note, many medications (especially ones you've been on long term) in the natural could be harmful to stop cold-turkey and are best to instead wean off of. That's in the natural of course, but it's something to strongly consider if you do decide to stop using a medication – you should give consideration in working with your doctor to wean off of it if that's your decision (of course, the doctor may try to convince you otherwise, so you need to know exactly what you are going to do). Do not stop taking a medication unless you are completely confident that you don't need it and can stand on the healing truths in the Word! If you have to ask me or a pastor or someone whether you should stop your medicine, then I can tell you right now that you should not. If you have to ask the question, you shouldn't stop it. But if you get the inward knowing in your heart where you just know that you know that your healing is done and you don't need the medicine, then that's something for you to consider with the Lord about whether to put your faith into action by stopping your medicine.

While talking about doctors and medicine, I also have to address a related area, which tends to be common among some Christians: natural or "alternative" medicine. Some people in realizing that doctors are fallible and often seem to be pushing drugs with lots of side effects to just try to treat symptoms, instead choose to embrace natural medicine. Natural medicine emphasizes a more holistic approach to your body and health and utilizes more natural substances, such as flowers and plants that God has given us to be a help to our bodies. I don't think there's anything wrong with seeing such doctors or taking such natural products. However, for the Christian, the same trap exists with them as exists for more conventional doctors and medicine, and perhaps even more so. Many people do not realize that natural medicine is actually the opposite side of the same coin. What happens is that people run to natural medicine to be their answer instead of conventional medicine. They look to a natural medicine doctor to be their healer or natural products to be their answer, instead of looking to God as their Healer and His Word as their answer. Just as our faith shouldn't be in a medication or a surgery or a conventional doctor, it shouldn't be in a natural medicine doctor or a natural product. Our faith is to be rooted in Jesus and what He's provided for us, not pills (natural or otherwise) or doctors (natural or otherwise). Again that doesn't mean we can't see such doctors or use such products – there are certainly natural products that could be helpful for you. Whether you see a doctor or use a product is a decision between you and God, but we do need to guard ourselves to not be looking to them as our Savior. You have one Savior, and His name is Jesus. And healing is one of your Savior's saving works.

Regardless of whether you see a doctor or not, the bottom-line is we want to be in a place of faith. This also affects our dietary choices. It is very common right now for people to avoid certain foods because they might be "bad" for them. Gluten, dairy, meat, sugar – all sorts of things are put on the "bad list" by well-meaning people, telling us of all the things we shouldn't be eating. There's even people that say we should only be eating raw food and so forth. I'm just going to say this: That's all based in fear, not faith. In the Bible, I see a lot of talk of people eating bread (that's gluten), milk (that's dairy), honey (that's sugar), and meat. The Israelites went to the land of "milk and honey" and not "almond milk and tofu." I'm just saying. Some argue that because of the way we produce our food today (such as being genetically modified and tainted from antibiotics), that our food's not the same now. That's probably true and it may complicate things. However, there still is the faith principle here.

> 1 Now the Spirit expressly says that in later times some will depart from the faith by devoting themselves to deceitful spirits and teachings of demons, 2 through the insincerity of liars whose consciences are seared, 3 who forbid marriage and require abstinence from foods that God created to be received with thanksgiving by those who believe and know the truth. 4 For everything created by God is good, and nothing is to be rejected if it is received with thanksgiving, 5 for it is made holy by the word of God and prayer. (1 Timothy 4:1–5 ESV)

You know what? You can pray over your food and trust God in faith that it will be life and health to your body, and even if it otherwise might not be, through faith it can be made so. That's awesome!

I do acknowledge that because humanity has been mucking around with the natural production of food and genetically modifying things that that can perhaps create issues. I also believe that faith is a stronger force than any of that. With that said, I concede that it can be a process to build our faith up and get rid of unbelief and God might have us avoid things in the process based on where we are at. I also acknowledge that there are certain things that wisdom would just say to avoid. So I'm not really trying to get on anyone's case here as much as to make the point that we need to not be led by fear when it comes to dietary choices, but to live (and eat) from a position of faith.

Sometimes operating in faith means doing things contrary to what our natural mind tells us we should do. There's an interesting story in John 9 about a blind guy where we see Jesus do something quite intriguing:

6 When He had said these things, He spat on the ground and made clay with the saliva; and He anointed the eyes of the blind man with the clay. 7 And He said to him, "Go, wash in the pool of Siloam" (which is translated, Sent). So he went and washed, and came back seeing. (John 9:6–7 NKJV)

Jesus spat on the ground to make mud and rubbed that mud in the man's eyes! Talk about an unusual method! Jesus then told the guy to go wash in the pool of Siloam. One could wonder all day long why Jesus did the whole spit/mud thing, but I do know this: Like many of the things Jesus did, He pushed the guy into making a faith decision. Here Jesus had just spat and made mud and put it on his eyes and then told him to go do something – to go to a specific pool and wash. Now, the man could have said: "Eww!! This is gross & crazy! Who do you think you are that you think mud on my eyes is going to heal me? Forget you!" And then he could have just rubbed it off – and he would have still been blind. But he didn't do that. He made a decision to take Jesus at His word and put His faith in Jesus, even if it seemed unusual or weird to him, and when He obeyed Jesus and did what Jesus told Him, that is when his healing occurred. Verse 7 tells us that he came back seeing after he did what Jesus told him. There's a lesson in this. Sometimes what Jesus asks of us seems unusual or weird and doesn't make any sense to our brain (or, I might add, to those around us), but as we put our faith into practice by trusting Him and doing what He says, we find our answer. Following Jesus in lots of areas sometimes involves putting aside or ignoring what our natural mind is telling us is best/right and to instead choose the "faith route" in trusting God and His Word even while our natural mind is screaming at us. Like the majority of other individual healing cases recorded for us, this man's own faith is shown to have played a part in his healing.

Sometimes standing in faith means doing things that seem contrary to our brain. Faith ultimately is about trusting God regardless of our symptoms/circumstances/feelings. It is choosing to put all your chips on God even when things don't seem good in the natural.

Sometimes you have to take a faith step that seems completely counter to your brain or human logic or other people.

Part of my story involves having had really bad allergic / immune system reactions to various environmental stimuli where my body would literally seize up in my chest and throat. A bad attack would make it feel like I couldn't breathe (even though I could) but make me feel like I was steps from death – it literally would make it feel like my heart might give out. The doctors never did figure any of that out with me. It had gotten so bad that literally all sorts of foreign environments could set me off: a movie theater or other businesses, churches, hotels/motels, and people's houses. Along my healing journey, at various points I have had to take faith actions that seemed absolutely ridiculous to be doing.

I took a trip to visit my sister out-of-state and taking that trip was a major faith battle for me because among other things it meant dealing with hotels and also my sister's house. I chose to stand in faith and believe God for the trip and I made a decision that no matter what, I was going to believe God and stand on His Word. I had made a decision that I couldn't live life in fear and I had to be able to live my life here and go places and do things – that if I couldn't do that, then I might as well just go "home" to Jesus because that's no way to live. Much of the way on the long drive up there, I listened to teaching on healing to help build up my faith and cast out doubt and unbelief. And I'll be honest with you, I had plenty of doubt and unbelief swirling around.

Well, I got to my sister's and on my first night in the bedroom, I had a bad attack. It absolutely felt like I was dying. Everything in my body and my brain screamed at me that I needed to get out of there. But I had already determined that I was going to make my stand on God's Word, come what may. In the natural, I figured one of two things was going to happen: Either I was going to go see Jesus or the Word would be proven true as I was believing and declaring it was. I declared healing scriptures over me like Psalm 118:7 that says "I shall not die, but live, and declare the works of the LORD." (KJV). I did a lot of praying, a lot of declaring Scripture, and a lot of speaking to my body. I specifically identified myself with Jesus' death and His resurrection – identifying with

Him in His position of authority in the Heavenlies and the life that I now have in Him, and applying and releasing that life to my physical body.

I remember at 3:00 in the morning lying there with all these bad symptoms and fear trying to have a field-day with me and I remember thinking: "This is where the rubber meets the road." See, it's nice to talk about faith in theoretical terms. But this is the kind of situation where when you have to make a choice to go by what you see and feel or go by faith and the potential risk is that you die, that's where your faith really gets tested, I assure you. I remember thinking that if I did by some chance fall asleep, that I might not wake up.

I cried out to God telling Him that I did everything I knew to do and was choosing to fully bank on Him and His Word. I remember telling Him something like: "God, I'm trusting solely in Your Word and the healing that you've provided for me and I'm believing that I am well in you. I'm doing everything I know to do. Now, I need you to work it out in my body." I ended up just reaching a place of peace where in choosing to rest in Jesus and His Word, I entrusted myself to His care. I put myself in His hands and that's where I made my stand to rest. I actually fell asleep, which was a miracle in itself because my body was absolutely on "overload."

Long story short, I obviously did wake up some hours later. I was still reeling from the effects of the attack throughout the following day, but from then on out, I was much better. Once I got past that first night, I did much better. I had "gone through" a faith test of sorts.

The truth is that night wasn't the first time I've had to do that. I've actually had several times that I've had similar experiences. I went to serve as a counselor at a camp for hurting kids and I really felt called to be there. But I had a bad attack the first night before the kids arrived and everything in me was screaming that I couldn't do the camp and needed to leave. I knew that once the kids arrived and I bonded with the kids under my charge that it would be terrible for them if I had to leave and it would also make things logistically hard on everyone else. So, if I was going to leave, the time to do it was then. I prayed about it and felt like I was supposed to stay and I made the decision to stand in faith and just commit it to God. Well, the long story short is that God took care of it, and I ended up having a great week where I felt like God really used me powerfully. Had I backed out because of fear, I would never have been used to help those kids.

The reason I bring these personal experiences up is because faith isn't just a nice "Christianny" word or a light concept. Sometimes acting in faith means doing things that are completely contrary to our natural senses.

I'm reminded of the story in the Old Testament book of 2 Kings where a large Syrian army came and surrounded Elijah the prophet:

> 15 When the servant of the man of God rose early in the morning and went out, behold, an army with horses and chariots was all around the city. And the servant said, "Alas, my master! What shall we do?" 16 He said, "Do not be afraid, for those who are with us are more than those who are with them." 17 Then Elisha prayed and said, "O LORD, please open his eyes that he may see." So the LORD opened the eyes of the young man, and he saw, and behold, the mountain was full of horses and chariots of fire all around Elisha. (2 Kings 6:15–17 ESV)

There was a huge Syrian army all around the city and Elisha's servant saw that and was terrified! But Elisha wasn't just looking at the natural circumstances. He saw beyond that by faith. He acknowledged the Syrian army, but he also saw the LORD's Army by faith. And out of that place, he asked the LORD to open his servant's eyes so that the servant also would see what he already saw through faith. If he hadn't been in faith, he might have been in fear just like his servant and he might have gone and run away. But he didn't do that. He didn't let the natural circumstances alone dictate his course of action because he realized there was more to the story than just what his natural senses were telling him.

There are times where you just need to "go for it" in faith and stand on the Word of God despite what the natural data around you says. When it comes to living the abundant life, I can guarantee you that you will face some "faith tests" at some point. Often times what happens is a person receives their healing or answer but then natural symptoms/circumstances try to come back on them and fear can start to rise up and they can be tempted to think things like: "Well, I guess it didn't really work." In moments like these, which I call "flashpoint moments", a decision has to be made: stand on the Word and trust God in faith and declare that those symptoms/circumstances must leave in Jesus' name, or give in to the fear. If a person gives in to the fear, the symptoms/circumstances can get amplified and next thing you know, the person is right back where they started.

Now while there are times where you need to stand in faith regardless of the circumstances, I do have to caution you that you really need to be led of the Lord in this. You also need to know deep down that you can stand before attempting to do so. Things can get "tricky" if you really aren't in a place to stand and you've got major circumstances come against you and you give in to the fear. You need to be honest with yourself and with God regarding where you are at in your faith, what you are believing, and any doubts you may have. If you don't feel like you're in a place to take a major stand, then don't beat yourself up for that. Just keep marinating in what the Bible teaches regarding these things until that changes. Perhaps consider going through this book again as there's a lot packed in it that might take a few reads to fully grasp. The resources in Appendix D of this book can also be very helpful. Keep growing and learning.

The number one most important thing I could say for you to do is to spend time talking with God and listening to Him. Be honest with Him and then let Him speak to you about what you are to do. Listen for His voice and follow Him. He wants you well too and as you genuinely ask, seek, and knock, He will reveal things to you and show you your next steps.

Don't beat yourself up for where you aren't at, and don't make decisions out of your flesh either. Don't let other people pressure you to take faith steps you aren't ready to take! But at the same time, you do need to be aware that faith does act and ultimately you need to put your faith into practice. Before David defeated Goliath, he first defeated lions and bears (1 Samuel 17:36). Wherever you are at at this moment, just go forward. Start taking the steps that you can take today. Believe God and stand on the promises of His Word!

Conclusion

It is my sincere hope and prayer that this book has helped you to realize all that Jesus died to give you; that the abundant life is real and is available for you to walk in every day through Jesus. I hope that this book has moved you to a deeper level of faith and trust in Jesus and putting that faith into practice in your life to live more of the abundant life.

If you thought you were going to pick this book up and read it and it was going to be your magic answer to make everything instantly right in your life, I'm sorry to disappoint but that's just not reality. The practical living out of the abundant life that Jesus has for us is a process as we learn and grow and exercise our faith.

The point of this book hasn't been for you to read it and then instantly have a perfect life here. The goal has been to help remove some major roadblocks and pave the road so that as you follow Jesus and put your faith into practice, you can experience more of the abundant life Jesus has for you in your day-to-day life.

The truth is that there is so much more that could be written about this subject. Each one of the chapters in this book in itself could be a whole other book. Yet, I believe God has a purpose for melding all these concepts together into a simplified and practically digestible form.

There is something really important I still have to say regarding this book. It presents important truths and I absolutely believe what I have written, but the actual implementation of those truths in our lives is sometimes kind of a messy affair. Sometimes things are not quite as simple as they might come across on a written page.

This book was in-process for a long time. I started writing it in October of 2014. At the time, I was dealing with significant health challenges. These were a continuation of issues I had been dealing with for years. I had originally gotten ahold of some of the truths in this book regarding health in 2011 and by putting my faith into practice, I did see tremendous turn-around. Yet there were a lot of things I did not understand as well, so it was a part-way implementation. Eventually I let unbelief and doubt and fear cloud out some of what I knew, and in mid-2013 I had a relapse that continued for several years. When that relapse occurred, it caused me to have to go much deeper and face things I needed to face.

Much of this book actually was written in the midst of this. There were some days I would be writing about health and wholeness and be in terrible physical pain. I remember one time I actually had a cold/flu type thing going on, and yet there I was typing away about how God wants us well while feeling like I had just been run over by a steamroller.

That probably will come across as hypocritical to some. And guess what? I sometimes felt that way too. I assure you I had thoughts like: "What business do I have telling people about health or wholeness if I myself am not fully walking in it?" In my own life, I had to ask myself hard questions like: "Why am I not seeing the results that I am praying for and say I'm believing for and am writing about?" "Why am I able to pray for someone else and they see a result, but yet I am not?"

Part of the reason this book took me so long to finish is that I kept going through periods where I just plain got discouraged. I'm being straight-up honest with you.

Here's the thing though: Just because I didn't always understand what was going on in my own life or even when looking at other people's situations, doesn't mean God's Word is any less true. I don't always understand why for instance it appears that some people pray in faith and see an instantaneous result on one thing and then on the next thing, it takes a long time for them to see it. I don't necessarily understand why some people don't seem to see the result of what they are believing God for at all, but yet they pray for someone else and that person does see a result. There are all sorts of things in this arena that we might be able to make some good guesses at as to why things are the way they are, but we might not fully understand. That doesn't mean there aren't reasons though, only that we might not see them or have all of the data. A lot of times we don't even see all the variables in play.

But at the end of the day, I do know this: The Word is true and what it says is ours, is ours. We have to be at a place where whether something seems to be working or not, or seems to be taking a long time or not, does not sway us from this fact. We need to keep our posture of faith. We can't let what we see or don't see move us from our position of faith in Jesus and His sacrifice for us that provided the abundant life for us.

I kept coming back to writing this book because what is in this book is truth based on the Word of God and that truth is truth whether I was at a place of fully seeing it in my own life or not.

You know what I did when it seemed like things weren't fully working for me? I just kept trying to learn and grow and continue soaking in the Word and putting my faith into action as best I could. And that is still what I am doing. I need this book myself! I do not consider myself the poster child for someone that's lived an abundant life. Again, I suppose that could seem hypocritical to some.

But here's the thing friends: this life is all a process and a journey, and I am definitely still in process and on that journey too. While I'm certainly further along then I used to be, if someone is looking at my life to 100% prove out what I've written, the focus is in the wrong place. I have to appropriate this abundant life that's been provided for me in Jesus the same as you do and I have made my share of mistakes and do not even remotely claim to have it down perfect. We are all learning and growing and at different stages and with different levels of knowledge and practical application of that knowledge; we are all in process. But the truth of God's Word is the truth whether we are fully experiencing it or not. It does not change and it does not need our experiences to validate it. If God's Word is not fully working in our life, the problem is not with the Word or with God and we just plain have to come to a place of settling that issue. I am not saying that to condemn; it's just the truth.

Don't assume that God is mad at you because things maybe haven't worked as you thought they would or should or in the timetable you expected. God is for you and He wants you well and living a full life more than you do. Keep looking to Him, keep standing on the facts of what is yours in Jesus, and keep declaring it forth.

God does not lie and the Word will be proven true. Don't lose heart. We are to "imitate those who through faith and patience inherit the promises." (Hebrews 6:12b NKJV). It is through both faith *and* patience. Don't give up! Keep pressing forward!

Friend, your God loves you and is for you and on your side. He's not some distant puppet-master up there just controlling your life, but He wants to be in a close relationship with you, working with you to see all the benefits that He has provided for you practically come to pass in your life. Look to Him, take hold of the truth of who you are in Jesus and what is yours because of that position, and receive the full abundant life that's yours.

Receive now, in Jesus' name!

A Request

Did you find this book to be helpful, insightful, and encouraging? If not, please accept my sincere apology as that was my desire. But if so, would you please consider sharing this book with those around you that you know so they can be blessed also? In addition to purchasing a copy for your friends and family, would you please consider sending one to your pastor as well?

There's millions of different books out there, and even a bunch of ones talking about how you can live or have a great life, but if you, like me, believe that the truths contained in these pages need to get out there in a greater degree, I humbly ask that you help and join with me in that process.

My heart is to help equip the Body of Christ to experience the fullness of life Jesus died to provide for us. And one of my admittedly really big goals is to see this book in the hands of every Christian pastor in the world, regardless of denomination. In order to hopefully accomplish that and also just fulfill the calling God has on my life, I am humbly asking you to pray about partnering with me and supporting my ministry efforts by purchasing books and donating finances. By partnering with me, you are helping to get this message out across the entire Body of Christ which I believe will then help elevate the practical daily-life experience of believers, which leads to us being a better witness, which I believe helps pave the way for many more unbelievers to come to a saving faith in Jesus. And big picture, that's really the main goal.

Please visit BodEquip Ministries on the Internet at www.bodequip.org At this site, in addition to an ability to purchase books or donate, you will find a bunch of free articles and encouraging songs that I hope will prove a blessing to you!

Thank you! Blessings and love to you in Jesus! :)
Chris

Appendix A – God's Answer for a Broken World

We all deep-down have questions about life such as:

Why am I here on this planet?
What is the purpose to us being here?
Why is there such evil and pain in the world?
What happens when we die?

Different people seek to answer those questions in different ways.

God has answers to each of those questions for us, but the problem is that so many people out there (including unfortunately some spiritual leaders) have misrepresented God to such a degree that it makes people untrusting of God and the Bible.

There is a God. He loves you. He is NOT mad at you. And He wants you to live a full and abundant life doing things that He has planned for you to do, and for you to be with Him forever. This is the message of the Bible, but that message has gotten perverted by some to instead make God all about a list of rules, and that if you step outside of His rules, He will pour out His wrath on you. Even if you think you've heard some of what the Bible has to say before, would you give me a few minutes to address this?

In the first book of the Bible (Genesis), we discover that there is a God and that He created the world. The first line is "In the beginning God created the heaven and the earth." (Genesis 1:1 KJV). This first sentence alone forces people to make a choice; it divides all of humanity into 2 camps: those who are willing to believe that there is a Being greater than them that created this world and those that are not.

People that believe what the Bible says, believe that there is a loving God that made this universe with perfect design and order. They look at the world with all of its intricacies and detail and order and realize that a being greater than them MUST have been involved. They realize that all of creation, even their own bodies –

down to the lines on their hands – testify of a being greater than them. They realize that all of the animals doing what they do, the plants doing what they do – all of creation – screams out "There is a God!" They look at the order and design of things (just think of a spider's web or a snowflake for instance!) and realize something had to order all of that.

People that do not believe what the Bible says are forced to explain things outside of God and try to come up with their own "theories" on how an ordered universe could come out of nothingness or disorder. Even though everything in our world showcases things going from order –> disorder (a result of sin which we'll get to in a moment), they are forced to explain that instead disorder –> order. Thus they come up with thoughts such as a "big bang" where out of nothing something appeared after millions and millions of years and then over more millions grew and "evolved" and developed legs and over more millions of years, eyes, and so forth – eventually evolving to the point of humans.

Honestly it takes MUCH more faith in my opinion to believe that everything came from nothing with no Designer behind it, then to believe in simplicity the Bible's first verse (Genesis 1:1) that there is a Being greater than me that made everything with purpose and design. And, actually, in a sense the Bible does support a notion of a "big bang" – that God SPOKE, and then BANG – It Was! But that's different from the theories floating around out there (which are often times taught like they are fact in the schools) that completely leave God out of the picture. Either there's a God and He was involved in creation, or not. We all have to choose. If the Bible really is truth and is a book from God to humanity and we're willing to believe what it says in its first sentence, then we need to take the rest of it just as seriously.

Continuing on in the Biblical account, we discover that originally the earth was created and humans were made to live in perfect fellowship with God. We discover that everything God created was declared to be "very good", including those first two humans. But God gave those two humans "choice" so they could choose to love and obey God or not. Had God not done this, we would be nothing more than mindless robots – but God wanted us to freely choose

Him and want Him. God put the humans over all the creation and allowed them to freely eat of anything, except one tree that He told them they would die from if they ate of it (Genesis 2:16–17). That tree had to be there for there to truly be a choice. The choice was even more real because the devil (an evil fallen angel) was allowed to tempt them. Those first humans chose to disobey God and instead listen to the lies of the devil, who convinced Eve (the first woman) that God had lied to them and was withholding good from them.

In doing this, they basically chose to disobey God and reject Him. This was sin and their disobedience brought sin into this world. The previously unbroken fellowship between God and mankind changed. A gap now existed between a holy, righteous God and sinful humans who rejected God and His ways. The result of that was that death entered the world. Shortly thereafter we read of the first recorded death where one of Adam & Eve's (the first two humans) sons kills their other son (Genesis 4:8). The horribleness of death and of pain became realized in a very tangible way.

God could have just ignored Adam & Eve's sin or just started over, but then our choices would be of no importance and thus we could not have any choice in whether we loved God and wanted to be with Him. God could also have just punished us forever with no hope. And yet, God's heart was to restore the broken fellowship. He wanted us to be with him forever.

Because God who is holy and pure also is a just and fair God, there had to be an act to satisfy God's justice. And yet, we could not satisfy it. God spent a long time from the time of those first humans until the time of Jesus, showing us that we as humans would never be good enough and could never do enough to cover our sins. We couldn't even keep 10 simple commandments from Him! Much of the Old Testament of the Bible showcases this very clearly and shows us our inability to save ourselves and proves to us that we NEED a Savior.

God loves each person on this planet. So, in His love, He Himself satisfied His justice by sacrificing Himself on our behalf. Jesus, who is referred to as "God's Son", but is also one of the 3 parts that makes up who God is (yes, there is a mystery in this), caused Himself to enter our world to fulfill His divinely orchestrated plan to save us.

Jesus, who lived a perfect, sinless life on this earth, was put to death by sinful humans on a cross. He then rose from the dead. Jesus Himself, speaking of His life, said "No one takes it from me, but I lay it down of my own accord. I have authority to lay it down, and I have authority to take it up again." (John 10:18a ESV). Jesus proved He was God by rising from the dead, because only the One who made the universe and had total authority over life and death itself could do it! He showed Himself to many after He was raised and history records that many of those people eventually ended up being put to death themselves for their faith and unwavering assertion of what had transpired.

It could not have been us dying on the cross because even if my death could satisfy God's justice, at best it could only satisfy His justice in regards to me because as a sinful human, I certainly could not atone for everyone else's sin. Only God Himself, perfect in every way, could atone for all mankind. Jesus, God's Son, came and paid the penalty for not just our own personal sins here and now, but for the sins of humanity – going back to that first sin in the Garden. In other words, Jesus paid for all sin, for all time.

Now just because Jesus did this, it doesn't mean that every person accepts this gift and makes it applicable to them. We may not have had a say as to whether we were born into this sinful world, but we do still get to make a choice. God never took back the gift of choice He gave humanity. Just as Adam & Eve had a choice to look to God and believe Him or not, we still get to make that same choice. We still get to choose whether we will look to God and believe Him or not. Jesus' sacrifice for humanity was a global human act and yet, it is very personal in application. If we do not WANT Jesus to pay for our sin, God will not force it.

Jesus alone is the bridge that closes the gap between sinful men and women in rebellion to God and a holy, just, righteous God who loves everyone and wants ALL to come to full repentance. Jesus Himself stated, "I am the way, and the truth, and the life. No one comes to the Father except through me." (John 14:6b ESV). The choice to believe that, or not believe that, is ours.

The reality is that God loves you and me deeply. When you read through the Bible, you don't get a picture of a harsh, angry God that's just out to get us or hurt us. No, you see a God that created us and loves us and is for us. What you do read though time after time is that people (starting with Adam & Eve) continually rejected God and His love for them. You see a picture of a brokenhearted Father that is grieved over what has happened to His kids. The whole Bible records story after story of people disobeying God and doing terrible wrong. Sometimes because of this disobedience, God just plain had enough and there would be punishment, usually after we see Him being extremely patient for a very long time – extending mercy and grace time after time after time. But the picture is never portrayed of a God that isn't love or good or want what's best for us. The picture that's portrayed is that people started running from God in the Garden of Eden and they've been running from Him ever since.

God is "merciful and gracious, longsuffering, and abundant in goodness and truth." (Exodus 34:6b KJV). We are told in 1 John 4:16 that God not only loves us, but that "God is love." The very essence of God is love. Love is for you, not against you.

Jesus told us: "For God so loved the world, that he gave his only Son, that whoever believes in him should not perish but have eternal life. For God did not send his Son into the world to condemn the world, but in order that the world might be saved through him. Whoever believes in him is not condemned, but whoever does not believe is condemned already, because he has not believed in the name of the only Son of God. And this is the judgment: the light has come into the world, and people loved the darkness rather than the light because their works were evil." (John 3:16–19 ESV).

God sent Jesus to bring us life and restore us to fellowship with Himself. God, in His love for us, provided an answer for the terrible predicament that we see when we look around at ourselves and our world that's full of such darkness. And yet, Jesus Himself declared that some people won't come to Him and want Him to be their Savior because they actually love the darkness rather than the light. The truth is that there are a lot of people in our world that are in this boat – they prefer the darkness. Notice that Jesus says about them that they are "condemned already." God has never sent a single person to hell. He didn't even intend for hell to be for people (the Bible tells us it was created for the devil). However, to use an analogy: If a person already has a disease and yet refuses the remedy that's offered to them, who's fault is it if they die? Certainly not the one that extended the remedy. In like manner, we all are already born into a diseased state of sin and darkness. We are ALL infected. And we all need the remedy that's offered to us. But if a person refuses to take it and ends up in hell, there's only one person to be blamed and that's the person themself, not God. There is not one person who will ever be in hell that God has not deeply loved and wanted with Him. But people have choice and some have chosen (and do choose) to reject Him. And it breaks God's heart.

But for those that will come to Jesus, the One who loves them deeply, and receive the gift He has provided for them, they can be restored to right fellowship with God and live an abundant life here (while still recognizing that we still dwell in a sinful and dark world that can affect us) and ultimately will have fullness of life with God forever. They will find the true meaning to their lives that they've been searching for.

Many try to deal with our obvious sin problem by turning to various religions. Even though Jesus stated that He was the ONLY way (John 14:6), there are lots of religions in the world that men have come up with to try to come to God another way. They can't all be right. People love to believe that all religions lead to being right with God: "You believe what you want to believe, I'll believe what I want to believe, and all is fine." Strictly speaking from just a logic perspective here: All religions can be wrong, but they can't all be right. Because most CLAIM to be the right and only way. When Jesus said "I am the way, and the truth, and the life. No one comes to the Father except through me." (John 14:6b ESV), He either was telling the truth or He wasn't. Using purely logic: All religions could be wrong, but they can't all be right. Somebody is right and the rest are wrong.

All man-made religions in one way or another are based in what you can DO to get right with God. If you do enough works, if you do enough good, if you do this and do that, then God will accept you. They appeal to us in our pride because we like the idea that WE can make it to heaven ourselves without any help or as some religions teach that we can become our own god. This is in stark contrast to Christianity which is not about what we can do, but about what God has DONE for us. Christians don't do good because we're trying to get to heaven – we do good out of our gratitude towards God because of what He's already done for us. Christianity is really all about having a personal, close relationship with the God that made us and loves us. It's all about relationship, not about trying to appease an angry God. Jesus has ALREADY appeased God for us! And if we simply choose to believe in Jesus and receive the gift He's provided for us, God sees us as being in Jesus and actually sees us as righteous! The Bible tells us that "For our sake he [God] made him [Jesus] to be sin who knew no sin, so that in him [Jesus] we might become the righteousness of God. (2 Corinthians 5:21 ESV, bracketed text added for clarity). This is the real good news of the Bible!

We must make a conscious choice to believe in Jesus and find our rightstanding with God through Jesus rather than banking on our own righteousness and arrogantly approaching God in our pride thinking that He has to accept us. In ourselves, we have sinned and broken God's standards, and there is not a single person that can stand before God on their own merits. This is why we all need Jesus. Neither your sin or your "relative goodness" as compared to other people is the deciding factor. You might be better or worse than some other human beings in regards to the things you've done, but compared to God we ALL fall short and we ALL need Jesus.

Friend, God does love you very much. God is FOR you, not against you. He wants a relationship with you and He has provided the way for that. If you want to finally stop running here and there and everywhere, and if you want real peace in your life, and if you want to really know your purpose in life and to fulfill all that you are here to fulfill, it starts with turning to Jesus.

The starting point is as simple as praying a prayer like this one, in faith. It isn't about the prayer but about the faith in your heart.

"Lord Jesus, I admit and confess that I am a sinner. I have done bad things and have hurt myself and others. I have been living for wrong reasons and bought the lie that I would be happy if I only had enough of what the world has to offer. I now realize that the world cannot satisfy me because it can't address my deep spiritual need of having peace with God. I repent and turn from my sin, and I believe Jesus that You came into this world and lived a perfect life to die for me and pay the penalty for my sin. I thank you for that and I receive your free gift of righteousness and eternal life. Please forgive me of my sin and come into my life today. Fill me with your peace and joy and love and help me to live rightly. Give me vision for my future and what You would have me do. Amen."

If you've prayed this prayer sincerely from a heart of faith, re-gardless of whether you instantly feel anything different or not, you become "born again" – meaning that you have passed from death to life. We're all born physically but are dead in our spirit. To be "born again" means that you literally become a new creation where your spirit becomes alive and fellowship with God is restored. The Bible says "Therefore, if anyone is in Christ, he is a new creation. The old has passed away; behold, the new has come. All this is from God, who through Christ reconciled us to himself..." (2 Corinthians 5:17–18a ESV).

God Himself actually comes to reside in you by His Spirit as a part of that fellowship restoration. He will help you to live an abun-dant life where you can obey God and live rightly and live a life where sin does not dominate you. It can be a process in working those things out (after all, we've all had lots of practice living wrongly) but He will work with you.

The Bible also tells you "For by grace you have been saved through faith. And this is not your own doing; it is the gift of God, not a result of works, so that no one may boast. For we are his workmanship, created in Christ Jesus for good works, which God prepared beforehand, that we should walk in them." (Ephesians

2:8–10 ESV). Through your faith in Jesus – God's gracious gift to you – you have been saved, and God has "good works" planned out special for you – plans and purposes for your life that He wants you to fulfill.

The next step is to seek out a local Christian church in your area that teaches the Bible and believes that all of it is the true Word of God. Tell them that you have just given your heart and life to Jesus and you would like their help to go forward. They will be glad to assist you.

Shattered Glass
(By Margaret Long)

All of Earth's children have a home –
Some of stone, some of grass...
But I lived in a house of glass;
Content to let the world slide past.
Illusion mirrored on every side,
Reflected in self-righteous pride.

Then one day my soul looked back,
And I smashed my fist through the glass –
To wrap my bleeding hands around
A blood-stained cross.

For Jesus died on Calvary,
To hold my soul and set me free.
No more to play a puppet's role,
Only Christ can make us whole!

Appendix B – Declarative Healing Prayer

This is a sample prayer to hopefully be an aid for you in putting your faith into tangible expression in regards to health and wholeness – particularly in regards to physical health. I emphasize the word "sample." Do NOT see this as a rote thing to do or as some magic prayer or formula for you to get your answers! This is NOT some magic prayer! This is merely an EXAMPLE of a faith-filled prayer that can be powerful for you IF you will mix your faith with it and truly believe what you are saying and personalize it for you. What matters is your faith, not merely repeating some words.

God, my Healer, I come before you and praise you because you are a good God that loves me. I believe that I am your beloved child and that you look upon me with compassion. Thank you for your love. I believe that you are a merciful God and that you want me well in my body and my mind.

I thank you that you have fearfully and wonderfully made me – that you designed every part of my body. Every organ, every system, every gland, and every cell was designed by you with a specific purpose. I ask you to help them all to perform their functions as you designed them to operate. Bring everything into proper balance and congruence in accordance with the perfect functioning that you intended for this body. Bring my body and soul into congruence with my spirit.

I look to you as my Healer. You are my source. I thank you that because Jesus bore my sickness and carried my disease away, that I don't have to bear what Jesus has already borne for me. I thank you that by the stripes of Jesus, I am right now healed and whole. I choose by an act of my will to see myself well. I believe that I am healed in you and that you are at work in this body bringing it into the full alignment with this truth.

You are faithful to your Word. You have told me that I will live and will not die and will declare your works. You have told me that it is better to trust in you than to put my confidence in man (or anything else). You have told me that those who hope in you will not be put to shame. You are NOT a liar. You are faithful and trustworthy and always have been in my life – and you are now. I choose to believe your words to me. I choose to trust you.

I submit this body and mind unto you God, and I resist the devil and therefore he must flee now. I believe that because I am in Jesus, that the devil has no place in me and I take authority over any demonic spirits that have been trying to come against me. Any foul spirits – you must leave me now in the name of Jesus! Any spirits of infirmity or sickness or disease, you must go now! All discouragement, depression, fear, anxiety, hopelessness, worry, negativity – I command you to leave – you are not welcome here. I don't want you. In the name of Jesus Christ, be gone and don't come back!

I believe that I have nothing to fear because God is my helper and is with me. Father, I choose to rest secure in You under the shadow of your wings – safe in the knowledge that you are my defender and protector and that nothing will harm me as I abide with you. I specifically cast off and reject all fear, worry, anxiety, and dread. I reject and eject from my life all negative thinking and negative imaginations. I envision myself well doing the works that you've prepared in advance for me to do [pause to do so]. I reject all hopelessness because I have tremendous hope in you. I choose Life! I choose to see myself well and healthy in you, living the abundant life that Jesus died for me to have.

I choose to rest in the sacrifice of Jesus. I believe that Jesus has provided salvation for me in every respect. It has already been done and provided for me, and I rest in that finished work. It is done and I appropriate everything purchased for me by faith. Where I have sinned God, I receive your forgiveness provided me by Jesus. I repent of [list anything you can think of]. Thank you that I am forgiven by the blood of Jesus that was shed for me. I declare that I am free from sin and have the victory over sin in Jesus because of what He's done for me. I declare and believe God that you see me right now as righteous because you are seeing Jesus' righteousness when you look at me. I ask you Holy Spirit for your daily help to live in accordance with the reality of who I am in Jesus.

I also receive healing and health in my body that was paid for by Jesus' body that was broken for me. Thank you Jesus for bearing my punishment and making the way for me to be whole in every part of my being. I receive the gracious gift of health and wholeness for this body.

Where I have been hurt in my soul, God, I ask for your love to come and bring healing and wholeness. I open the door for your love to come into those deep places. I choose to let go of past hurts and regrets. I give them to you. Just as you have forgiven me, I choose to forgive those that have hurt me and go forward with you in the beautiful future that you have for me.

I believe that I have been set free from the law of sin and death. I am under the law of the Spirit of Life. Your Spirit brings life to every part of me. I believe that I am blessed in you. I am not cursed or under the curse – I have been set free from that. Because I am in Christ, I receive all the blessings of Christ. I am healed. Healing is the children's bread, and I am your child. So I declare and believe that healing is mine.

I choose to put on the life of Jesus today. My old man is dead and buried, and I have risen to newness of life in Jesus and my life is hidden with Christ in God. I declare that this physical body must come in line with the truth that the life of Jesus is in this body. Jesus is in me and I am in Him. Jesus is not sick, so this body cannot be sick either. We are one flesh – a one flesh union. This is the temple of the Holy Spirit and I believe Jesus is sweeping this temple clean of anything impure. Sickness cannot stay in this atmosphere. It must flee! I command you sickness and disease to flee now – to leave this body in the name of Jesus. I reject and eject from this body all sickness and disease. [Name whatever problem you have been dealing with] – I command you to go in Jesus' name! I receive healing and health in this body.

I declare that no weapon formed against me will prosper. Any bacteria or foreign invaders in this body that have been trying to harm this body, you yourself are dying now and leaving this body in the name of Jesus. Any cells that are not as you are supposed to be and that are harming this body, I command you to die and leave this body in Jesus' name. I command you body to have the proper levels and balance of cells, and that only cells that are healthy and in the places they are supposed to be, in accordance with God's design for you, are permitted. In the mighty name of Jesus – the name that is above every name including above any names of any diseases – this is so!

I believe right now God that your life is flowing throughout my body – that your Spirit is bringing life to all my flesh. You are righting everything and putting all into perfect balance and order. Every organ is working as you intend for it to work. Every function and component of this body is doing exactly what it is supposed to do. Every chemical, nerve, organ, cell, system, and every part of this body is brought into congruence with the truth of Your Word that declares me well and whole.

I declare now that I am healed. This body is in perfect health and wholeness in accordance with the Word of God.

God, You are my God. I am your child. I believe that you love me. I receive and rest in that love. I love you. Thank you for the healing and wholeness that you have provided for me. I AM healed and this is where I stand. I praise you God!! I pray all of this in the wonderful, mighty name of Jesus. Hallelujah!!!

Appendix C – Healing Scriptures

Here are some passages of Scripture that you can go through and meditate on as it relates to the area of health and wholeness. This is far from an exhaustive list, but are just some to get you started.

"It is better to trust in the LORD than to put confidence in man." (Psalm 118:8 KJV)

"The LORD is my light and my salvation; whom shall I fear? the LORD is the stronghold of my life; of whom shall I be afraid?" (Psalm 27:1 KJV)

"The Lord is at hand; do not be anxious about anything, but in everything by prayer and supplication with thanksgiving let your requests be made known to God. And the peace of God, which surpasses all understanding, will guard your hearts and your minds in Christ Jesus." (Philippians 4:5b–7 ESV)

"You keep him in perfect peace whose mind is stayed on you, because he trusts in you." (Isaiah 26:3 ESV)

"Fear not, for I have redeemed you; I have called you by name, you are mine. When you pass through the waters, I will be with you; and through the rivers, they shall not overwhelm you;" (Isaiah 43:1b–2a ESV)

"God is our refuge and strength, a very present help in trouble." (Psalm 46:1 KJV)

"I shall not die, but live, and declare the works of the LORD... he hath not given me over unto death." (Psalm 118:17,18b KJV)

"Bless the Lord, O my soul, and forget not all his benefits: Who forgiveth all thine iniquities; who healeth all thy diseases; Who redeemeth thy life from destruction; who crowneth thee with lovingkindness and tender mercies; Who satisfieth thy mouth with good things; so that thy youth is renewed like the eagle's." (Psalm 103:2–5 KJV)

"Because he holds fast to me in love, I will deliver him; I will protect him, because he knows my name. When he calls to me, I will answer him; I will be with him in trouble; I will rescue him and honor him. With long life I will satisfy him and show him my salvation." (Psalm 91:14–16 ESV)

"I am afflicted very much: quicken me, O LORD, according unto thy word." (Psalm 119:107 KJV)

"This *is* my comfort in my affliction, For Your word has given me life." (Psalm 119:50 NKJV)

"He sent his word, and healed them, and delivered them from their destructions." (Psalm 107:20 KJV)

"Do not be wise in your own eyes; Fear the LORD and depart from evil. It will be health to your flesh, And strength to your bones." (Proverbs 3:7–8 NKJV)

"My son, attend to my words; incline thine ear unto my sayings. Let them not depart from thine eyes; keep them in the midst of thine heart. For they are life unto those that find them, and health to all their flesh." (Proverbs 4:20–22 KJV)

"He giveth power to the faint; and to them that have no might he increaseth strength." (Isaiah 40:29 KJV)

"Heal me, O LORD, and I shall be healed; save me, and I shall be saved: for thou art my praise." (Jeremiah 17:14 KJV)

"You shall serve the LORD your God, and he will bless your bread and your water, and I will take sickness away from among you. None shall miscarry or be barren in your land; I will fulfill the number of your days." (Exodus 23:25–26 ESV). This was part of an Old Testament covenant. If this was their covenant right prior to Jesus, how much more ours in the New Covenant with Jesus.

"Behold, I will bring to it health and healing, and I will heal them and reveal to them abundance of prosperity and security." (Jeremiah 33:6 ESV)

"Surely he hath borne our griefs, and carried our sorrows: yet we did esteem him stricken, smitten of God, and afflicted. But he was wounded for our transgressions, he was bruised for our iniquities: the chastisement of our peace was upon him; and with his stripes we are healed." (Isaiah 53:4–5 KJV)

"That evening they brought to him many who were oppressed by demons, and he cast out the spirits with a word and healed all who were sick. This was to fulfill what was spoken by the prophet Isaiah: 'He took our illnesses and bore our diseases.'" (Matthew 8:16–17 ESV)

"For this purpose the Son of God was manifested, that he might destroy the works of the devil." (1 John 3:8b KJV)

"How God anointed Jesus of Nazareth with the Holy Ghost and with power: who went about doing good, and healing all that were oppressed of the devil; for God was with him." (Acts 10:38 KJV)

"Jesus Christ is the same yesterday and today and forever." (Hebrews 13:8 ESV)

"Whatever you ask in my name, this I will do, that the Father may be glorified in the Son. If you ask me anything in my name, I will do it." (John 14:13–14 ESV)

"Assuredly, I say to you, whatever you bind on earth will be bound in heaven, and whatever you loose on earth will be loosed in heaven." (Matthew 18:18 NKJV). Bind up/forbid sickness and loose health and healing in your body.

"Again I say to you, if two of you agree on earth about anything they ask, it will be done for them by my Father in heaven." (Matthew 18:19 ESV). A prayer of agreement is a powerful thing.

"Have faith in God. Truly, I say to you, whoever says to this mountain, 'Be taken up and thrown into the sea,' and does not doubt in his heart, but believes that what he says will come to pass, it will be done for him. Therefore I tell you, whatever you ask in prayer, believe that you have received it, and it will be yours." (Mark 11:22b–24 ESV)

"Behold, I give unto you power to tread on serpents and scorpions, and over all the power of the enemy: and nothing shall by any means hurt you." (Luke 10:19 KJV)

"For the law of the Spirit of life in Christ Jesus has made me free from the law of sin and death." (Romans 8:2 NKJV)

"If the Spirit of him who raised Jesus from the dead dwells in you, he who raised Christ Jesus from the dead will also give life to your mortal bodies through his Spirit who dwells in you." (Romans 8:11 ESV). This is one of my favorite healing scriptures! It's a great one to memorize.

"Now to Him who is able to do exceedingly abundantly above all that we ask or think, according to the power that works in us," (Ephesians 3:20 NKJV). What is this power that works in us? The power of the Spirit – the same Spirit that raised Jesus from the dead!

"Always bearing about in the body the dying of the Lord Jesus, that the life also of Jesus might be made manifest in our body." (2 Corinthians 4:10 KJV). We need to identify with Christ's death and burial – realizing that we died with Him. But we also identify with his resurrection life – realizing that we were raised with Him – and Christ's life can thus flow through your body bringing it to health.

"He that spared not his own Son, but delivered him up for us all, how shall he not with him also freely give us all things?" (Romans 8:32 KJV). That includes health and healing...

"Beloved, I wish above all things that thou mayest prosper and be in health, even as thy soul prospereth." (3 John 1:2 KJV)

"For God has not given us a spirit of fear, but of power and of love and of a sound mind." (2 Timothy 1:7 NKJV)

"No weapon formed against you shall prosper, And every tongue *which* rises against you in judgment You shall condemn. This *is* the heritage of the servants of the LORD, And their righteousness *is* from Me," Says the LORD." (Isaiah 54:17 NKJV)

"The LORD opens *the eyes of* the blind; The LORD raises those who are bowed down; The LORD loves the righteous." (Psalm 146:8 NKJV) Who's righteous? Us through Jesus – our righteousness is given to us as a gift by God as shown in the Isaiah 54 verse above.

"You have turned for me my mourning into dancing; You have put off my sackcloth and clothed me with gladness," (Psalm 30:11 NKJV)

"The LORD is good, a strong hold in the day of trouble; and he knoweth them that trust in him... affliction shall not rise up the second time." (Nahum 1:7,9b KJV)

Appendix D – Additional Resources

There are a bunch of great recommendations for additional resources for you to check out. However, so that I have flexibility to update recommendations and related info, I've decided to make them as an extra of sorts that's only available via the Internet.

You can access them at the website for this book at:
www.bodequip.org/life

Consider this a "bonus" – there's no guarantee that this site or list of resources will always be available and it is subject to change at any time.

Notes

Chapter 1

1. From a 2001 survey: "The Leadership survey on Pastors and Internet Pornography" in Christianity Today's Leadership Journal. Winter 2001 issue. Available online at: http://www.christianitytoday.com/le/2001/winter/12.89.html. Accessed October 16, 2014. In the survey, 43% of pastors admitted to having viewed a pornographic website, and 36% said it was within the previous year. This was a 2001 survey, which when it comes to such things, seems like forever ago – I would bet a whole lot that these numbers would be even higher now – probably substantially higher.

Chapter 2

1. I've chosen not to name the movie for a few different reasons, one of which is that it is really irrelevant to my point. There's lots of movies out there I could have used – I just picked this one because it was a relatively recent (at the time I first wrote this chapter anyway) and clear example. My goal in giving this example wasn't to try and single it out, but to use it to highlight a pattern of thinking that undergirds a LOT of Christian media out there. Naming the movie would only serve to obfuscate this purpose by putting the focus on one specific movie rather than the underlying theology platform that it is based upon.

2. I cannot recollect the origin of this quote but I am fairly certain that I personally read it/heard it many years ago (like in the 1990's). It is also found attributed to Dr. Dobson (James C. Dobson) on several Internet websites including: http://www.frankjuelich.in/Illustrations%20-%20C.htm. Accessed October 16, 2014. Use of this quote is not at all meant to imply that Dr. James Dobson has read or endorses this book.

3. From a sermon (unknown date) entitled "God is Good". Use of this quote is neither meant to imply that I endorse everything in that sermon or that Chuck Smith would have endorsed this book. The

quote I shared skipped part of the quote after where he says "God loves me." The full sentence is: "I understand God loves me, and that God is in control." I skipped the part about God being in control, because while I agree that is true in an overarching sense, it could be confusing given some of the other things I say in the chapter and it wasn't critical to the point of me sharing the quote. Chuck has been home with Jesus for several years now, but I am forever grateful for how the Lord used him in recent church history and I'm sure he's brightening up Heaven now with his giant smile! (and I for one miss seeing it here!).

4. I'm not going to name the pastor as I am not interested in shaming him or putting the focus on that pastor specifically. The reality is that I've heard many sermons from many different pastors with similar content over the years (perhaps not as bluntly, but the same underpinnings). Like my decision not to mention the movie I referenced at the beginning of the chapter, naming the pastor would only serve to distract by putting the focus on a specific individual when the real issue is a wrong underlying theology platform that is shared by many.

Chapter 7
1. Lyrics are taken from a song called "Back to Eden" (just like the name of this chapter) and this song is a great corollary to this chapter. You can possibly find the song, along with a bunch of other songs, available to listen to at the website given in Appendix D. If you like modern rock music, I also recommend another song that is simply called "Eden" by artist Phil Wickham from his excellent album titled "Heaven & Earth". Similar to my time-machine portrayal, his song paints a picture of pre-Fall Garden of Eden in a very vivid way.

Technical Info About This Book

The style and formatting of this book could be seen as simplistic or non-conforming to some standard book publishing practices, including some practices within the Christian publishing world. This is actually by design and I believe is largely just the way it is supposed to be. I think God likes to just shake things up a bit sometimes. :) Much like some of the content of this book could be considered "counter" to some of the norms out there, so are some other facets as well in the way this book is constructed. Call me a rebel, but as a general rule, I chose not to let style or style rules interfere in any way with the purpose of this book, even if it meant breaking some norms.

This book is pretty theology-heavy but is written in a straight-forward, conversational, folksy type style (that's really just how I write by default). Most Christian non-fiction books have a different type of feel and follow conventional norms of splitting up the chapters into various subsections, making it more visually appealing and easy to read little sections at a time to take in chapters in smaller nuggets. This book, by contrast, is mostly formatted more like a fiction book would be in reading as a narrative, even though it is dealing with theological content. Many of the chapters build steadily throughout the chapter like a train chugging along trying to get to the station. Putting in divisions would interrupt that flow and provide more likelihood for people to lose some of the built-up momentum by stopping reading at one of the division points instead of the end of the chapter.

In addition, the text itself tends to have lengthier paragraphs than one might expect to see. I tend to group thoughts together into their own paragraph, regardless of size, even though conventional wisdom might say to split up those paragraphs into multiple smaller ones. Again, to me, especially when building a theological case (as this book does), once I'm going on a certain train of thought, I don't like to interrupt that thought for a new paragraph where I feel that could lend to being more disrupting to the flow for readers.

Stylistically, the interior of this book is also quite "plain" looking. Although I reviewed many different font choices (including many of the ones that non-fiction books are commonly printed in), when it came down to it, out of all the choices I looked at anyway, trusty Times New Roman provided the absolute best readability in my opinion. Given that this book does have a lot of text in many of the chapters, and that it is not uncommon to see longer paragraphs of text, I decided it was more important that this book "read well" with less chance for "fatigue" than it was for it to look pretty. I do understand that Times New Roman is a very recognizable font and that it might at first glance seem I was lazy in using it (or come across "amateurish") but rest assured, it was actually a thought-out choice.

Because of the length of the book, on a practical level, it was also not really feasible for me to use 1.5 or double line spacing as is commonly used for non-fiction books if I wanted to keep the book in any realm of the physical size of common non-fiction books. Same rationale for no line breaks between paragraphs, even though I actually prefer them. I felt that making the book appear physically "too big" could be more of an initial turn-off than utilizing single line spacing and no paragraph line breaks. Plus it would serve to significantly increase printing costs.

Taking it all together, stylistically this is not a particularly "pretty" book to look at when looking at the text, but I decided that content and readability of that content was more important than having a "pretty face". I do realize that at first glance this book might not initially look as "inviting" in comparison to some other non-fiction books, but I am trusting that people will be able to look past that to see that this is a substantive book that is relying more on its actual content.

Some of the editorial decisions made for this book also fly against conventional wisdom. This book uses a mix of U.S. and U.K. style. For instance, punctuation is usually handled as U.S. style but sometimes uses U.K. style where that seemed to flow better. Also, because my writing style uses a fair amount of dashes, the U.K. style of using en-dashes instead of the em-dashes just visually made more sense. Emphasis is communicated in several different ways: italics are usually used as a "light emphasis" and UPPER CAPS are usually used when the goal is to really make a word or phrase stand out in a very forceful manner or when being used in a Scripture quotation. Any existing italics in Bible translations that utilize that were retained when quoting verses. I did not really want to do this and I consider this practice confusing because readers could easily assume I am trying to emphasize something in the passage (I tried to counter that by alerting readers upfront of this book's practice). As far as I know, the vast majority of Christian books do not retain the italics precisely because it could be confusing, but unfortunately I felt a bit boxed in on this based on an interaction I had with someone.

Regarding Bible verses, it is relatively common in Christian publishing to abbreviate verse references. I chose for the most part not to do this. It is also commonly accepted publishing practice to quote only parts of Bible verses but yet just give the verse reference without indicating a partial quotation. Given the importance in this book of reliance on the Bible to make its points and also given that the subject matter of this book lends towards more people reading skeptically, I purposely tried to be as transparent as possible when quoting verses. Thus if I used only part of a verse, I typically indicate that with a designator "a" or "b" at the end of the verse reference depending on whether I used the beginning of the verse or a part after the beginning. Even if I merely omitted one word at the start for grammatical reasons for fitting with the sentence structure, I still typically use the "b" designator in that case. I also sometimes use 3 dots/ellipsis at the beginning to indicate if I've started a quote in the midst of a verse where there is notable text before the portion I'm quoting. Again, even though that's not necessarily in line with how some books handle quoting Bible verses, I feel it adds clarity and transparency. Exceptions to all of this might be in brief references to portions of a verse, especially popularly known verses, that are not generally being used for making a central point.

This book capitalizes words referring to God, and does not capitalize words referring to the devil. To me, the devil doesn't deserve any honor that might be implied by a capital "D". Note however that I do not change the capitalization as used in quotations from Bible translations. Some translations I have used capitalize names referring to God and/or the devil and some do not. Although that produces some inconsistency, I have chosen to just let it be.

The bottom line regarding editorial style is that while I know that there are publishing norms for different regions and so-forth, I'm not really super interested in following certain norms simply because that's the way it's always been done. If a grammatical or style rule gets in the way of my communicating what I'm trying to communicate or just makes something look out of place, then I have no problem just doing it how I feel works best for my type of writing whether it technically breaks a rule or not. In the final analysis, while some "grammar nazi's" might nitpick certain elements of this book, I believe stylistically it is perfectly fine for all English-speaking regions.

About the Author

This is where I'm supposed to tell you how great I am and make you think "WOW! This Christopher Long guy's somebody real important!" The truth is that while I have ministered to thousands of believers from all parts of the Body of Christ for over twenty years through a daily online ministry, basically I'm just a follower of Jesus that tries to do my part in whatever way God would have me do so. While I do have a bit of Bible college training, I don't have any fancy degrees to impress you with. I'm just someone that's been through some stuff and that God I believe has revealed some things to for myself and then to pass on to others.

In 2004, the Lord showed me that He had given me a "pastor's heart" and gifted me in this area. My primary life calling I believe is to encourage and help equip the Body of Christ to walk in the fullness of all God would have. As a part of that, I've established BodEquip Ministries (www.bodequip.org).

It is common for Christians to want to know what theological framework an author is operating under. While I think that's understandable (I myself am this way), far too often I think the reality is that we really are just looking for a label so we can decide whether we should instantly dismiss them or not according to our preconceived notions of that label.

Knowing this, and particularly because I believe this book is one that God intends for all of His Body regardless of label, I suppose I'm going to disappoint a bit. I truly just consider myself a Christian, and the theological framework I operate under is the Bible. I have been a follower of Jesus since 1995 and I support the historic doctrines of the Christian faith that are rooted in the Bible, including those found in the Apostle's Creed. If you really must know more, you can read the Statement of Faith as found on the BodEquip Ministries website given above, but spoiler alert: there's nothing unbiblical or weird in it.

Made in USA - Crawfordsville, IN
40699_9781734845747
04.29.2020 2118